Bioactive Medicinal Plants

Bioactive Medicinal Plants

Editor

Dharamvir Hota

GENE TECH

2015

Gene-Tech Books

New Delhi - 110 002

ISBN 81-89729-19-5
ISBN 978-81-89729-19-6

Published by : **GENE-TECH BOOKS**
4762-63/23, Ansari Road, Darya Ganj,
NEW DELHI - 110 002
Phone: 41562849
e-mail: genetechbooks@yahoo.co.in

Printed at : **Chawla Offset Printers**
New Delhi – 110 052

PRINTED IN INDIA

Preface

Medicinal plants are plants whose extracts can be used directly or indirectly for the treatment of different ailments. The use of traditional medicine and medicinal plants in most developing countries, as a basis for the maintenance of good health, has been widely observed. In the world more than 30 per cent of the pharmaceutical preparations are based on plants. Scientists throughout the world are trying to explore the precious assets of medicinal plants to help the suffering humanity.

An increasing reliance on the use of medicinal plants in the industrialised societies has been traced to the extraction and development of several drugs and chemotherapeutics from these plants. The medicinal values of these plants are due to the presence of small doses of active compounds which produces physiological actions in the human and animal body. Some of the important bioactive compounds found in medicinal plants are alkaloids, glycosides, resins, gums, mucilages etc.

The present book explores the recent developments in the field of botanical medicine. It provides vital information on various bioactive compounds present in plants and their use in the synthesis of pharmaceuticals. Educated readers, practitioners, and academics of natural sciences will be benefited by the contents of this work.

Editor

Contents

1

Therapeutic Value of Medicinal Plants

Medicinal plants are an integral component of ethnoveterinary medicine. Medicinal plants, since times immemorial, have been used in virtually all cultures as a source of medicine. The widespread use of herbal remedies and healthcare preparations, as those described in ancient texts such as the Vedas and the Bible, and obtained from commonly used traditional herbs and medicinal plants, has been traced to the occurrence of natural products with medicinal properties. The use of traditional medicine and medicinal plants in most developing countries, as a normative basis for the maintenance of good health, has been widely observed.

Furthermore, an increasing reliance on the use of medicinal plants in the industrialised societies has been traced to the extraction and development of several drugs and chemotherapeutics from these plants as well as from traditionally used rural herbal remedies. Moreover, in these societies, herbal remedies have become more popular in the treatment of minor ailments, and also on account of the increasing costs of personal health maintenance. Indeed, the market and public demand has been so great that there is a great risk that many medicinal plants today, face either extinction or loss of genetic diversity.

As defined by WHO, health is a state of complete physical, mental, and social well being and not merely the absence of disease or infirmity. Medicine, in several developing countries, using local traditions and beliefs, is still the mainstay of health care. The practise of traditional medicine is widespread in China, India, Japan, Pakistan, Sri Lanka and Thailand. In China about 40% of the total medicinal consumption is attributed to traditional tribal medicines. In Thailand, herbal medicines make use of legumes encountered in the Caesalpiniaceae, the Fabaceae, and the Mimosaceae.

In the mid-90s, it is estimated that receipts of more than US$2.5 billion have resulted from the sales of herbal medicines. And, in Japan, herbal medicinal preparations are more in demand than mainstream pharmaceutical products. Africa is a rich source of medicinal plants. Perhaps, the best known species is Phytolacca dodecandra. Extracts of the plant, commonly known as endod, are used as an effective molluscicide to control schistosomiasis. Other notable examples are Catharanthus roseus, which yields anti-tumour agents such as vinblastine and vincristine; and Ricinus communis, which yields the laxative--castor oil.

In Botswana, Lesotho, Namibia and South Africa, Harpagophytum procumbens is produced as a crude drug for export. Similarly, Hibiscus sabdariffa is exported from Sudan and Egypt. Other exports are Pausinystalia yohimbe from Cameroon, Nigeria and Rwanda, which yields yohimbine; and Rauwolfia vomitoria, from Madagascar, Mozambique and Zaire, which is exploited to yield reserpine and ajmaline. The use of medicinal plants like Eupatorium perfoliatum (bonest), Podophyllum peltatum (mayapple), and Panax quinquefolium (ginseng) has long been associated with the American Indians. These plants have also been appreciated and recognised for their aesthetic and ornamental value.

In Central America medicinal plants have been widely used—by the Maya Indians in Mexico, the Miskitos and Sumus in Honduras and Nicaragua, the Pech, Lencas, and Xicaques in Honduras, the Pipiles in El Salvador, the Talamancas in Costa Rica, and the Guaymis and Kunas in Panama. In Europe, some 1500 species of medicinal and aromatic plants are widely used in Albania, Bulgaria, Croatia, France, Germany, Hungary, Poland, Spain, Turkey, and the United Kingdom. The Maltese islands constitute an apt example where medicinal plants are widely used in every day life as part of folk medicinal remedies.

Ethnobotanical information is leading to the discovery of novel phytopharmaceuticals and other phytoproducts. This trend has made their commercialisation a necessity. Therefore, industries based on medicinal and aromatic plants have been established all over the world with a view to manufacture the so-called green products to satisfy the growing demand.

The development of formulation of drugs of plant origin involves botanical identification of the vegetable drug, cultivation and post-harvest procedures, extraction procedures, standardisation of extracts and pharmaceutical formulation. This means that the phytotherapeutics are in the hands of personnel from different disciplines. The production of phytotherapeutics or drugs from plants needs the co-operation of a big team of horticulturists, botanists, ecologists, taxonomists, phyto-chemists, pharmacists, pharmacologists, pharmaceutical specialists, marketing and distribution specialists, etc.

The modern development of phytotherapy requires the integration of scientific results of different disciplines, namely, ethno-botanical, agro-technical, biomedical, industrial, registration and marketing, and education and dissemination Doubtless this puts the issue of medicinal plants and phytotherapeutics in a critical situation as the synchronised cooperation among these specialists is not an easy task.

The plant products available in the commercial market still lack, to some extent, quality certificates that inform us about the content of the active ingredients or about a necessary standardisation procedure. Standardisation is more difficult with drugs which active principles are not well known. No one is prepared to take plant products seriously unless certain elementary quality control criteria have been fulfilled.

Also, physicians are not prepared to prescribe the raw plant drugs. A full acceptance of phytopharmaceuticals and the integration of phytotherapy into the concepts of classical medicine can be achieved only if phytopharmaceuticals meet the same criteria of quality as synthetic pharmaceuticals.

Adulterated phytopharmaceuticals have been put on the market in different countries. Moreover, we should be aware of the problems with contaminants like pesticides. The safety and quality of phytopharmaceuticals must be guaranteed, even if efficacy is already recognised and traditionally accepted The development of medicinal and aromatic plants is hindered by lack of technical and economic data.

It is interesting to note that in many countries all over the world the drugs are exhibited in the shops in a more or less similar manner. Trade in the drugs obtained from wild plants is very common everywhere. However, there is no proper attention paid to its socio-economical aspects in the developing countries.

History of Medicinal Plants

As early as 3000 B.C., the ancient Egyptians put much

confidence in plants for curing many diseases. Up till now, the same confidence is still existing among the contemporary Egyptians and a "turn-back" to "remedy by herbs" is now becoming a global rather than regional or national request. This is strongly favoured, since the natural drugs have little or no side effects as do the chemically synthesised medications.

In view of the diversity of the habitats and the climate of the country, the biota exhibits considerable diversity. The plant resources, despite the climatic aridity, are diverse and some of them could be unexpected food or remedy for the natives. The medicinal plants growing in the various habitats in Egypt represent a major and important component of these plants, which are threatened and some are on the brink of extinction.

Since times immemorial, the use of plants for curing human diseases has been in practice everywhere. Such use of plants is a part of the human history in Egypt as well as in all the countries of N. Africa and the Middle East. The people in the region depended mainly on traditional medicine for their health care needs and the ailments of their animals. The folk medicine in the region is full of receipes for curing various diseases.

The term "Attar" in Egypt and "Herb's seller" in Tunisia denotes the persons who sell drugs and medicinal plants for curing diseases or for health care. The shops of attarin occur in the narrow lanes of the old part of the city in any Arab country. It is the quarter of the city which represented the core of the old city, with mosques. The drugs and the medicinal plants, from every corner of the world, are exhibited in a very attractive way. The beautiful colours are attractive, and the odour is characteristic of the whole quarter.

One smells cumin, cardamom, coriander, cinnamon, pepper, liquorice, etc.; all mixed together with perfumes.

This is not in a particular city, but it observed in all the cities of the Arab World. For instance, in Argentine, on can see the same exhibition in the city of Mendoza. In Egypt, the famous Ebers Papyrus, written in 1550 B.C., gives 842 prescriptions, that are not explicitly magical, they are made of 328 different ingredients. Among them are plant species growing in Egypt or other N. African countries, e.g. Artemisia absinthium, Acacia spp., Balanites aegyptiaca, Bryonia spp., Hyoscyamus muticus, Myrtus communis, Onopordon spp., Ziziphus spp., etc. Dioscorides, in his Materia Medica, gave the names of many plants from Egypt (Acacia nilotica, the Egyptian thorn) and Cyrenaica (Dorema ammoniacum).

The Muslim herbalists wrote over centuries many books and treatises on medicinal plants in the Islamic World, including Egypt. In view of the vast area occupied by the Islamic nation, the names of these plants were given in Arabic, Amazighy (Berber), Greek, Persian, Hindi and other languages. Writing about medicinal plants became very common. Institutes, universities and research centres hosted many studies on the medicinal plants of the different countries in Egypt and other countries in the Middle East and North Africa. Phytochemical screening and search for active principles in wild plants represent common projects in the different countries. Ecological, taxonomic and floristic studies of medicinal plants took place.

In 1960 a book on the medicinal plants in arid zones was published by UNESCO. Both the botanical and pharmacological aspects of medicinal plants growing in the arid zones were presented in that book Later, in 1983, Boulos wrote a book on the medicinal plants in North Africa in which he gives information about these plants and their therapeutic uses in folk medicine. Scientists from the region wrote many books and articles about the medicinal plants.

Nevertheless, there are gaps of knowledge about the medicinal plants in the region, e.g., their autecology, distribution, productivity, possibility of cultivation. In view of the rapid extensive exploitation of the wild medicinal plants in the region. It is indispensable to undertake studies on these plants and investigate methods and measures of conservation.

Wild Medicinal Plants

The conspicuous habitat diversity in the country, as a result of geographical, physiographic, edaphic and climatic conditions, is reflected upon the plant life. More than two thousand species grow wild in Egypt. Doubtless, man has been using hundreds of these species for their therapeutic value or as condiments. There is no complete inventory of medicinal plants of the region.

Pharmacopoeial wild medicinal plants: These are plants used in folk medicine since a long time ago. Recent and modern studies on these plants proved the occurrence of active principles in them. Their pharmacological activity had been investigated. They are among the pharmacopoeial drugs in different pharmacopoeias; either in the Arab countries or abroad.

Plants used in folk medicine: There are numerous plant species which are collected from the field to be sold in the "Attarin" or the herb's seller shops.

Plants of Potential Medicinal Value: Many plant species were investigated for their active constituents. This has been done depending on the information of the folk use of these plants, or in species with relatives of species, genera or he same family, known from other countries to have active constituents.

The great surge of public interest in the use of plants, as well as some animal products, as medicines is based on the assumption that the plants will be available on a continuing basis. However, no concerted effort has been made to ensure this, in the face of the threats posed by increasing demand of vastly increasing human population and extensive destruction of plant-rich habitats.

Drugs obtained from these plants are sold in the markets all over the region. Shops selling these drugs, either fresh or dried, are widespread in the main cities of the country. Usually, these shops are found in the old part of the city. All over the Arab, and also the Islamic World, one finds that these shops are in the old part of the city. These shops occur in narrow lanes and are full of drugs obtained from the same country or imported from different countries.

The fragrant odours of the powders of the drugs and condiments can be smelled in the area where these shops are located. The visitors to these shops are diverse, with different educational backgrounds; everybody is asking the help of the attar and his advice for the treatment of some diseases, or for fattening or reducing weight. After birth, the woman needs nutritive drinks, which can be obtained by decoctions from compound drugs and materials mixed by the attar.

The most famous prescriptions by the attar include those drugs for cough, urinary stones, abdominal pains, diabetes, rheumatism, spasms, aphrodisiac, constipation, headache, liver problems, skin diseases, etc. The continuous use of these plants impose a considerable pressure on the naturally growing plants in the deserts and semi-deserts of the region. In such habitats, the rate of exploitation is more than the rate of establishment in the harsh desert environment.

Value of Phytomedicines

The world-wide sales of over-the-counter phytomedicines

to be $ 10 billion, with an annual growth of 6.5%. The US market for botanical medicine is estimated to exceed $ 2 billion at retail sales in 1997. Due to this demand, both universities and pharmaceutical companies devote themselves to the research of medicinal plants.

The European market for Herbal Medicinal Products (HMP) represents $7 billion of the $ 14 billion global retail market. Based on thousands of years of herbal tradition, business conditions in Europe are very favourable. There are well established guidelines and regulations to register HMP as drugs in many European countries. Germany is the leading market with approx. 50% of the sales in Europe, followed by France and Italy. In Germany still 50% of the HMP are prescribed by physicians and reimbursed by the heath insurance system.

Some multinational pharmaceutical companies like Boehringer Ingelheim, Bayer, Novartis and Roche are active in the field of HMP. On the other hand, in developing countries, there are no reliable available data on the economy of the medicinal plants. The problem is more significant in the case of wild medicinal plants. However, these are the plants subjected to degradation and may be to extinction within a few years. In view of the consequences of the GAAT, it is important to assess the value of these plants as an important biological resource and to document the intellectual property rights.

Medicinal plants are an important health and economic component of the floras in developed as well as developing countries. Increasing world-wide interest in herbal remedies, expanding reliance of local health care of traditional remedies, and a renewed interest in the development of pharmaceuticals from plant sources have greatly increased trade in medicinal plant materials. Important populations of medicinal plants are found not only in the regions and ecosystems with high biological diversity but also in less diverse floras and in floristic communities that are not a common focus of conservation efforts.

For instance, in the arid and semi-arid zones of the Middle East, the floras comprise very important genetic resources of crop and medicinal plants. The conservation of medicinal plant species in the wild is indispensable. While little is known about the population status of the majority of medicinal plant species, it is clear that most medicinal plants are collected from wild populations, and many are seriously threatened with extinction by lack of local harvest controls and habitat degradation.

The current focus of attention on biodiversity prospecting has diverted attention from the more serious environmental threat posed by large-scale harvest of medicinal plants for phyto-medicine production. Efforts to comprehend conservation needs and provide incentives for long-term sustainable harvest of medicinal plants are few. National and international regulation and protection may have some effect, but the most important role and responsibility for sustainable use belongs to industry and consumer support for local conservation.

The great surge of public interest in the use of plants as medicines is based on the assumption that the plants will be available on a continuing basis. However, no concerted effort has been made to ensure this, in the face of threats posed by increasing demand of vastly increasing human population and extensive destruction of plant rich habitats.

The disappearance of the medicinal plants from their natural habitats has an unseen consequence. This is the knowledge of the medicinal healers. In some parts of Egypt, as well as other Arab countries, this healer is known as a "doctor" or hakim. Those traditional doctors usually have a long and inherited experience. The erosion of such important genetic resource and their deterioration are accompanied with the disappearance of knowledge and traditional experience.

Consequently, a loss of the intellectual property rights. There is a great need to provide a framework for the conservation and sustainable use of plants in medicine. Ethnobotanical studies should be encouraged which represent basic studies to help implementing conservation programmes. Drugs obtained from these plants are sold in the market, they are sold either fresh or dried. Shops selling these drugs, either fresh or dried, are found in the old part of the cities in the Arab region, and also in the Islamic countries.

These shops are full of drugs obtained from the same country or imported from different countries. All over the Arab, and also the Islamic World, One finds that these shops are in the old part of the city. These shops occur in narrow lanes and are full of drugs, which may be obtained from the same country or imported from different countries. The continuous use of these plants impose a considerable pressure on the naturally growing plants in the deserts and semi-deserts of the region. In such habitats, the rate of exploitation is more than the rate of establishment of new stands of the collected plants. Doubtless, this has consequences affecting the components of the environment, including the biodiversity.

Production of Medicinal Plants

The production of medicinal and aromatic plants requires an understandings of plant growth, ecology, business, economics, law, conservation, and a lot of other subjects related to tillage and gathering plants, While developments such as machinery, fertilizers, and pesticides, have helped farmers meet demands for quality materials at affordable prices, the balance with farming costs, and labour compels society to set directions and establish limits.

The technology of producing plants continues to evolve with the movement of laboratory and field experiments to firms and forests with the expectation that advancements create better farming. The current task is to examine and measure farming methods according to established principles in accordance with the common needs of communities. By taking advantage of progress in biology, engineering, and other disciplines, medicinal and aromatic plant growers can undoubtedly continue to harvest high-yielding crops.

Use of wild desert plants and their cultivation is not a new practice. It has been common in many countries all over the world. In U.S.A., Mexico, India and many other countries, such plants have been cultivated over varied areas and produced considerable economic return. The wild medicinal plants growing in the desert region of Egypt can be a good source for cultivating vast areas in the desert with the least ecological consequences in addition to the conservation of such resource.

Conservation of Water:

— Desert plants have low water consumption. The wild medicinal plants, as other desert ones, are endowed with characteristics and adaptations making them drought resistant and/or drought tolerant.

— One can make use of seepage water along the margins of the farms and irrigation canals. The yield can be a reasonable cash crop for the farmers in the desert.

— The wild plants are able to tolerate the unavailability of continuous exogenous water supply for reasonable periods.

Sustainable Development

— Cultivation of wild plants do not introduce new weeds or other new pests to the ecosystem.

— Many wild plants do not need the use of pesticides. This is a privilege of plants cultivated under desert conditions, i.e. under almost their natural habitat conditions.

— Minimal ecological consequences for the agro-ecosystem o Minimal degradation, salinisation, soil erosion, waterlogging, etc.

Improvement of the economy of wasteland:

a) Environmental protection

— Dune stabilisation

— Wildlife habitat

— Biodiversity conservation

b) Economical improvement:

— Fill a gap in the domestic needs such as folk medicine and pharmaceutical industries.

— Potential for exports, especially pharmacoepial drug plants o Potential for creation of small industries in cutting, drying, grinding, extraction, packing, etc..

— Provides cash (crop) income for settlers in newly reclaimed land and desert areas.

Issues

Traditional and folklore medicine bequeathed from generation to generation is rich in domestic recipes and communal practice. Encompassing concepts and methods for the protection and restoration of health, traditional medicine has served as a fount of alternative medicine, new pharmaceuticals, and healthcare products. The best known examples of traditional medicine, differing in concept and protocol, are well-developed systems such as acupuncture and ayurvedic medicine that have been widely used to conserve human health in China and India.

Developed countries, in recent times, are turning to the use of traditional medicinal systems that involve the use of herbal drugs and remedies. About 1400 herbal preparations are used widely, according to a recent survey in Member States of the European Union. Herbal preparations are popular and are of significance in primary healthcare in Belgium, France, Germany and the Netherlands. Such popularity of healthcare plant-derived products has been traced to their increasing acceptance and use in the cosmetic industry as well as to increasing public costs in the daily maintenance of personal health and well being.

Examples of such beauty-oriented therapeuticals are skin tissue regenerators, anti-wrinkling agents and anti-age creams. Most dermaceuticals are derived from algal extracts that are rich in minerals and the vitamin B group. Skincare products such as skin creams, skin tonics, etc. derived from medicinal plants are grouped together as dermaceuticals. Also, amongst the poor, cures and drugs, derived from plants, constitute the main source of healthcare products.

Gorman drew attention to the power of Chinese folk medicinal potions in treating maladies from eczema and malaria to respiratory disorders. In the quest for new medicines to treat old and emergent diseases such as malaria and AIDS, attention is now being given to discovering the active ingredients encountered in the treasury of over 5,000 Chinese herbs, plants and roots that have been used routinely and traditionally. Quinghaosu and Chaihu are two such examples. Whereas the former, called artemisinin and obtained from Artemisia annua is expected to yield, in the coming millennium, a potent new class of antimalarials, the latter, obtained from Bupleurum chinense and used as a popular remedy for hepatitis is the focus of intense research by the Japanese pharmaceutical industry. More recently, the biochemistry of tianhuafen or cucumber is being studied in the USA to decipher the identity of compound Q, an extract used in China and credited with remedial and relief properties in AIDS sufferers.

Farmers and pastoralists in several countries use medicinal plants in the maintenance and conservation of the healthcare of livestock. Intestinal disorders in cows, in Mexico, are treated with herbal extracts of Polakowskia tacacco. Dietary supplements such as vitamin A in poultry feeds in Uganda are supplied through enrichments of amaranth (Amaranthus sp.). It is estimated that medicinal plants, for several centuries, have been widely used as a primary source of prevention and control of livestock diseases. In fact, interest of such use in the veterinary sector has resulted primarily from the increasing cost of livestock maintenance and the introduction of new technology in the production of veterinary medicines and vaccines.

Some of the researchers surveying the use of spice and their medicinal properties around the world, concluded that spices serve the adaptive purpose of reducing food-borne disease. In reviewing relevant texts ranging from the preservative properties of spices against food spoilage to the presence of antimicrobial substances that lay claim to the elimination of pathogenic organisms in food preparations, the case is made for a more objective analysis and study of the medicinal properties of spices in victu rather than in victo. A whole range of plant-derived dietary supplements, phytochemicals and pro-vitamins that assist in maintaining good health and combating disease are now being described as functional foods, nutriceuticals and nutraceuticals.

Despite the increasing use of medicinal plants, their future, seemingly, is being threatened by complacency concerning their conservation. Reserves of herbs and stocks of medicinal plants in developing countries are diminishing and in danger of extinction as a result of growing trade demands for cheaper healthcare products and new plant-based therapeutic markets in preference to more expensive target-specific drugs and biopharmaceuticals. Such concerns have stimulated positive legal and economic interest.

Issues concerning intellectual property rights, compensation for loss of finance-rich biodiversity resources, and the acquisition and safeguarding of traditional healthcare knowledge are no longer neglected. Bioprospecting of new drugs from medicinal plants and the exploitation of unprotected traditional knowledge in starting-up potentially new bioindustries are the focus of new monitoring measures. Indeed, programmes dealing with medicinal plant conservation, cultivation, community involvement and sustainable development being initiated elsewhere, could benefit immensely from the Chinese and Indian experiences.

Genetic biodiversity of traditional medicinal herbs and plants is continuously under the threat of extinction as a result of growth-exploitation, environment-unfriendly harvesting techniques, loss of growth habitats and unmonitored trade of medicinal plants. Medicinal herbs, possessing penile potency properties and anti-cancer principles are the focus of smuggling to import markets in Germany, France, Switzerland, Japan, the U.K., and the U.S.A. The best known example, in recent times, is that of tetu lakda. Commonly encountered in southern India and Sri Lanka, the herb is exploited as a source of anti-cancer drugs.

The industrial uses of medicinal plants are many. These range from traditional medicines, herbal teas, and health foods such as nutriceuticals to galenicals, phytopharmaceuticals and industrially produced pharmaceuticals. Furthermore, medicinal plants constitute a source of valuable foreign exchange for most developing countries, as they are a ready source of drugs such as quinine and reserpine; of galenicals like tinctures and of intermediates (e.g. diosgenin from Discorea sp.) in the production of semi-synthetic drugs. The world market for plant-derived chemicals—pharmaceuticals, fragrances, flavours, and colour ingredients, alone exceeds several billion dollars per year.

Classic examples of phytochemicals in biology and medicine include taxol, vincristine, vinblastine, colchicine as well as the Chinese antimalarial—artemisinin, and the Indian ayurdevic drug-forkolin. Trade in medicinal plants is growing in volume and in exports. It is estimated that the global trade in medicinal plants is US$800 million per year. The botanical market, inclusive of herbs and medicinal plants, in USA, is estimated, at retail, at approximately US$1.6 billion p.a. China with exports of over 120,000 tonnes p.a., and India with some 32,000 tonnes p.a. dominate the international markets. It is estimated that Europe, annually, imports about 400,000 t of medicinal plants with an average market value of US$ 1 billion from Africa and Asia.

A growing awareness of this new contributor to the foreign-exchange reserves of several national treasuries is beginning to emerge. To satisfy growing market demands, surveys are being conducted to unearth new plant sources of herbal remedies and medicines. In several industrialised societies, plant-derived prescription drugs constitute an element in the maintenance of health. Medicinal plants are an integral component of research developments in the pharmaceutical industry. Such research focuses on the isolation and direct use of active medicinal constituents, or on the development of semi-synthetic drugs, or still again on the active screening of natural products to yield synthetic pharmacologically-active compounds.

For example, in Germany over 1500 plant species encountered in some 200 families and 800 genera have been processed into medicinal products. In South Africa, likewise, some 500 species are commercialised trade products. Today, Bulgaria, Germany and Poland are recognised as major exporters of plant-based medicinal products.

The development and commercialisation of medicinal plant-based bioindustries in the developing countries is dependent upon the availability of facilities and information concerning upstream and downstream bioprocessing, extraction, purification, and marketing of the industrial potential of medicinal plants. Absence of such infrastructure compounded by lack of governmental interest and financial support restricts the evolution of traditional herbal extracts into authenticated market products. Furthermore the absence of modernised socio-economic and public healthcare systems reinforces reliance of rural and lower-income urban populations on the use of traditional medicinal herbs and plants as complementary aids to routine pharmaceutical market products.

The prophylactic and therapeutic effects of plant foods and extracts in reducing cardiovascular disease has been reviewed. Non-nutrient phytochemicals are increasingly being recognised as potential health promoters in reducing the risks of cardiovascular disease and atherosclerosis. Prominent herbs identified were Achillea millefolium (yarrow), Allium sativum (garlic), Convallaria majalis (lily of the valley), Cratageus laevigata (hawthorn), Cynara scolymus (globe artichoke), Gingko biloba (gingko) and Viburnum opulus (cramp bark).

Medicinal plants can make an important contribution to the WHO goal to ensure, by the year 2000, that all peoples, worldwide, will lead a sustainable socio-economic productive life. The Centre for Science and Technology of the Non-Aligned and other Developing Countries in India organised an international workshop on Tissue Culture of Economic Plants in April, 1994, as a means of using modern biotechnological techniques to nurture and conserve medicinal plants. In late 1997, the World Bank, within the framework of the Global Environmental Facility, provided a US$ 4.5 million grant for the Sri Lanka Conservation of Medicinal Plants Project which focuses on the conservation of medicinal plant populations, their habitats, and their sustainable use in Medicinal Plant Conservation Areas (MPCAs).

Inventories with emphasis on the management, research and conservation of rare and endangered species of medicinal plants are the main programmes at MPCAs at Ritigala, Naula, Rajawaka, Kanneliya, and Bibile. Aspects of policy and research concerning the cultivation of non-tropical and tropical medicinal plants and their genetic improvement; their conservation in botanical gardens; their storage in liquid nitrogen; their economic potential in international pharmaceutical trade; and their vulnerability to over-exploitation and extinction have been dealt with authoritatively.

Moreover, such concerns and issues are addressed through a variety of programme activities and projects conducted, and promoted by several international, regional, and non-governmental organisations. Recent and renewed interest in medicinal plants coupled to developments in information technology has fuelled an explosion in the range and content of electronic information concerning medicinal plants as a re-emergent health aid. Recently reviewed diverse sources of such information in traditional abstracting services as well as in a variety of online electronic databases. As a result of such developments, access to indigenous peoples and cultures concerning medicinal plants are greatly facilitated.

2

Plant-based Biopharmaceuticals

The term "biopharmaceutical" was originated in the 1980s, when a general consensus evolved that it represented a class of therapeutics produced by means of modern biotechnologies. Biopharmaceuticals, which are large molecules produced by living cells, are currently the mainstay products of the biotechnology industry.

Indeed, biologics such as Genentech's human growth factor somatropin or Amgen's recombinant erythropoietin (EPO) have shown that biopharmaceuticals can benefit a huge number of patients and also generate big profits for these companies at the same time.

Biopharmaceuticals can benefit a huge number of patients and also generate big profits for these companies at the same time. The single most lucrative product is EPO and combined sales of the recombinant EPO products "Procrit" and "Epogen" have reportedly surpassed the $6.5 billion mark. The 10 monoclonal antibodies on the market consume more than 75% of the industry's manufacturing capability.

And there are up to 60 more that are expected to reach the market in the next six or seven years. Altogether, there are about 1200 protein-based products in the pipeline with a 20% growth rate and the market for current and late stage is estimated to be US$42 billion in 2005 and even US$100 billion in 2010. But, there are obvious limitations of large-scale manufacturing resources and production capacities—and pharmaceutical companies are competing. To circumvent this capacity crunch, it is necessary to look into other technologies rather than the established ones, like, for example, Escherichia coli or CHO (Chinese Hamster Ovary) cell expression.

One solution to avoid these limitations could be the use of transgenic plants to express recombinant proteins at low cost, in GMP (Good Manufacturing Practice) quality greenhouses. Plants therefore provide an economically sound source of recombinant proteins, such as industrial enzymes, and biopharmaceuticals. Furthermore, using the existing infrastructure for crop cultivation, processing, and storage will reduce the amount of capital investment required for commercial production.

The active pharmaceutical compounds have been primarily small molecules, however. One of the most popular examples is aspirin (acetylsalicylic acid) to relieve pain and reduce fever. First isolated natural salicin (a chemical relative of the compound used to make aspirin) from white willow bark in 1829. Advances in genetic engineering are now allowing for the production of therapeutic proteins (as opposed to small molecules) in plant tissues.

Expression of recombinant proteins in plants has been well documented since the 1970s and has slowly gained credibility in the biotechnology industry and regulatory agencies. The first proof of concept has been the incorporation of insect and pest resistance into grains. For example, Bt corn contains genes from Bacillus thuringensis and is currently being grown commercially. Genetic engineering techniques are now available for the manipulation of almost all commercially valuable plants.

Easy transformation and cultivation make plants suitable for production of virtually any recombinant protein.

Plants have a number of advantages over microbial expression systems, but one of them is of outmost importance: they can produce eukaryotic proteins in their native form, as they are capable of carrying out post translational modifications required for the biological activity of many such proteins. These modifications can be acetylation, phosphorylation, and glycosylation, as well as others. Per se, there is no restriction to the kind of proteins that can be expressed in plants: vaccines (e.g. pertussis or tetanus toxins), serum proteins (e.g. albumin), growth factors (e.g. vascular endothelial growth factor (VEGF), erythropoietin), or enzymes (e.g. urokinase, glucose oxidase, or glucocerebrosidase).

However, enzymes sometimes have very complex cofactors, which are essential for their catalytic mode of action, but cannot be supplied bymost expression systems. This is why, for the expression of some enzymes, expression systems with special features and characteristics need to be developed. Another very important class of proteins is the antibodies (e.g. scFv, Fab, IgG, or IgA). More than 100 antibodies are currently used in clinical trials as therapeutics, drug delivery vehicles, in diagnostics and imaging, and in drug discovery research for both screening and validation of targets. Again, plants are considered as the system of choice for the production of antibodies (plantibodies) in bulk amounts at low costs.

Since the initial demonstration that transgenic tobacco (Nicotiana tabacum) is able to produce functional IgG1 from mouse, full-length antibodies, hybrid antibodies, antibody fragments (Fab), and single-chain variable fragments (scFv) have been expressed in higher plants for a number of purposes. These antibodies can serve in health care and medicinal applications, either directly by using the plant as a food ingredient or as a pharmaceutical or diagnostic reagent after purification from the plantmaterial. In addition, antibodiesmay improve plant performance, for example, by controlling plant disease or by modifying regulatory and metabolic pathways.

Plant Expression Systems

Chinese Hamster Ovary (CHO) cells are the most widely used technology in biomanufacturing because they are capable of expressing eukaryotic proteins (processing, folding, and posttranslational modifications) that cannot be provided by E. coli. A long track record exists for CHO cells, but unfortunately they bring some problems along when it comes to scaling up production.

Transport of oxygen (and other gases) and nutrients is critical for the fermentation process, as well as the fact that heat must diffuse evenly to all cultured cells. According to the Michaelis-Menten equation, the growth rate depends on the oxygen/nutrient supply; therefore, good mixing and aeration are a prerequisite for the biomanufacturing process and are usually achieved by different fermentation modes. But the laws of physics set strict limits on the size of bioreactors.

To compound the problem, regulators in the United States and Europe demand that drugs have to be produced for the market in the same system used to produce them for the final round of clinical trials, in order to guarantee bioequivalence (e.g. toxicity, bioavailability, pharmacokinetics, and pharmacodynamics) of the molecule. So, companies have to choose between launching a product manufactured at a smaller development facility or building larger, dedicated facilities for a drug that might never be approved.

Therefore, alternative technologies are used for the expression of biopharmaceuticals, some of them also at lower costs involved. One such alternative is the creation of transgenic animals ("pharming"), but this suffers from the disadvantage that it requires a long time to establish such animals. In addition to that, some of the human biopharmaceuticals could be detrimental to the mammal's health, when expressed in the mammary glands. This is why ethical debates sometimes arise from the use of transgenic mammals for production of biopharmaceuticals.

Although there are no ethical concerns involved with plants, there are societal ones that will be addressed later. Another expression system utilizes transgenic chicken. The eggs, from which the proteins are harvested, are natural protein-production systems. But production of transgenic birds is still several years behind transgenic mammal technology. Intensive animal housing constraints also make them more susceptible to disease.

In the light of development time, experience, costs, and ethical issues, plants are therefore the favoured technology, since such systems usually have short gene-to-protein times (weeks), some are already well established, and as mentioned before, the involved costs are comparatively low.

SWOT Analysis

The different expression systems regarding their strengths, weaknesses, opportunities, and threats (SWOT), the advantages of plants and their potential to circumvent the worldwide capacity limitations for protein production became quite obvious.

Comparison of transgenic animals, mammalian cell culture, plant expression systems, yeast, and bacteria shows certain advantages for each of the systems. In the order in which the systems were just mentioned, we can compare them in terms of their development time (speed).

Transgenic animals have the longest cycle time (18 months to develop a goat), followed by mammalian cell culture, plants, yeast, and bacteria (one day to transform E. coli).

If one looks at operating and capital costs, safety, and scalability, the data show that plants are beneficial: therefore, in the comparison, they are shown on the right-hand side already. But even for glycosylation, multimeric assembly and folding (where plants are not shown on the right-hand side, meaning other systems are advantageous), some plant expression systems are moving in that direction.

This system performs proper folding and assembly of even such complex proteins like the homodimeric VEGF. Even the sugar pattern could successfully be reengineered from plant to human like glycosylation. In addition to the potential of performing human glycosylation, plants also enjoy the distinct advantage of not harboring any pathogens, which are known to harm animal cells (as opposed to animal cell cultures and products), nor do the products contain any microbial toxins, TSE (Transmissible Spongiform Encephalopathies), prions, or oncogenic sequences.

In fact, humans are exposed to a large, constant dose of living plant viruses in the diet without any known effects/illnesses. Plant production of protein therapeutics also has advantages with regard to their scale and speed of production. Plants can be grown in ton quantities (using existing plant/crop technology, like commercial greenhouses), be extracted with industrial-scale equipment, and produce kilogram-size yields from a single plot of cultivation. These economies of scale are expected to reduce the cost of production of pure pharmaceutical-grade therapeutics by more than 2 orders of magnitude versus current bacterial fermentation or cell culture reactor systems.

Heterologous proteins were successfully produced in a number of plant expression systems with their manifold advantages, there are also obvious downsides. The main concerns of using plant expression systems are societal ones about environmental impacts, segregation risk, and contamination of the food chain. But these threats can be dealt with, using nonedible plants (nonfood, nonfeed), applying advanced containment technologies (GMP greenhouses, bioreactors) and avoiding open-field production. Owing to the obvious strengths of plant expression systems, there has been explosive growth in the number of start-up companies.

Since the 1990s, a number of promising plant expression systems have been developed, and in response to this blooming field big pharmaceutical companies have become more interested. Now, the plant expression field is ripe for strategic alliances, and, in fact, the last year has seen several major biotech companies begin partnerships with such plant companies.

Contingency Measures

For a number of reasons, including the knowledge base developed on genetically modifying its genome, industrial processes for extracting fractionated products and the potential for large-scale production, the preferred plant expression system has been corn. However, the use of corn touches on a potential risk: some environmental activist groups and trade associations are concerned about the effect on the environment and possible contamination of the food supply.

These issues are reflected in the regulatory guidelines and have been the driving force to investigate other plants as well. While many mature and larger companies have been working in this area for many years, there are a number of newcomers that are developing expertise as well. These smaller companies are reacting to the concerns by looking at the use of nonedible plants that can be readily raised in greenhouses.

All potential risks have to be assessed and contingency measures need to be established. Understanding the underlying issues is mandatory to make sophisticated decisions about the science and subsequently on the development of appropriate plant expression systems for production of biopharmaceuticals. Ongoing public fears from the food industry and the public, particularly in Europe could have spillover effects on plant-derived pharmaceuticals.

Mistakes and misunderstandings have already cost the genetically enhanced grain industry hundreds of millions of dollars. The only way to prevent plant expression systems from suffering the same dilemma is to provide the public with appropriate information on emerging discoveries and newly developed production systems for biopharmaceuticals.

Real and theoretical risks involve the spread of engineered genes into wild plants, animals, and bacteria (horizontal transmission). For example, if herbicide resistance was transmitted to weeds, or antibiotic resistance was to be transmitted to bacteria, superpathogens could result. If these genetic alterations were transmitted to their progeny (vertical transmission), an explosion of the pathogens could cause extensive harm.

An example of this occurred several years ago, when it was feared that pest-resistant genes had been transmitted from Bt corn to milkweed—leading to the widespread death of Monarch butterflies. Although this was eventually not found to be the case, the public outcry over the incident was a wake-up call to the possible dangers of transgenic food technology.

To avoid the same bad perception for biopharmaceuticals expressed in plants, there is the need for thorough risk assessment and contingency planning. One method is the employment of all feasible safety strategies to prevent spreading of engineered DNA (genetic drift), like a basic containment in a greenhouse environment.

Although no practical shelter can totally eradicate insect and rodent intrusion, this type of isolation is very effective for self-pollinators and those plants with small pollen dispersal patterns. The use of species-specific, fragile, or poorly transmissible viral vectors is another strategy. Tobacco mosaic virus (TMV), for example, usually only infects a tobacco host.

It requires an injury of the plant to gain entry and cause infection. Destruction of a field of TMV-transformed tobacco requires only plowing under or application of a herbicide. These factors prevent both horizontal and vertical transmission. In addition, there is no known incidence of plant viruses infecting animal or bacterial cells. Another approach is to avoid stable transgenic germlines and therefore most uses of transforming viruses do not involve the incorporation of genes into the plant cell nucleus.

By definition, it is almost impossible for these genes to be transmitted vertically through pollen or seed. The engineered protein product is produced only by the infected generation of plants. Another effective way to reduce the risk of genetic drift is the use of plants that do not reproduce without human aid. The modern corn plant cannot reproduce without cultivation and the purposeful planting of its seeds.

If a plant may sprout from grain, it still needs to survive the wintering-over process and gain access to the proper planting depth. This extinction process is so rapid, however, that the errant loss of an ear of corn is very unlikely to grow a new plant. Another very well-known example of self-limited reproduction is the modern banana. It propagates almost exclusively through vegetative cloning (i.e. via cuttings).

Pollination is the natural way for most plants to spread their genetic information, make up new plants, and to deliver their offspring in other locations. The use of plants with limited range of pollen dispersal and limited contact with compatible wild hosts therefore is also very effective to prevent genetic drift. Corn, for example, has pollen, which survives for only 10 to 30 min and, hence, has an effective fertilizing radius of less than 500 m.

In North America, it has no wild-type relatives with which it could cross-pollinate. In addition to being spatially isolated from nearby cornfields, transgenic corn can be temporally isolated by being planted at least 21 days earlier or 21 days later than the surrounding corn, to ensure that the fields are not producing flowers at the same time.

For soybeans, the situation is different, since they are virtually 100% self-fertilizers and can be planted in very close proximity to other plants without fear of horizontal spread. Another option is the design of transgenic plants that have only sterile pollen or—more or less only applicable for greenhouses—completely prevent cross-pollination by covering the individual plants. One public fear regards spreading antibiotic resistance from one (transgenic donor) plant to other wildtype plants or bacteria in the environment.

Although prokaryotic promoters for antibiotic resistance are sometimes used in the fabrication and selection of transgenic constructs, once a transgene has been stably incorporated into the plant genome, it is under the control of plant (eukaryotic) promoter elements. Hence, antibiotic-resistance genes are unable to pass from genetically altered plants into bacteria and remain functional.

Another common fear is the creation of a super bug. The chance of creating a supervirulent virus or bacterium from genetic engineering is unlikely, because the construction of expression cassettes from viral or bacterial genomes involves the removal of the majority of genes responsible for the normal function of these organisms. Even if a resultant organism is somewhat functional, it cannot compete for long in nature with normal, wild-type bacteria of the same species.

As one can see from the aforementioned safety strategies, considerable effort is put into the reduction of any potential risk from the transgenic plant for the environment. In general, the scientific risk can be kept at a minimum, if common sense is applied—in accordance that "Science is simply common sense at its best." For example, protein toxins (for vaccine production) should never be grown in food plants. Additionally, the following can be employed as a kind of risk management to prevent the inappropriate or unsafe use of genetically engineered plants:

— An easily recognised phenotypic characteristic can be coexpressed in an engineered product (e.g. tomatoes that contain a therapeutic protein can be selected to grow in a colourless variety of fruit).

— Protein expression can be induced only after harvesting or fruit ripening. For example, CropTech's inducible expression system in tobacco, MeGA-PharM, leads to very ef.cient induction upon leaf injury (harvest) and needs no chemical inducers. This system possesses a fast induction response and protein synthesis rate, and thus leads to high expression levels with no aged product in the .eld (no environmental damage accumulation).

— Potentially antigenic or immunomodulatory products can be induced to grow in, or not to grow in, a certain plant tissue (e.g. root, leaf/stem, seed, or pollen). In this way, for example, farmers can be protected from harmful airborne pollen or seed dusts.

— Although no absolute system can prevent vandalism or theft of the transgenic plants, a very effective, cheap solution has been used quietly for many years now in the United States. Plots of these modified plants are being grown with absolutely no indication that they are different from a routine crop.

In the Midwest, for example, finding a transgenic corn plot among the millions of acres of concurrently growing grain is virtually impossible. The only question here is, if this approach really helps facilitating a fair and an open discussion with the public. Asking the same question for the EU is not relevant: owing to labelling requirements, this approach would not be feasible, as, in general, it is much more difficult to perform open-field studies with transgenic plants.

Plant production of therapeutic proteins has many advantages over bacterial systems. One very important feature of plant cells is their capability of carrying out post translational modifications. Since they are eukaryotes (i.e. have a nucleus), plants produce proteins through an ER (endoplasmatic reticulum) pathway, adding sugar residues also to the protein—a process called glycosylation. These carbohydrates help determine the three-dimensional structures of proteins, which are inherently linked to their function and their efficacy as therapeutics.

This glycosylation also affects protein bioavailability and breakdown of the biopharmaceutical; for example, proteins lacking terminalsialic acid residues on their sugar groups are often targeted by the immune system and are rapidly degraded. The glycosylation process begins by targeting the protein to the ER. During translation of mRNA (messenger RNA) into protein, the ribosome is attached to the ER, and the nascent protein fed into the lumen of the ER as translation proceeds.

This glycosylation process continues into the Golgi apparatus, which sorts the new proteins, and distributes them to their final destinations in the cell. Bacteria lack this ability and therefore cannot be used to synthesise proteins that require glycosylation for activity. Although plants have a somewhat different system of protein glycosylation from mammalian cells, the differences usually prove not to be a problem.

Some proteins, however, require humanlike glycosylation—they must have specific sugar structures attached to the correct sites on the molecule to be maximally effective. Therefore, some efforts are being made in modifying host plants in such a way that they provide the protein with human glycosylation patterns.

Tobacco and Moss

To further elaborate on improving glycosylation and downstream processing, three interesting plant expression systems. All systems share the advantage of utilizing nonedible plants (nonfood and nonfeed) and can be kept in either a greenhouse or a fermenter to avoid any segregation risk. Another obvious advantage is secretion of the protein into the medium so that no grinding or extraction is required. This is very important in light of downstream processing: protein purification is often as expensive as the biomanufacturing and should never be underestimated in the total COGS equation.

Harnessing Tobacco Roots to Secrete Proteins

Phytomedics uses tobacco plants as an expression system for biopharmaceuticals. Besides the advantage of being well characterised and used in agriculture for some time, tobacco has a stable genetic system, provides highdensity tissue (high protein production), needs only simple medium, and can be kept in a greenhouse.

Optimised antibody expression can be rapidly verified using transient expression assays (short development time) in the plants before creation of transgenic suspension cells or stable plant lines (longer development time). Different vector systems, harboring targeting signals for subcellular compartments, are constructed in parallel and used for transient expression. Applying this screening approach, high expressing cell lines can rapidly be identified.

High Protein Yields Utilizing Viral Transfection ICON Genetics (Halle, Germany) has developed a protein-production system that relies on rapid multiplication of viral vectors in an infected tobacco plant. Viral transfection systems offer a number of advantages, such as very rapid (1 to 2 week) expression time, possibility of generating initial milligram quantities within weeks, high expression levels, and so on.

However, the existing viral vectors, such as TMV-based vectors used by, for example, Large Scale Biology Corp for production of single-chain antibodies for treatment of non-Hodgkin lymphoma, had numerous shortcomings, such as inability to express genes larger than 1 kb, inability to coexpress two or more proteins (a prerequisite for production of monoclonal antibodies, because they consist of the light and heavy chains, which are expressed independently and are subsequently assembled), low expression level in systemically infected leaves, and so on.

ICON has solved many of these problems by designing a process that starts with an assembly of one or more viral vectors inside a plant after treating the leaves with agrobacteria, which deliver the necessary viral vector components. ICON's proviral vectors provide advantages of fast and high-yield amplification processes in a plant cell, simple and inexpensive assembly of expression cassettes in planta, and full control of the process.

The robustness of highly standardised protocols allows the use of inherently the same safe protocols for both laboratory-scale as well as industrial production processes. In this system, the plant is modified transiently rather than genetically and reaches the speed and yield of microbial systems while enjoying post translational capabilities of plant cells.

De-and reconstructing of the virus adds some safety features and also increases efficiency. There is no physiology conflict, because the growth phase is separated from the production phase, so that no competition occurs for nutrients and other components required for growth and also for expression of the biopharmaceutical at the same time.

This transfection-based platform allows the production of proteins in a plant host at a cost of US$1 to 10 per gram of crude protein. The platform is essentially free from limitations (gene insert size limit, inability to express more than one gene) of current viral vector-based platforms. The expression levels reach 5 g per kilogram of fresh leaf tissue (or some 50% of total cellular protein!) in 5 to 14 days after inoculation.

Since the virus process (in addition to super high production of its own proteins, including the protein of interest) leads to the shutoff of the other cellular protein synthesis, the amount of protein of interest in the initial extract is extremely high. It thus results in reduced costs of downstream processing. Milligram quantities can be produced within two weeks, gram quantities in 4 to 6 months, and the production system is inherently scalable. Anumber of high-value proteins have been successfully expressed, including antibodies, antigens, interferons, hormones, and enzymes .

Simple Moss Performs Complex Glycosylation

An innovative production system for human proteins. The system produces pharmacologically active proteins in a bioreactor, utilizing a moss (Physcomitrella patens) cell culture system with unique properties. It was stated before that posttranslational modifications for some proteins are crucial to gain complete pharmacological activity.

Since moss is the only known plant system that shows a high frequency of homologous recombination, this is a highly attractive tool for production strain design. By establishing stable integration of foreign genes (gene knockout and new transgene insertion) into the plant genome, it can be programmed to produce proteins with modified glycosylation patterns that are identical to animal cells.

The moss is photoautotrophic and therefore only requires simple media for growth, which consist essentially of water and minerals. This reduces costs and also accounts for signi.cantly lower infectious and contamination risks, but in addition to this, the system has some more advantages:

- The transient system allows production of quantities for a feasibility study within weeks—production of a stable expression strain takes 4 to 6 months.
- On the basis of transient expression data, the yield of stable production lines is expected to reach 30 mg L^{-1} per day. This corresponds to the yield of a typical fed-batch culture over 20 days of 600 mg L^{-1}.

— Bacterial fermentation usually requires addition of antibiotics (serving as selection marker and to avoid loss of the expression vector). Formoss cultivation, no antibiotics are needed—this avoids the risk of traces of antibiotics having a signi.cant allergenic potential in the finished product.

— Genetic stability is provided by the fact that the moss is grown in small plant fragments and not as protoplasts or tissue cultures avoiding somaclonal variation.

— As a contained system, the moss bioreactor can be standardised and validated according to GMP standards mandatory in the pharmaceutical industry.

— Excretion into the simple medium is anothermajor feature of the moss bioreactor, which greatly facilitates downstream processing.

The first step to get humanlike glycosylation in plants is to eliminate the plant glycosylation, for example, the attachment of β-1-2-linked xylosyl and α-1-3-linked fucosyl sugars to the protein, because these two residues have allergenic potential. Greenovation was able to knockout the relevant glycosylation enzymes xylosyl transferase and fucosyl transferase, which was confirmed by RT-PCR (reverse transcriptase PCR).

And indeed, xylosyl and fucosyl residues were completely removed from the glycosylation pattern of the expressed protein as confirmed by MALDI-TOF (matrix assisted laser desorption ionization time of fiight) mass spectroscopy analysis. A very challenging protein to express is VEGF because this homodimer consists of two identical monomers linked via a disulfide bond. To produce VEGF in an active form, the following need to be provided:

— Monomers need to be expressed to the right level.
— Monomers need to be correctly folded.
— Homodimer needs to be correctly assembled and linked via a disulfide bond.
— Complex protein needs to be secreted in its active form.

Other Systems Used for Plant Expression

Several different plants have been used for the expression of proteins in plants. All these systems have certain advantages regarding edibility, growth rate, scalability, gene-to-protein time, yield, downstream processing, ease of use, and so on. A selection of different expression systems is listed:

Alfalfa	Ethiopian mustard	Potatoes
Arabidopsis	Lemna	Rice
Banana	Maize	Soybean
Cauliflower	Moss	Tomatoes
Corn	Oilseeds	Wheat

Some of these systems have been used for research on the basis of their ease of transformation, well-known characterisation, and ease to work with. However, they are not necessarily appropriate for commercial production. Which crop is ultimately used for full-scale commercial production will depend on a number of factors including

— time to develop an appropriate system (gene-to-protein);
— section of the plant expressing the product/possible secretion;
— cost and potential waste products from extraction;
— aged product/ease of storage;

— long-term stability of the storage tissue;
— quantities of protein needed (scale of production).

Depending on the genetic complexity and ease of manipulation, the development time to produce an appropriate transgenic plant for milligram production of the desired protein can vary from 10 to 12 months in corn as compared to only weeks in moss. Estimates for full GMP production in corn are 30 to 36 months and approximately 12 months for moss.

Expression of the protein in various tissues of the plant can result in a great variationin yield. Expression in the seed can often lead to higher yields than in the leafy portion of the plant. This is another explanation for the high interest in using corn, which has a relatively high seed-to-leaf ratio.

Extraction from leaf can be costly as it contains a high percentage of water, which could result in unavoidable proteolysis during the process. Proteins stored in seeds can be desiccated and remain intact for long periods of time. The purification and extraction of the protein is likely to be done by adaptations of current processes for the extraction and/or fractionation.

For these reasons, it is anticipated that large-scale commercial production of recombinant proteins will involve grain and oilseed crops such as maize, rice, wheat, and soybeans. In general, the use of smaller plants that can be grown in greenhouses is an effective way of producing the biopharmaceuticals and alleviating concerns from environmental activist groups that the transgenic plant might be harmful to the environment (food chain, segregation risk, genetic drift, etc.).

Analytical Characterisation

Validated bioanalytical assays are essential and have to

be developed to characterise the biopharmaceuticals during the production process (e.g. in-process control) and to release the final product for use as a drug in humans. These assays are applied to determine characteristics such as purity/impurities, identity, quantity, stability, specificity, and potency of the recombinant protein during drug development.

Since the very diverse functions of different proteins heavily depend on their structure, one very valuable parameter in protein characterisation is the elucidation of their three-dimensional structure. Although over the last couple of years a lot of effort was put into a method for improving the elucidation of protein structures, it is still very time consuming to solve the 3-D structure of larger proteins.

This is why despite the high degree of information that can be obtained from the protein structure, this approach cannot be applied on a routine basis. Therefore, tremendous efforts are put into the development of other assays to guarantee that a potent biopharmaceutical drug is indeed ready for use in humans.

3

Identification of Bioactive Compounds in Plants

The biological diversity of our world is great. In some areas diversity may be more valuable in its natural state than when used for pasture or timber. For example, one highly valued marketable commodity of tropical areas is medicinal products. At the present time, half the drugs on the market are derived from natural sources and 47 marketed drugs have been derived from 39 tropical forest plants. Clearly, bioactive molecules from botanicals can continue to be derived from the tropics.

Methods to identify medicinal plant leads from tropical areas include random screening, taxonomic collecting (sampling by botanical family), or ethnobotanical collecting. It has been shown that ethnobotanically-derived compounds have greater activity than compounds derived from random screening and therefore a greater potential for product development.

Many issues have caused an erosion of the tropical regions of our planet, but for many years only the biological factors associated with this loss have received investigation. Recently, it has been recognised that areas of great biological diversity overlap with those of cultural diversity; when either is disturbed the other is compromised. Some of the researchers established that the conservation of plants alone was inadequate to maintain an ecosystem because humans are a critical component. Plants are nurtured and manipulated by their human co-inhabitants and only when both are considered as an integral functional group can preservation and conscientious use of species occur.

Ethnobotany

Ethnobotany is a multidisciplinary science defined as the interaction between plants and people. The relationship between plants and human cultures is not limited to the use of plants for food, clothing, and shelter but also includes their use for religious ceremonies, ornamentation, and health care. In the past, ethnobotanical research was predominately a survey of the plants used by villagers. A trained botanist identified the plants and recorded their uses.

Sometimes an anthropologist was present to translate the disease descriptions, but rarely was a physician available to identify the disease. The results generated a list of plants and their uses which was published in a professional journal, usually in the country of the scientist. Nothing was communicated or returned to the cultural group in exchange for their participation in the survey, nor was any environmental or cultural status or concerns included in the survey.

Basic quantitative and experimental ethnobotany includes basic documentation, quantitative evaluation of use and management, and experimental assessment. Today, ethnobotanical surveys include applied projects that have the potential to ameliorate poverty levels of these people, allowing them to make more educated decisions about their future directions. These new approaches enhance the quality of the science, provide compensation for the cultural groups, and take into account environmental concerns. This modern approach is based on an interdisciplinary team usually composed of an ethnobotanist, an anthropologist, an ecologist, and a physician. Some of these team members are in-country colleagues who have arranged the details of the expedition as well as the contractual agreements for reciprocal programmes of the village or community.

Ethnobotanical Expedition Organisation

The initial steps to this approach are critical. Any errors will jeopardise the entire project. To aggressively enter a community or even a country and take out the information is rarely a successful process. However, abiding by the in-country federal requirements will support the goals of a long-term, mutually productive relationship. The negotiations can be done through a trusted colleague, either a person who has worked within the country and is familiar with these procedures or an in-country person. All permits and permissions must be in order prior to the expedition. This process can taken months or years, but regardless of the time period, must be done properly.

Many countries are limiting their genetic resources from scientists because of unhappy past experiences and are slowly devising new guidelines. Some, such as the Philippines, are initiating federal legislation which incorporates reciprocity while most others negotiate on an individual basis. Prior to the expedition, the in-country collaborator can communicate with the village to find out if they have any immediate needs. For example, a five-member team entering a small village must either provide its own food or shelter or provide funds for the villagers to acquire these things. Sensitivity to the community's needs will lay the groundwork for a trusting relationship.

The process should be considered as the normal good manners of invited guests. On a scientific level a sincere relationship is needed to ascertain the real data. A superficial personal relationship will yield a superficial scientific relationship. Many plants are used in village pharmacopoeias, but only a few powerful ones will make it as pharmaceuticals or powerful dietary supplements. When a research team arrives at the village a customary welcoming ceremony should occur. This is when permission to work with the healers is requested from the village leader or chief. It is most appropriate at this time to demonstrate your support by offering reciprocity for the information you are about to receive.

Reciprocity can be clean water systems, books for their schools, health professionals to visit on a regular basis, or any other programme they request. The key here is that it be their request. Most of these requests are not exorbitant, certainly not in excess of $5,000, but this is in addition to payment for the herbs you will be collecting. Be aware of the cultural requirements for payment of the plant collections. Ask your in-country liaison because there are some places where payments are unacceptable and initiate divisiveness between community members.

How the ethnobotanical information is gathered is often a pre-planned technique of the anthropologist or ethnobotanist. The technique depends on whether you want to concentrate on particular disease categories or a general survey, have time for just an interview, or can participate in the process for several months. Using signs and symptoms to describe the disease allows for an equal exchange of information. Titles and names can be misleading and unknown. Some native people are often eager to be helpful and may respond positively even if the answer is incorrect. Visual aids are helpful vehicles.

As the healers identify the plants they use to treat specific diseases, data is recorded, the plants are collected, and voucher specimens are taken. Not all expeditions collect plants, but vouchers are always taken and numbered correlations can be made to the collections. A minimum of one of the collected vouchers needs to be left within the country, another archived at an herbarium for positive identification, and the final one stored under appropriate conditions in the researcher's laboratory.

The recording of detailed information during the expedition is crucial for isolating the active molecule and obtaining reliable and reproducible collections for a potential product. No detail is expendable. All the data is entered into a database for future and continual use and returned to all collaborators. After the plants have been identified to genus, and hopefully species, it is extracted and tested biologically for activity. The critical path is to include the ethnobotanical data into these laboratory processes. The natives are the ethnobotanical technicians and translation of their technical knowledge is required for the discovery of ethnobotanically derived medicines.

If there is a separation of the field data from the chemistry and biological laboratory assays, the ethnobotanically derived molecule may never be found, or worse, activity could be null. From this point on the process involves chemical and biological assays to isolate the active molecule. This can take from one to nine months or more depending upon the complexity of the molecule and the efficiency and technical competence of the research team. During this time you may need to be acquiring more of the raw botanical material. This allows time to collect more data and compare shipments.

When isolation and identification of the bioactive molecule is completed and activity is demonstrated, synthesis still may be infeasible or impractical, necessitating further research. Plants have evolved wondrous systems to protect themselves, and it is these "secondary metabolites" that provide flavors and healing substances. However, many plant species have similar metabolic pathways. Running searches to find plants which contain the greatest amount of the same active compound may offer you a choice of species to work with. In some cases, this is very desirable because the plant may be endangered or difficult to import from the country in which it was first found. In these cases the compensation package must reflect these situations.

Sustainable Crop Production

If you are to acquire more material of a plant already researched, then the challenge begins. If the quality of science was high in your original fieldwork then you have all the details you need to expand the horticultural aspects of the project. If not, collect the missing data on the return to the field. This new data may not have been obvious to the healers or yourself before, yet is important at this stage of the project's development. People have different concepts of time and business so these differences need to be taken into consideration in your scientific planning.

At this point, research funds are needed to determine the factors that may enhance the yield of the bioactive molecule. One needs to speak with the healers and understand how, when, and where they harvest, details about drying, and any other particulars about the plant's collection and use. The subtleties are important. We assume or forget that most native peoples in the tropics are excellent managers of their natural resources and the best approach may be to observe and integrate their traditional practices into your sustainable programme.

Additional studies on distribution and density surveys, soil sampling, and multiple plant part sampling are all needed parameters within the design of an ecologically productive programme. A less obvious goal for most agriculturists is a verification of a potential market for this commodity in-country. Many of the plants being investigated may not yield the "pharmaceutical magical bullet" that is desired and having alternative uses such as dietary supplements may offer your collaborators a viable commodity if your goals change.

Regardless of the product's end point, the ethnobotanical process can still enhance cultural values and this can have a long-term consequence. This occurs by expanding markets, initiating market economies for the community, and demonstrating to the youth of the community the validity of the elder's plant knowledge. Several options exist to proceed once the raw data about the plant is compiled. Extractive reserves provide forest dwelling peoples an ecologically managed decentralised system of collection. The indigenous groups or communities, if adequate lands are made available, can grow or actively manage economically valuable plant populations within this reserve.

Land can also be dedicated as an ecological buffer zone and comparative study plots can be implemented. These plots would demonstrate if the collections were sustainable by comparing the populations in the buffer preserved zone to the actively managed area. The effect of increasing or decreasing a specific plant's density and diversity in secondary forests will be visible and cultural methods that have little impact on the forest can be designed from the data.

Another approach is to work with individual land owners to grow or manage their lands to provide the desired crop. Working with one person who has acquired land allows for direct and responsive communication. Compensation requirements are simplified. They include paying land and community taxes, require participation in community functions, and direct payment to individuals for services or products rendered. The employment of the local community members offers physical protection for the land and often others begin to request participation onto their parcels. The pride and knowledge this creates will assist you in protecting and developing the land, crop, and future product. Another approach is to work within a community to provide adequate raw botanicals. Once the community has been identified, an all inclusive meeting needs to be convened through the governing body.

Culturally sensitive and environmentally sensitive programmes are required to successfully acquire data from primitive tropical areas. Valid approaches will become more evident as more collaborative attempts are completed. However, at present, there are not enough data to know which programmes are environmentally and socially appropriate. Different programmes that are species specific may be required for sustainable production. Very little is known at present on how to even define sustainability. However, we now know that there is a potential for many natural products and that there are many communities who are eager to open their lives to market economies to provide more opportunities for themselves.

Ethnobotanical expeditions can be conducted anywhere that contacts are available and participants agree to cooperate. However, ethnobotanical collecting is a multidisciplinary effort that requires sensitivity to both land and people. The discovery and exploitation of natural products must be a shared programme for maximum success. Agricultural programmes have other needs and there are many complex decisions that must be analysed before ascertaining the most appropriate and rewarding approach.

Berberis Lyceum Royle Justicia Adhatodal

Berberis lyceum is locally known as simbuli or simbulu

belonging to family Berberidaceae. It is about 4-6 feet in height with thorny branches. The leaves are somewhat obviate, with ciliated teeth on their margins. The flowers are drooping racemes, with yellow petals. The berries (fruit) grow in loose bunches. Recently, a study was conducted by some researchers to find out the bioactive compounds in Berberis Lyceum.

In the study, Berberis lyceum was valued mainly for its fruits and roots, which contain alkaloids like berberine and plamitine. These alkaloids are effective against eye diseases, febrifuge, and piles. Whereas, an extract made from its roots (known as 'rasaunt') which is being used against many infections including eye's disorders. Whereas in some areas of India and Pakistan fruits are mostly used as a tonic against liver and heart diseases. Furthermore it showed antihistaminic activity, also possesses stomachic, astringent, antipyretic and diaphoretic properties.

Justicia adhatoda is one of the most important specie and dominant vegetation of hilly areas of Rawalpindi, Islamabad and extended up to NWFP. It belongs to family Acanthaceae, subclass Asteridae and specie Adhatoda. It is evergreen, gregarious shrub 3-6 m long, large leaves lanceolate 10-20 by 4-8 cm.Whereas flowers are white or purple in short, dense auxiliary penduncullate.

Chemical compounds found in leaves and roots of this plant includes essential oils, fats, resins, sugar, gum, amino acids, proteins and vitamin-C etc. The medicinal properties of Adhatoda vasica Nees are well known in India and several other countries for many years. The leaves contained an essential oil and the alkaloids quinazoline, vasicine, vasicinone and deoxyvasicine. The roots contained vasicinolone, vasicol, peganine and 2'-hydroxy-4-glucosyl-oxychalcone. The flowers contained -D-glucoside, kaempferol and its glucosides, as well as the bioflavonoid, namely quercetin.

The leaves are mostly used in the treatment of respiratory disorders in Ayurveda. The alkaloids, vasicine and vasicinone present in the leaves, possess respiratory stimulant activity. Whereas, vasicine, at low concentrations, induced bronchodilation and relaxation of the tracheal muscle. However, at high concentrations, vasicine offered significant protection against histamine-induced bronchospasm in guinea pigs. Vasicinone, the auto-oxidation product of vasicine has been reported to cause bronchodilatory effects both in vitro and in vivo.

Both roots and fruits samples were analyzed for protein, carbohydrate, lipid, vitamins, and fibers. Sodium, Potassium, Calcium, phosphorus.Sulphur, Iron and Zinc by routine chemical analysis. Whereas alkaloids of these valuable plants species were separated by chemical extraction methods followed by Column and thin layer chromatography.

In order to extract and purifying alkaloids from roots, leaves and fruits samples, following procedure were adopted.

Fifty grams (each of roots, fruits and leaves) samples were soaked in the ethanol (80%) for 24 hours and filtered. The ethanol was evaporated and half volume of NaOH (3-4%) was added. The pH of the mixture was adjusted to 10 with NaOH. The mixture was run through a column using silica gel to separate the alkaloids through column chromatography, those were further identified on thin layer chromatography using reference standards.

The concentration level of these alkaloids was determined with the help of spectrophotometer at 650 nm and that was compared with standard alkaloid compounds. Finally the PH of alkaloids were obtained and were compared with standard alkaloids.

Structures of Alkaloids

Results of biochemical compounds found in roots, leaves and fruits of Berberis lyceum and Justicia adhatoda is given in tables 1-5 whereas comparison of these Bio active compounds are given in Figure 1 and 2.

Higher concentration of alkaloids was found in roots as compared to the fruits. Furthermore, high concentration of proteins (4.5 %), fat (2.6 %), fiber (2.5%),sodium (1.5%) calcium (2.2%), sulphur (0.2%), iron (0.3% zinc (0.3%), palmitine (3.1%) and berberine (4.5% were present in the roots. However, the level of these chemicals was low in fruits except sugar (4.5 %), and vitamin C (0.8%) was high in fruits as compared to roots (Table 1, 2).

Table 1: Analysis of Bioactive compounds from roots of Berberis lyceum.

Constituent	Percentage	Constituent	Percentage
Dry matter	61.2	Calcium	2.2
Moisture	20.5	Sodium	1.5
Protein	4.5	Sulphur	0.2
Fat	2.6	Iron	0.3
Sugar	3.5	Zinc	0.2
Fiber	2.5	Berberine	4.5
Palmatine	3.1	Vitamin C	0.3

Table 2. Analysis of bioactive compounds from fruits of Berberis lyceum.

Constituent	Percentage	Constituent	Percentage
Dry matter	62.5	Calcium	1.8
Moisture	12.5	Sodium	0.6
Protein	2.5	Sulphur	0.1
Fat	1.8	Iron	0.2
Sugar	4.5	Zinc	0.8
Fiber	1.5	Berberine	2.9

Table 3: Analysis of Bioactive compounds from roots of Justicia adhatoda.

Constituent	Percentage	Constituent	Percentage
Dry matter	66.4	Calcium	3.1
Moisture	24.6	Sodium	2.4
Protein	8.5	Sulphur	1.2
Fat	2.5	Iron	0.7
Sugar	2.6	Zinc	0.5
Fiber	5.2	Berberine	0.3
Vasicine	7.5	Vitamin C	5.2

Table 4: Analysis of Bioactive compounds from leaves of Justicia adhatoda.

Constituent	Percentage	Constituent	Percentage
Dry matter	50.4	Calcium	1.5
Moisture	15.3	Sodium	1.4
Protein	6.5	Sulphur	1.3
Fat	1.6	Iron	1.2
Sugar	16.4	Zinc	0.6
Fiber	6.4	Vasicinone	3.5
Vasicine	4.5	Vitamin C	1.5

Table 5: Spectrophotometric analysis of various alkaloids at 470nm and their PH values.

Alkaloids	Concenteration	PH
1	0.724	7.8
2	0.668	7.9
3	0.716	7.7
4	0.163	6.9
5	0.113	7.0
6	0.097	6.9
7	0.58	7.2
8	0.51	6.7
9	0.95	7.6

The pH values and concentration level (mg/l) of various bioactive compounds (Alkaloids) are given in table

5.Which shows that bioactive compounds observed in higher amount in these valuable plants and could be used against various infections and diseases.

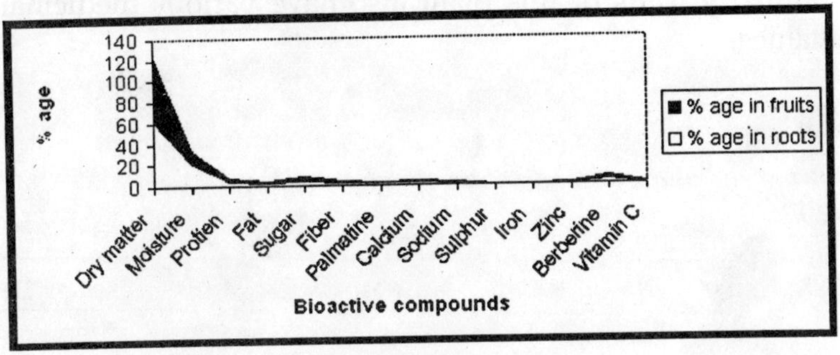

Figure 1: Comparison of bioactive compounds in roots and fruits of Berberis lyceum.

It was observed that roots of Justicia adhatoda contained higher concentration of protein fat and alkaloids like vasicine and vasicinone. The leaves of Justicia adhatoda contained higher concentration of sugar and vitamin C. It was observed that roots, leaves and fruit of both plant species contained higher concentrations of chemicals those can be used against various disorders in human population.

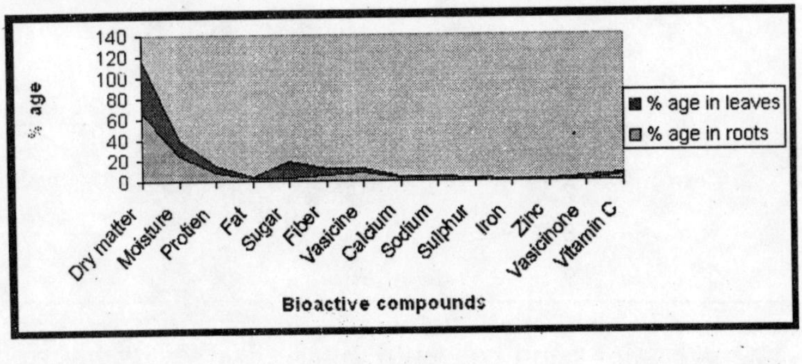

Figure 2: Comparison of bioactive compounds in roots and leaves of Justicia adhatoda.

The extract of roots and leaves of Justicia adhatoda are commonly used by rural population against diabetes, cough and certain liver disorders. The roots of Berberis lyceum are commonly used by people for their body pain to repair cut, wounds and also against high grade fever. Similarly fruits of this plant also have various medicinal values.

4

Plant-based Antimicrobials

Plants produce a diverse range of bioactive molecules, making them a rich source of different types of medicines. Higher plants, as sources of medicinal compounds, have continued to play a dominant role in the maintenance of human health since ancient times. Over 50% of all modern clinical drugs are of natural product origin and natural products play an important role in drug development programmess in the pharmaceutical industry.

There has been a revival of interest in herbal medicines. This is due to increased awareness of the limited ability of synthetic pharmaceutical products to control major diseases and the need to discover new molecular structures as lead compounds from the plant kingdom. Plants are the basic source of knowledge of modern medicine. The basic molecular and active structures for synthetic fields are provided by rich natural sources. This burgeoning worldwide interest in medicinal plants reflects a recognition of the validity of many traditional claims regarding the value of natural products in health care.

The relatively lower incidence of adverse reactions to plant preparations compared to modern conventional pharmaceuticals, coupled with their reduced cost, is encouraging both the consuming public and national health care institutions to consider plant medicines as alternatives to synthetic drugs. Plants with possible antimicrobial activity should be tested against an appropriate microbial model to confirm the activity and to ascertain the parameters associated with it. The effects of plant extracts on bacteria have been studied by a very large number of researchers in different parts of the world. Much work has been done on ethnomedicinal plants in India.

Interest in a large number of traditional natural products has increased. It has been suggested that aqueous and ethanolic extracts from plants used in allopathic medicine are potential sources of antiviral, antitumoral and antimicrobial agents. The selection of crude plant extracts for screening programmess has the potential of being more successful in initial steps than the screening of pure compounds isolated from natural products.

Plants have forever been a catalyst for our healing. In order to halt the trend of increased emerging and resistant infectious disease, it will require a multi-pronged approach that includes the development of new drugs. Using plants as the inspiration for new drugs provides an infusion of novel compounds or substances for healing disease. Evaluating plants from the traditional system of medicine, provides us with clues as to how these plants can be used in the treatment of disease.

Infectious diseases account for approximately one-half of all deaths in tropical countries. In industrialised nations, despite the progress made in the understanding of microbiology and their control, incidents of epidemics due to drug resistant microorganisms and the emergence of hitherto unknown disease-causing microbes, pose enormous public health concerns. Historically, plants have provided a good source of antiinfective agents; emetine, quinine, and berberine remain highly effective instruments in the fight against microbial infections. Phytomedicines derived from plants have shown great promise in the treatment of intractable infectious diseases including opportunistic AIDS infections.

Plants containing protoberberines and related alkaloids, picralima-type indole alkaloids and garcinia biflavonones used in traditional system of medicine, have been found to be active against a wide variety of micro-organisms. The profile of known drugs like Hydrastis canadensis (goldenseal), Garcinia kola (bitter kola), Polygonum sp., Aframomum melegueta (grains of paradise) will be used to illustrate the enormous potential of antiinfective agents from higher plants. Newer drugs such as Xylopia aethiopica, Araliopsis tabouensis, Cryptolepis sanguinolenta, Chasmanthera dependens and Nauclea species will be reviewed.

World wide, infectious disease is the number one cause of death accounting for approximately one-half of all deaths in tropical countries. Perhaps it is not surprising to see these statistics in developing nations, but what may be remarkable is that infectious disease mortality rates are actually increasing in developed countries. The increases are attributed to increases in respiratory tract infections and HIV/AIDS. Other contributing factors are an increase in antibiotic resistance in nosicomial and community acquired infections.

Furthermore, the most dramatic increases are occurring in the 25-44 ear old age group. These negative health trends call for a renewed interest in infectious disease in the medical and public health communities and renewed strategies on treatment and prevention. Proposed solutions are outlined as a multi-pronged approach that includes: prevention, (such as vaccination); improved monitoring; and the development of new treatments. It is this last solution that would encompass the development of new antimicrobials.

Historically, plants have provided a source of inspiration for novel drug compounds, as plant derived medicines have made large contributions to human health and well-being. Their role is two fold in the development of new drugs: (1) they may become the base for the development of a medicine, a natural blueprint for the development of new drugs, or; (2) a phytomedicine to be used for the treatment of disease. There are numerous illustrations of plant derived drugs. Some selected examples, including those classified as antiinfective, are presented below.

The isoquinoline alkaloid emetine obtained from the underground part of Cephaelis ipecacuanha, and related species, has been used for many years as and amoebicidal drug as well as for the treatment of abscesses due to the spread of Escherichia histolytica infections. Another important drug of plant origin with a long history of use, is quinine. This alkaloid occurs naturally in the bark of Cinchona tree. Apart from its continued usefulness in the treatment of malaria, it can be also used to relieve nocturnal leg cramps.

Currently, the widely prescribed drugs are analogs of quinine such as chloroquine. Some strains of malarial parasites have become resistant to the quinines, therefore antimalarial drugs with novel mode of action are required. Similarly, higher plants have made important contributions in the areas beyond antiinfectives, such as cancer therapies. Other cancer therapeutic agents include taxol, homoharringtonine and several derivatives of camptothein. For example, a well-known benzylisoquinoline alkaliod, papaverine, has been shown to have a potent inhibitory effect on the replication of several viruses including cytomegalovirus, measles and HIV.

Most recently, three new atropisomeric naphthylisoquinoline alkaloid dimers, michellamines A, B, and C were isolated from a newly described species tropical liana Ancistrocladus korupensis from the rainforest of Cameroon. The three compounds showed potential anti-HIV with michellamine B being the most potent and abundant member of the series. These compounds were capable of complete inhibition of the cytopathic effects of HIV-1 and HIV-2 on human lymphoblastoid target cell in vitro.

Phytomedicines Development

The first generation of plant drugs were usually simple botanicals employed in more or less their crude form. Several effective medicines used in their natural state such as cinchona, opium, belladonna and aloe were selected as therapeutics agents based on empirical evidence of their clinical application by traditional societies from different parts of the world. Following the industrial revolution, a second generation of plant based drugs emerged based on scientific processing of the plant extracts to isolate "their active constituents."

The second-generation phytopharmaceutical agents were pure molecules and some of the compounds were even more pharmacologically active than their synthetic counterparts. Notable examples were quinine from Cinchona, reserpine from Rauvolfia, and more recently taxol from Taxus species. These compounds differed from the synthetic therapeutic agents only in their origin. They followed the same method of development and evaluation as other pharmaceutical agents.

The sequence for development of pharmaceuticals usually begins with the identification of active lead molecules, detailed biological assays, and formulation of dosage forms in that order, and followed by several phases of clinical studies designed to established safety, efficacy and pharmacokinetic profile of the new drug. Possible interaction with food and other medications may be discerned from the clinical trials.

In the development of "Third Generation" phytotherapeutic agents a top-bottom approach is usually adopted. This consists of first conducting a clinical evaluation of the treatment modalities and therapy as administered by traditional doctors or as used by the community as folk medicine. This evaluation is then followed by acute and chronic toxicity studies in animals. Studies should, when applicable, include cytotoxicity studies. It is only if the substance has an acceptable safety index would it be necessary to conduct detailed pharmacological/ biochemical studies.

Formulation and trial production of the dosage forms are structured to mimic the traditional use of the herb. The stability of the finished product is given careful attention during the formulation of the final dosage form. This is a unique blend of the empiricism of the earlier first generation botanicals with the experimental research used to prove the efficacy and safety of second generation isolated pure compounds. Several pharmaceuticals companies are engaged in the development of natural product drugs through the isolation of the so-called active molecules from plant extracts.

Present Use of Plants

It is estimated that today, plant materials are present in, or have provided the models for 50% Western drugs. Many commercially proven drugs used in modern medicine were initially used in crude form in traditional or folk healing practices, or for other purposes that suggested potentially useful biological activity. The primary benefits of using plant derived medicines are that they are relatively safer than synthetic alternatives, offering profound therapeutic benefits and more affordable treatment.

Therapeutic benefit

Much of the exploration and utilisation of natural products as antimicrobials arise from microbial sources. It was the discovery of penicillin that led to later discoveries of antibiotics such as streptomycin, aureomycin and chloromycetin. Though most of the clinically used antibiotics are produced by soil microorganisms or fungi, higher plants have also been a source of antibiotics. Examples of these are the bacteriostatic and antifugicidal properties of Lichens, the antibiotic action of allinine in Allium sativum, or the antimicrobial action berberines in goldenseal.

Plant based antimicrobials represent a vast untapped source for medicines. Continued and further exploration of plant antimicrobials needs to occur. Plants based antimicrobials have enormous therapeutic potential. They are effective in the treatment of infectious diseases while simultaneously mitigating many of the side effects that are often associated with synthetic antimicrobials. They are effective, yet gentle. Many plants have tropisms to specific organs or systems in the body. Phytomedicines usually have multiple effects on the body. Their actions often act beyond the symptomatic treatment of disease. An example of this is Hydrastis canadensis. Hydrastis not only has antimicrobial activity, but also increases blood supply to the spleen promoting optimal activity of the spleen to release mediating compounds.

Economic benefit

World wide, there has been a renewed interest in natural products. This interest is a result of factors such as:

consumer's belief that natural products are superior; consumer's dissatisfaction with conventional medicines; changes in laws allowing structure-function claims which results in more liberal advertising; aging baby boomers; national concerns for health care cost. Sales of products in this market have increased dramatically in the last decade. Many plants that were previously wildcrafted will need to be grown domestically to meet the demands of the consumer. This represents many opportunities for the cultivation of crops for this industry.

A market based illustration of the need for plant based antimicrobials is demonstrated by the dissection of the herbal products market. In reviewing the top botanicals used as antiinfectives, the primary botanical used as an antimicrobial is Hydrastis with sales of 4.7% in 1995. While antiinfectives agents make up 24 % of the pharmaceutical market. A similar, analysis of Hypericum (St. John's wort), demonstrates the value of such an evaluation. Though Hypericum is an antiviral, it is primarily used for its antidepressant activity. In 1995 it was not among the top selling herbs.

However, by 1997, it had become an overnight success, with sales increasing over 20,000% in the mass market sector. The meteoric increase in the sales of Hypericum is multifactorial, but one factor in its in popularity was the existence of an unexploited market opportunity. In 1994 21% of pharmaceuticals sold were for the conditions affecting the central nervous system. Most of the drugs sold in this category are for depression. During this period of time, none of the top selling herbs sold had a primary indication for depression. This market hole, coupled with the media exposure produced a market success.

Many market holes exist. When using the same strategy to look at antimicrobial agents there is a similar gap. If the market dissection for antiinfectives is viewed in the same light as the Hypericum analogy, then perhaps this market is prime for receiving new plant based antimicrobials. The potential for developing antimicrobials into medicines appears rewarding, from both the perspective of drug development and the perspective of phytomedicines. The immediate source of financial benefit from plants based antimicrobials is from the herbal products market. This market offers many opportunities for those cultivating new crops, as many of the plants that are wildcrafted today must be cultivated to match the demands of this market.

Again Hydrastis, one of the top selling antimicrobials in the herbal market, represents an example of a herb that has undergone domestication. Originally this plant, native to eastern North America, was wild crafted. Hydrastis, has been used by Native Americans for many conditions, including as an antimicrobial for infections. Efforts to cultivate this plant were undertaken in order to supply the demands of the herbal products market and to battle it's threatened extinction. It is vital to be in the position to capitalise on the phytomedicine market, providing environmentally responsible solutions to public health concerns presented by new trends in infectious disease. In order to be prepared, the industry must be able to sustainably harvest and supply the herbal market. That means we must be able to anticipate the market needs and develop products to satisfy this market.

Plants containing protoberberines and related biflavones used in traditional African system of medicine have been found to be active against a wide variety of micro-organisms. Many medicinal plants of Africa have been investigated for their chemical components and some of the isolated compounds have been shown to posses interesting biological activity. Some of these plants are discussed below.

Garcinia kola, bitter kola (Guttiferae): Garcinia kola, is found in moist forest and grows as a medium size tree, up to 12 m high. It is cultivated and distributed throughout west and central Africa. Medicinal uses include, purgative, antiparasitic, antimicrobial. The seeds are used in the treatment of bronchitis and throat infections. They are also used to prevent and relieve colic, cure head or chest colds and relieve cough. Also the plant is used for the treatment of liver disorders and as a chewing stick.

The constituents include-biflavonoids, xanthones and benzophenones. The antimicrobial properties of this plant are attributed to the benzophenone, flavanones. This plant has shown both anti-inflammatory, antimicrobial and antiviral properties. Studies show very good antimicrobial and antiviral properties. In addition, the plant possesses antidiabetic, and antihepatotoxic activities.

Aframomum melegueta Grains of Paradise: This is a spicy edible fruit that is cultivated and occurs throughout the tropics. It is a perennial herb. The medicinal uses of Aframomum include aphrodisiac, measles, and leprosy, taken for excessive lactation and post partem hemorrhage, purgative, galactogogue and anthelmintic, and hemostatic agent. The constituents are essential oils-such as gingerol, shagaol, paradol. Studies show antimicrobial and antifungal activity and effective against schistosomes.

Xylopia aethiopica, Ethiopian Pepper (Abbibacceae): An evergreen, aromatic tree growing up to 20 m high with peppery fruit. It is native to the lowland rainforest and moist fringe forest in the savanna zones of in Africa. Medicinal uses of the plant are, as a carminative, as a cough remedy, and as a post partum tonic and lactation aid. Other uses are stomachache, bronchitis, biliousness and dysentery. It is also used externally as a poultice for headache and neuralgia. It is used with lemon grass for female hygiene. It is high in copper, manganese, and zinc.

Key constituents are diterpenic and xylopic acid. In studies, the fruit as an extracts has been shown to be active as an antimicrobial against gram positive and negative bacteria. Though it has not been shown to be effective against E. coli. Xylopic acid has also demonstrated activity against Candida albicans.

Cryptolepis sanguinolenta Lindl. Schltr. (Periplocaceae): A shrub that grows in the rainforest and the deciduous belt forest, found in the west coast of Africa. Related species appear in the east and southern regions of the continent. Its main medicinal use is for the treatment of fevers. It is used for urinary tract infections, especially Candida. Other uses are inflammatory conditions, malaria, hypertension, microbial infections and inflammatory conditions, stomach aches colic.

Active principals identified are indo quinoline alkaloids. Studies show inhibition against gram negative bacteria and yeast. Additionally studies have shown this plant to have bactericidal activity and extracts of the plant were effective in parasitemia. Recent in vitro study shows activity against bacteria specifically, enteric pathogens, most notably E. coli (but also staphylococcus, C. coli, C. jejuni, pseudomonous, salmonella, shigella, streptococcus, and vibrio) and some activity against candida. It has shown histamine antagonism, hypotensive, and vasodilatory activities. In addition it has demonstrative antihyperglcyemic properties.

Chasmanthera dependens Hoschst (Menispermaceae): A woody climber that grows wild in forest margins and savanna. The plant is cultivated. It is used medicinally for venereal disease, topically on sprained joints and bruises and as a general tonic for physical and nervous debilities. The constituents include berberine type alkaloids, palmatine, colombamine, and jateorhizine. Studies show that the berberine sulfate in the plant inhibits lieshmania.

Nauclea Latifolia Smith (Rubiaceae): It is a shrub or small spreading tree that is a widely distributed savanna plant. It is found in the forest and fringe tropical forest. Medicinal uses are as a tonic and fever medicine, chewing stick, toothaches, dental caries, septic mouth and malaria., diarrhea and dysentery. Key constituents are indole-quinolizidine alkaloids and glycoalkaloids and sapponins. There are studies showing the root has antibacterial activity against gram positive and negative bacteria and antifungal activity. It is most effective against Corynebacterium diphtheriae, Streptobacillis sp., Streptococcus sp., Neisseria sp., Pseudomonas aeruginosa, Salmonella sp.

Araliopsis tabouensis (Rutaceae): It is a large evergreen tree found throughout west tropical Africa. Its medicinal use is for the treatment of sexually transmitted diseases. The bark infusion is drunk for gonorrhea in the Ivory Coast. Its major constituents are alkaloids. Seven alkaloids have been isolated from the root and stem bark.

In a recent study on antibacterial activity of medicinal plants, conducted by, R.Nair, T. Kalariya and Sumitra Chandra, a few medicinal flora were screened for potential antibacterial activity. Details of the study described below.

Sapindus Emarginatus: Sapindus emarginatusVahl. belongs to the family Sapindaceae. This tree is 8 to 10 m high and has many branches with leaves and leaflets. Its flowers are white, and its fruits are round. It contains saponin and glucose. The seed contains oil. Traditionally, it is used as anti-inflammatory and antiprurutic. It is used to purify the blood. The seed is in intoxicant and the fruit rind has oxytropic action. Its powder is used as a nasal insufflation.

Hibiscus rosa-sinensis: Hibiscus rosa-sinensis belongs to the family Malvaceae. The roots are cylindrical, 5-15 cm in length and 2 cm in diameter, off white and with light brown transverse lenticles. The roots taste sweet and are mucilaginous. The leaves are simple ovate or ovatelancolate, and are entire at the base and coarsely toothed at the apex. The flowers are pedicillate, actinomorphic, pentamerous and complete. The corolla consists of 5 petals, red and about 8 cm in diameter. Traditionally this plant is used for the control of dysfunctional uterine bleeding and as an oral contraceptive. Some of the chemical constituents isolated from this plant are cyanidin, quercetin, hentriacontane, calcium oxalate, thiamine, riboflavin, niacin and ascorbic acid. Flavonoids are also present.

Mirabilis jalapa: Mirabilis jalapaLinn. belongs to the family Nyctaginaceae. It is a large herbaceous plant grown in gardens throughout India. This plant is 50-100 cm high. It has antifungal, antimicrobial, antiviral, antispasmodic, antibacterial, diuretic, carminative, cathartic, hydragogues, purgative, stomachic, tonic and vermifuge properties This plant contains alanine, alphaamyrins, arabinose, beta-amyrins, campesterol, daucosterol and dopamine, and is used to treat conjunctivitis, edema, fungal infections, inflammation, pains and swellings.

Rheo discolorHance: Rheo discolor Hance belongs to the family Commelinaceae. It is commonly grown in gardens, and is usually known as Tradescantia. The leaves are large, imbricated, green above and purple beneath.

Nyctanthes arbortristis: Nyctanthes arbortristis Linn. belongs to the family Oleaceae. The tree measures up to 3-10 m in height. The leaves face forwards and are 10-12.5 cm long. The leaf juice is used to treat loss of appetite, piles, liver disorders, biliary disorders, intestinal worms, chronic fever, obstinate sciatica, rheumatism and fever with rigours. The seeds are used as anthelmintics and in alopecia. It is antibilious and an expectorant, and is also useful in bilious fevers.

Colocasia esculenta: Colocasia esculenta Schott. belongs to the family Araceae. The plant is a hearty succulent herb, with clusters of long heart or arrowhead- shaped leaves that point earthwards. It grows on erect stems that may be green, red black or variegated. The stems are a few meters high. The species is thought to be a native of India. The young leaves are rich in Vitamin C, and the roots are rich in starch. It contains thiamine, riboflavin, niacin, oxalic acid, calcium oxalate and sapotoxin. The tubers contain aminoacids and proteins. The corms contain the anthocyanins perlargonidin 3-glucoside, cyaniding 3-rhamnoside and cyaniding 3-glucoside. Traditionally it is used to settle the stomach, to prevent swelling and pain and to reduce fever. It is also used as a poultice on infected sores.

Gracilaria corticata: Gracilaria corticata belongs to the family Rhodophyceae. These algae are multicellular, forming well-developed branched thalli.

Dictyotaspp: Dictyota spp. belong to the family Phaeophyaceae. The brown algae vary in size from microscopic plants with a few cells to very large plants some 70 m in length. Most brown algae possess a holdfast, stipe and blade.

Pulicaria wightiana: Pulicaria wightiana belongs to the family Asteraceae. The leaves are sessile, and pubescent on both sides.

Aqueous Extraction: Fresh plant materials were washed under running tap water, air dried and then homogenised to fine powder and stored in airtight bottles. For aqueous extraction, 10 g of air-dried powder was placed in distilled water and boiled for 6 h. At intervals of 2 h it was filtered through 8 layers of muslin cloth and centrifuged at 5000 x g for 15 min. The supernatant was collected. After 6 h, the supernatant was concentrated to make the final volume one-fourth of the original volume. Finally 10 g of material was extracted in 25 ml of distilled water giving a concentration of 40 mg/0.1 ml. It was then autoclaved at 121°C and 15 lbs pressure and stored at 4°C.

Table 1: Screening of some medicinal plants for potential antibacterial activity.

No.	Botanical name	Family	Vernacular name	Parts used
1.	Sapindus emarginatus	Sapindaceae	Aritha	Leaf
2.	Hibiscus rosa-sinensis	Malvaceae	Jasud	Leaf
3.	Mirabilis jalapa	Nyctaginaceae	Gulbas	in toto
4.	Rheo discolor	Commelinaceae	–	Leaf
5.	Nyctanthes arbortristis	Oleaceae	Parijatak	Leaf
6.	Colocasia esculenta		Araceae	Leaf
7.	Gracilaria corticata	Rhodophyaceae	–	in toto
8.	Dictyota spp.	Phaeophyaceae	–	in toto
9.	Pulicaria wightiana	Asteraceae	Shinshoria	in toto

Solvent extraction: Ten grams of air dried powder was placed in 100 ml of organic solvent (methanol) in a conical flask, plugged with cotton and then kept on a rotary shaker at 190-220 rpm for 24 h. After 24 h, it was filtered through 8 layers of muslin cloth and centrifuged at 5000 x g for 15 min. The supernatant was collected and the solvent was evaporated to make the final volume one-fourth of the original volume, giving a concentration of 40 mg/0.1 ml. It was stored at 4°C in airtight bottles for further studies.

Test Microorganisms: The microbial strains are identified strains and were obtained from the National Chemical Laboratory (NCL), Pune, India. The bacterial strains studied are Pseudomonas testosteroni NCIM 5098,

Staphylococcus epidermidisATCC 12228, Proteus morganiiNCIM 2040, Bacillus subtilis ATCC 6633, Micrococcus flavus ATCC 10240 and Klebsiella pneumoniaeNCIM 2719.

A loop full of the strain was inoculated in 30 ml of nutrient broth in a conical flask and incubated on a rotary shaker for 24 h to activate the strain. Mueller Hinton Agar No. 2 was prepared for the study. The assay was performed using 2 methods. Agar disk diffusion for aqueous extract and Agar ditch diffusion for solvent extract. The media and the test bacterial cultures were poured into Petri dishes (Hi-Media).

The test strain (0.2 ml) was inoculated into the media (inoculum size 108 cells/ml) when the temperature reached 40-42°C. Care was taken to ensure proper homogenisation. The experiment was performed under strict aseptic conditions. For the Agar disk diffusion method, the test compound (0.1 ml) was introduced onto the disk (0.7 cm) (Hi-Media) and then allowed to dry. Thus the disk was completely saturated with the test compound. Then the disk was introduced onto the upper layer of the medium with the bacteria. The plates were incubated overnight at 37°C. For the Agar ditch diffusion method, after the medium was solidified, a ditch was made in the plates with the help of a cup-borer (0.85 cm). The test compound was introduced into the well and the plates were incubated overnight at 37°C.

Microbial growth was determined by measuring the diameter of the zone of inhibition. Methanol and distilled water were used as the control. The control activity was deducted from the test and the result obtained was plotted. The antibacterial activity of S. emarginatus leaf extract of both solvents (aqueous and methanolic) against Ps. testosteroni, K. pneumoniae, M. flavus, P. morganii, B. subtilis and S. epidermidis is shown in Figure 1a. The methanolic extract showed considerably more activity than the aqueous extract. Maximum antibacterial activity was shown against M. flavus, followed by S. epidermidis and P. morganii. Neither of the extracts were able to inhibit Ps. testosteroni or K. pneumoniae.

The antibacterial activities of H. rosa-sinensis and M. jalapa are shown in Figure 1b and Figure 1c, respectively. Neither aqueous non methanolic extracts were able to inhibit any of the tested bacterial strains. In Figure 2a the antibacterial activity of R. discolor against the tested bacterial strains is shown. Neither of the extracts (aqueous or methanolic) were able to inhibit any of the tested bacterial strains. The antibacterial activity of N. arbortristis against the tested strains is shown in Figure 2b. The aqueous extract showed some activity against Ps. testosteroni, but showed negligible activity against the other bacterial strains.

This plant, i.e. N. arbortristis, extract (methanolic), was unable to inhibit any of the bacterial strains studied. The antibacterial activity of C. esculenta is shown in Figure 2c. The aqueous extract did not show any activity against any of the bacterial strains. The methanolic extract showed inhibitory activity against K. pneumoniae only, and none of the other bacterial strains were affected. The antibacterial activity of G. corticata is shown in Figure 3a. Neither of the extracts were able to inhibit any of the tested bacterial strains.

In Figure 3b, the antibacterial activity of Dictyota spp. is shown. The aqueous extract showed slight activity against S. epidermidis and B. subtilis, whereas methanolic extract showed activity against B. subtilis only. Both the extracts showed activity against B. subtilis. Neither of the extracts were able to inhibit Ps. testosteroni, P. morganii, M. flavus or K. pneumoniae. In Figure 3c the antibacterial activity of P. wightiana is shown. The methanolic extract

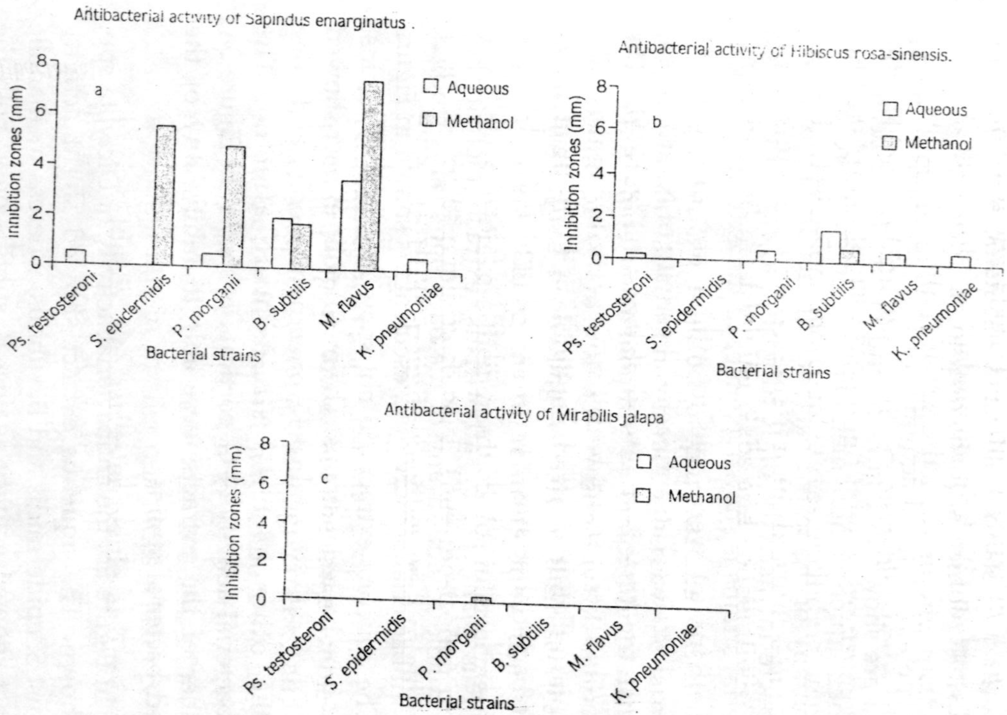

Figure 1: Antibacterial activity of Sapindus emarginatus (a) Hibiscus rosa-sinensis (b) and Mirabilis jalapa (c) in aqueous and methanol extracts against some bacterial strains.

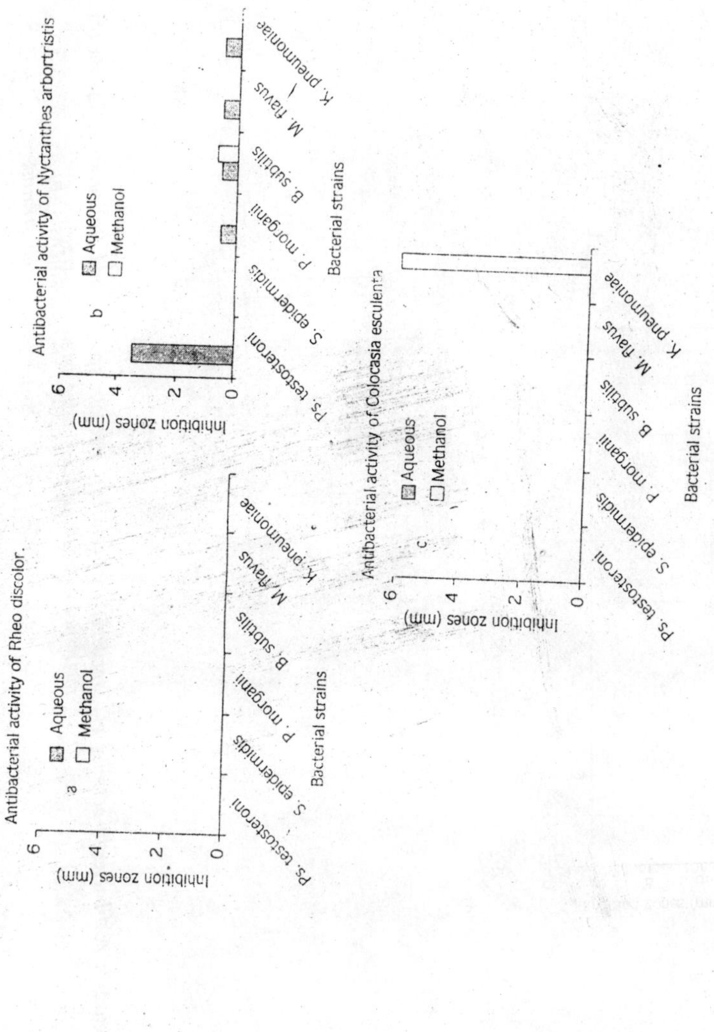

Figure 2: Antibacterial activity of Rheo discolor (a) Nyctantes arbortristis (b) and Colocasia esculenta (c) in aqueous and methanol extracts against some bacterial strains.

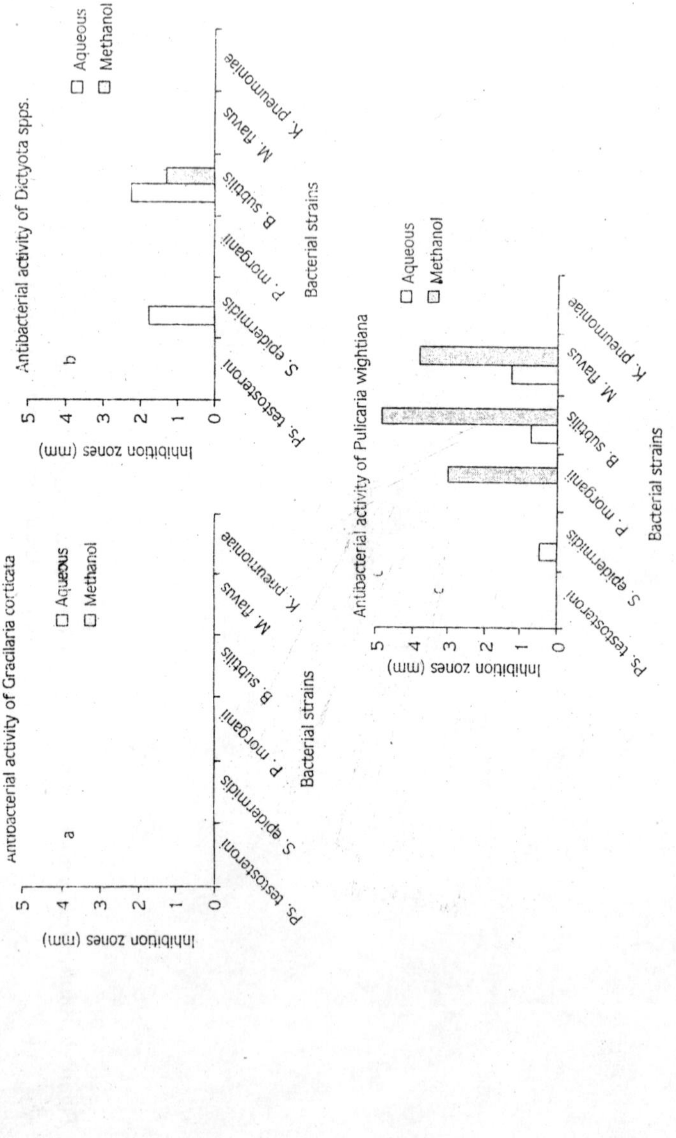

Figure 3: Antibacterial activity of Gracileria corticata (a) Dictyota spp. (b) and Pulicaria wightiana (c) in aqueous and methanol extracts against some bacterial strains.

showed more activity than the aqueous extract. The greatest activity of the methanolic extract was against B. subtilis, followed by M. flavusand P. morganii. The other 2 bacteria were not affected. The aqueous extract showed negligible activity.

The aqueous extract appears to have less antibacterial activity than the methanolic extract. This is interesting in that the traditional method of treating a bacterial infection was by administering a decoction of the plant or a part there of by boiling it in water, whereas according to the researchers results an organic solvent is better; hence this may be more beneficial. Amongst the 6 bacterial strains investigated Ps. testosteroniand K. pneumoniaewere the most resistant. It was also evident that Gram negative bacteria were more resistant than Gram positive bacteria. It can be concluded that plant extracts have great potential as antimicrobial compounds against microorganisms and that they can be used in the treatment of infectious diseases caused by resistant microorganisms.

S. emarginatus showed maximum antibacterial activity and so this plant can be used to discover bioactive natural products that may serve as leads for the development of new pharmaceuticals that address hither to unmet therapeutic needs. Such screening of various natural organic compounds and identifying active agents is the need of the hour, because successful prediction of lead molecule and drug like properties at the onset of drug discovery will pay off later in drug development.

5

Validity of Ethnomedicines

Fossil records date human use of plants as medicines at least to the Middle Paleolithic age some 60,000 years ago. From that point the development of traditional medical systems incorporating plants as a means of therapy can be traced back only as far as recorded documents of their likeness.

Ethnomedicine is defined as the use of plants by humans as medicines, is a highly diversified approach to drug discovery that involves observation, description, and experimental investigation (screening) for possible biological/medicinal properties from indigenous drugs. It is based on botany, chemistry, biochemistry, pharmacology, physiology and other disciplines such as anthropology, archaeology and history that contribute to the discovery of natural products with medicinal activity.

According to the World Health Organisation, more than 60 % of the world's population use ethnomedicine as part of their primary health care. Being given that plants have been used by humans (often hundreds or thousands of years), one could therefore expect any bioactive compounds obtained from such plants to have low human toxicity. Therefore the goals of using plants as possible leads for therapeutic agents are four folds:

— to isolate and characterise bioactive compounds for possible use as drugs, e.g., the cardiac drug, digoxin, as well as morphine andtaxol;

— to produce bioactive compounds of novel or known structures as lead compounds for semisynthesis to produce pharmaceuticals that may display lower toxicity and for which patents can be acquired, e.g., metformin, verapamil, and amiodarone;

— to use agents as pharmacologic tools; and

— to use the whole plant or part of it as a herbal remedy, e.g., garlic, bitter melon.

With the use of traditional plants as herbal remedies over the centuries, some of these plants obviously may be toxic within a given endemic culture that has no reporting system to document these effects. It is unlikely, however, that acute toxic effects following the use of a plant in these cultures would go unnoticed or unreported. The plant would then be used cautiously or even lose its importance in the local usage. However it is worth mentioning that in case of chronic toxic effects, the symptoms may be less likely apparent at the early onset. Should be plant(s) prove to possess such undesirable properties; its use should be immediately discontinued.

In addition, many of the plants, which are use for their medicinal properties, possess an array of chemical diversity of secondary metabolites as a result of evolution. These medicinal properties that the secondary metabolites could possess may be equal or superior to that found in synthetic combinatorial chemical libraries.

The development of traditional medical systems incorporating plants as a means of therapy can be traced back to the Middle Paleolithic age some 60,000 years ago. Plants have long been a very important source of drugs and many plant species (like microbes) have been screened to see if they contain substances with therapeutic activity. Many plant drugs of long-standing were discovered by investigating the scientific basis of old folk remedies to determine the active ingredient in the concoction. The discovery digoxin from foxgloves (an old discovery) used to treat heart failure is a classical example whilst a recent discovery in the form of paclitaxel (discovered in yew leaves) has shown promising anti-cancerous properties.

In earlier times, all drugs and medicinal agents were derived from natural substances, and most of these remedies were obtained from higher plants. Drug development is a complex process, and only companies with a consequent investment in research and development can afford to bring drugs from conception to market. Today, many new chemotherapeutic agents are obtained synthetically, based on "rational" drug design. The study of natural products has many advantages over synthetic drug design. The former leads to materials having new structural features with novel biological activity. Plants continue to serve as possible sources for new drugs, but chemicals derived from the various parts of these plants can also be extremely useful as lead structures for synthetic modification and optimisation of bioactivity.

The starting materials for about one-half of the medicines we use today come from natural sources. There is no doubt that the future of plants as sources of medicinal agents for use in investigation, prevention, and treatment of diseases is very promising. In the context of isolation and screening for chemicals that may possess medicinal properties from plants, different approaches can be used. The following is a brief discription of the current approaches being used by scientists to isolate and characterise these agents.

Random selection followed by chemical screening: This technique is also known as phytochemical screening approaches whereby the plants are analysed for alkaloids, terpenes and flavonoids etc. This approach has been used in the past and is still being used in the developing countries. The tests are simple to perform, but false-positive and false-negative tests often render results difficult to assess. More important, it is usually impossible to relate one class of phytochemicals to specific biological targets; for example, the alkaloids or flavonoids produce a vast array of biological effects that cannot be usually predicted well in advance.

Random selection followed by one or more biological assays: In the past, plant extracts were evaluated mainly in experimental animals, primarily mice and rats. The most extensive of these programmes were sponsored by the National Cancer Institute (NCI) in the United States and the Central Drug Research Institute (CDRI) in India. More than 35,000 species have been screened in vitro primarily. However between the period 1960-1981, the NCI has sponsored in vivo screening for biological properties emanating from these plants. Two major pharmaceutical agents namely taxol and camptothecin were discovered through the programme.

Several other plant-derived compounds has turned out to unsuccessful in human studies. The above process has been discontinued since 1986 onwards by the NCI who has from then on embarked on to continue to collect and screen plants using a battery of 60 human tumour cell lines and also initiated a screening of plants for anti-HIV activity in vitro. Calanolide A, has been discovered through this programme and is currently in its Phase I clinical trials.

Follow-up of biological activity reports: These reports showed that the plant extracts had interesting biologic activity, but the extracts were not studied for their active principles. The literature from the 1930s through the 1970s contains these types of reports.

Follow-up of ethnomedical (traditional medicine) uses of plants: Several types of ethnomedical information are available especially in the different cultures mainly in the Asian and African continents. It is of no denying facts that plants used in organised traditional medical systems. Ayurveda and traditional Chinese medicine have flourished as systems of medicine in use for thousands of years. These systems which include practice and theory are still in place today because of their organisational strengths, and they focus primarily on multicomponent mixtures.

There are still certain beliefs in though Western medical science that still view such systems as lacking credibility and validity despite the fact that these plants are undeniably still being widely used by a wide section of the population of poorer countries on this planet. One should however recognise that adverse effects from those widely used plants are not well documented, and efficacy of these plants and plant mixtures is more difficult to assess by Western scientific methods.

Importance of Ethnomedicine

At first interest in the western countries especially the United States, was directed toward antifungal and of antiviral agentsfrom traditional medicinal plants. The approach was to send scientist including botanist as well as physician teams to tropical areas to assess firsthand the use of plants by traditional healers and to collect interesting plants and assess them for validity in the Shaman laboratories. It is extremely difficult to assess the value of any approach to the use of higher plants to develop new drugs. Several active compounds were discovered. Unfortunately many failed to live up to the promise.

Many plants/extracts were either toxic or failed in the clinic. Priorities were then shifed or re-toward screening for possible antidiarrhoeal activity. A successful candidate that emerged from such programmes is SP-303, an oligomeric proanthocyanidin. SP-303 has proven to be clinically efficacious and is currently marketed as a dietary supplement for diarrhoea. In addition, a major effort has also been directed toward discovery of novel antidiabetic agents, which resulted in the discovery of several patented compounds: cryptolepine, maprouneacin.

During the past decade, traditional systems of medicine have become a topic of global importance. Current estimates suggests that, in many developing countries just like Mauritius, a large proportion of the population relies heavily on traditional practitioners and medicinal plants to meet primary health care needs. Although modern medicine may be available in these countries, herbal medicines (phyto-medicines) have often maintained popularity for historical and cultural reasons. Concurrently, many people in developed countries have begun to turn to alternative or complementary therapies, including medicinal herbs.

Even with this vast array of data, few medicinal plant species have been scientifically evaluated for their possible medical application. Safety and efficacy data are available for even a few plants, their extracts and their active ingredients, and the preparations containing them. Furthermore, in most countries the herbal medicine market is poorly regulated and herbal products are often neither registered nor controlled. Assurance of safety, quality and efficacy of medicinal plants and herbal products has now become a key issue in industrialised and in developing countries. Both the general consumer and health-care professionals need up-to-date information on the safety and efficacy of medicinal plants.

The goals of using plants as sources of therapeutic agents are;

a) to isolate bioactive compounds for direct use as drugs, e.g., digoxin, digitoxin, morphine, reserpine, taxol, vinblastine, vincristine;

b) to produce bioactive compounds of novel or known structures as lead compounds for semisynthesis to produce patentable entities of higher activity and/or lower toxicity, e.g., metformin, nabilone, oxycodon (and other narcotic analgesics), taxotere, teniposide, verapamil, and amiodarone, which are based, respectively, on galegine, Δ^9-tetrahydrocannabinol, morphine, taxol, podophyllotoxin, khellin, and khellin;

c) to use agents as pharmacologic tools, e.g., lysergic acid diethylamide, mescaline, yohimbine; and

d) to use the whole plant or part of it as a herbal remedy, e.g., cranberry, echinacea, feverfew, garlic, ginkgo biloba, St. John's wort, saw palmetto.

The number of higher plant species (angiosperms and gymnosperms) on this planet is estimated at 250,000 , with a lower level at 215,000 and an upper level as high as 500,000. Of these, only about 6% have been screened for biologic activity, and a reported 15% have been evaluated phytochemically. With high throughput screening methods becoming more advanced and available, these numbers will change, but the primary discriminator in evaluating one plant species versus another is the matter of approach to finding leads.

There are some broad starting points to selecting and obtaining plant material of potential therapeutic interest. However, the goals of such an endeavor are straightforward. Plants have an advantage in this area based on their long-term use by humans (often hundreds or thousands of years). One might expect any bioactive compounds obtained from such plants to have low human toxicity. Obviously, some of these plants may be toxic within a given endemic culture that has no reporting system to document these effects. It is unlikely, however, that acute toxic effects following the use of a plant in these cultures would not be noticed, and the plant would then be used cautiously or not at all.

In addition, chemical diversity of secondary plant metabolites that results from plant evolution may be equal or superior to that found in synthetic combinatorial chemical libraries. It was estimated that in 1991 in the United States, for every 10,000 pure compounds (most likely those based on synthesis) that are biologically evaluated (primarily in vitro), 20 would be tested in animal models, and 10 of these would be clinically evaluated, and only one would reach U.S. Food and Drug Administration approval for marketing. The time required for this process was estimated as 10 years at a cost of $231 million (U.S.).

Most large pharmaceutical manufacturers and some small biotechnology firms have the ability to screen 1,000 or more substances per week using high throughput in vitro assays. In addition to synthetic compounds from their own programmes, some of these companies screen plant, microbial, and marine organisms. Thus, the challenges facing these companies in acquiring organisms and extracts (vide infra) usually result in a failure to consider collection of plants, especially if the acquisitions are based on ethnomedical use. It is time-consuming to collect specific plants having an ethnomedical history.

Despite these problems, one cannot discount the past importance of plants as sources of structurally novel drugs. Ethnomedicine may be defined broadly as the use of plants by humans as medicines; but this use could be called more accurately ethnobotanic medicine. Traditional medicine is a broad term used to define any non-Western medical practice. Ethnopharmacology is a highly diversified approach to drug discovery involving the observation, description, and experimental investigation of indigenous drugs and their biologic activities. It is based on botany, chemistry, biochemistry, pharmacology, and many other disciplines (anthropology, archaeology, history, and linguistics) that contribute to the discovery of natural products with biologic activity.

Different Approaches to Drug Discovery

Several reviews pertaining to approaches for selecting plants as candidates for drug discovery programmes have been published; however, most concern screening plants for anticancer or anti-HIV activity. Researchers outline these approaches briefly before concentrating on the ethnomedical approach.

Random selection followed by chemical screening. These so-called phytochemical screening approaches have been used in the past and are currently pursued mainly in the developing countries. The tests are simple to perform, but false-positive and false-negative tests often render results difficult to assess. More important, it is usually impossible to relate one class of phytochemicals to specific biologic targets; for example, the alkaloids or flavonoids produce a vast array of biologic effects that are usually not predictable in advance.

Random selection followed by one or more biologic assays. In the past, plant extracts were evaluated mainly in experimental animals, primarily mice and rats. The most extensive of these programmes were sponsored by the National Cancer Institute (NCI) in the United States and the Central Drug Research Institute (CDRI) in India. More than 35,000 species were screened in vitro and later in vivo at NCI from 1960 to 1981. Taxol and camptothecin were discovered in this programme as well as several other plant-derived compounds that were unsuccessful in human studies. In 1986 the NCI programme abandoned this approach and continued to collect and screen plants using a battery of 60 human tumour cell lines and also initiated a screening of plants for anti-HIV activity in vitro.

The CDRI evaluated approximately 2,000 plant species for several biologic activities, including antibacterial, antidiabetic, antifertility, antifungal, antihypercholesteremic, anti-inflammatory, antitumour, cardiovascular, central nervous-system depressant, cytotoxicity, diuretic, and others. To date no biologically active drugs for human use have arisen from that programme, even though a large number of known and novel bioactive compounds were isolated from the active plants.

Follow-up of ethnomedical (traditional medicine) uses of plants. Several types of ethnomedical information are available:

Plants used in organised traditional medical systems: Ayurveda, Unani, Kampo, and traditional Chinese medicine have flourished as systems of medicine in use for thousands of years. Their individual arrangements all emphasise education based on an established, frequently revised body of written knowledge and theory. These systems are still in place today because of their organisational strengths, and they focus primarily on multicomponent mixtures. Even though Western medical science views such systems as lacking credibility, undeniably they are used widely by most people on this planet. Adverse effects from those widely used plants are not well documented in the literature, and efficacy of these plants and plant mixtures is more difficult to assess by Western scientific methods.

Herbalism, folklore, and shamanism: These center on an apprenticeship system of information passed to the next generation through a shaman, curandero, traditional healer, or herbalist. The plants that are used are often kept secret by the practitioner, so little information about them is recorded; thus there is less dependence on scientific evidence as in systems of traditional medicine that can be subject to scrutiny. The shaman or herbalist combines the roles of pharmacist and medical doctor with the cultural/spiritual/religious beliefs of a region or people, which are often regarded as magic or mysticism. This approach is widely practiced in Africa and South America.

6

Evaluation of Plant Extracts

Plants contain thousands of constituents and are a valuable source of new and biologically active molecules. For their investigation, it is important to have the necessary tools at hand. These include suitable biological assays and chemical screening methods. Bioassays should be as simple as possible and attempts should be made to have access to a large number of different tests so that many biological properties can be screened. The bioassays summarised here involve antifungal, antibacterial and antioxidant/radical scavenging activities. They are most effective when used in conjunction with chemical screening methods so that ubiquitous and unimportant compounds can be excluded.

When one considers that a single plant may contain up to thousands of constituents, the possibilities of making new discoveries become evident. The crucial factor for the ultimate success of an investigation into bioactive plant constituents is thus the selection of plant material.

Chemical Screening

Isolation of pure, pharmacologically active constituents from plants remains a long and tedious process. For this reason, it is necessary to have methods available which eliminate unneccesary separation procedures. Chemical screening is thus performed to allow localisation and targeted isolation of new or useful types of constituents with potential activities. This procedure enables recognition of known metabolites in extracts or at the earliest stages of separation and is thus economically very important.

Thin-layer chromatography (TLC) is the simplest and cheapest method of detecting plant constituents because the method is easy to run, reproducible and requires little equipment. However, for efficient separation of metabolites, good selectivity and sensitivity of detection, together with the capability of providing on-line structural information, hyphenated high performance liquid chromatographic (HPLC) techniques are preferred. They play an important role as an analytical support in the work of phytochemists for the efficient localisation and rapid characterisation of natural products.

HPLC coupled to a UV photodiode array detector (LC/UV) has been widely used for the analysis of crude plant extracts. The UV spectra of natural products obtained on-line by LC/UV give useful information on the type of constituents and in the case of certain classes of compound, such as the polyphenols, indications of oxidation patterns. HPLC coupled to mass spectrometry (LC/MS) is a newer hyphenated technique. Mass spectrometry is one of the most sensitive methods of molecular analysis and yields information on the molecular weight as well as on the structure of the analytes.

However, it has been difficult to achieve on-line coupling of HPLC and MS. These problems have now been overcome with the introduction of different LC/MS interfaces. For the HPLC screening of crude plant extracts, three interfaces have been used in our laboratory: thermospray (TSP), continuous flow fast atom bombardment (CF-FAB) and electrospray (ES). They cover the ionisation of relatively small non-polar products to highly polar molecules. LC/TSP-MS allows satisfactory ionisation of moderately polar constituents such as polyphenols or terpenoids in the mass range 200-800 amu. For larger, polar molecules such as saponins, CF-FAB or ES are the methods of choice.

HPLC coupled to a NMR spectrometer (LC/NMR) has, until recently, been little used mainly because of its lack of sensitivity. However, progress in pulse field gradients and solvent suppression, together with improvements in probe technology and the construction of high field magnets now allow many applications of the technique. LC/NMR has important potential for online structure identification of natural products. Indeed, NMR spectroscopy is by far the most powerful spectroscopic technique for obtaining detailed structural information about organic compounds in solution. Coupling to a HPLC instrument is straightforward and solvent suppression techniques enable the use of non-deuterated solvents (methanol or acetonitrile) under reversed-phase conditions. Water is replaced by D_2O.

Biological Screening

Screening programmes for biologically active natural products require the right bioassays. Detection of compounds with the desired activity in complex plant extracts depends on the reliability and sensitivity of the test systems used. Bioassays are also essential for monitoring the required effects throughout activity-guided fractionation: all fractions are tested and those continuing to exhibit activity are carried through further isolation and purification until the active monosubstances are obtained.

The search for promising plant extracts and subsequent activityguided isolation put specific requirements on the bioassays to be used. They must be simple, inexpensive and rapid in order to cope with the large number of samples—including extracts from the screening phase and all fractions obtained during the isolation procedure. They must also be sensitive enough to detect active principles which are generally present only in small concentrations in crude extracts. Their selectivity should be such that the number of false positives is reasonably small.

Here emphasis will be placed on TLC autographic assays, which combine TLC with a bioassay in situ and allow localisation of active constituents in a complex matrix. The number of available targets for biological screening is limited. Furthermore, bioassays are often not reliaby predictive for clinical efficiency. For these reasons, it is extremely helpful to have chemical screening techniques available as a complementary approach for the discovery of new molecules which might serve as lead compounds. Chemical screening also serves for dereplication purposes.

TLC Screening

TLC screening for antifungal and antibacterial compounds: The use of immunosuppressive drugs and the spread of AIDS have resulted in an increasing occurrence of opportunistic systemic mycoses. The infections commonly observed in the immunecompromised host include candidiasis (Candida albicans and related species) of the oesophagus and mouth, cryptococcosis (Candida neoformans) and aspergillosis.

As there are few really effective antifungal preparations currently available for the treatment of systemic mycoses and as the efficacy of existing drugs is rather limited, it is important to find new sources of antifungal agents. Plant-derived natural products may offer potential leads for novel agents which act against these mycoses. There is also a need to screen plants for constituents which have activity against plant pathogenic fungi: fungal attack can be economically devastating in agriculture.

Bioautography is a very convenient and simple way of testing plant extracts and pure substances for their effects on both human pathogenic and plant pathogenic microorganisms. It can be employed in the target-directed isolation of active constituents. Three bioautographic methods have been described : agar diffusion, direct TLC bioautographic detection and agar-overlay.

Direct bioautography is applicable to microorganisms that can grow directly on the TLC plate. The agar-overlay technique is a hybrid of the two other methods and is applicable to a broad spectrum of microorganisms. It produces well defined zones of inhibition and is not sensitive to contamination. Active compounds are transferred from the stationary phase to the agar layer (which contains the microorganism) by a diffusion process. After incubation, the plate is sprayed with a tetrazolium salt (e.g. MTT) which is converted to a formazan dye by the microorganism. Inhibition zones are observed as clear spots against a purple background.

Direct bioautographic procedures have been described for spore producing fungi such as Aspergillus, Penicillium and Cladosporium and also for bacteria. Numerous antifungal compounds have been characterised using Cladosporium cucumerinum in a routine assay. The agar-overlay assay has been used for yeasts such as Candida albicans and can also be applied to bacteria such as Bacillus subtilis. If phenol red is incorporated into media containing 0.6% agar and the plates are sprayed with MTT, clearer results are obtained, with dark red coloured inhibition zones appearing against a blue background. This method works successfully with a range of microorganisms, including Candida albicans, Escherichia coli, Pseudomonas aeruginosa and Staphylococcus aureus.

TLC screening for radical scavengers and antioxidants: Another use of TLC for biological testing is as a means for discovering new antioxidants in higher plants. These can be detected on a TLC plate by spraying with 2,2-diphenyl-1-picrylhydrazyl (DPPH) radical. Antioxidants reduce the radical, producing white spots on a purple background. Alternatively, the bleaching of crocin (which normally gives a yellow colour on the plate) can be used to distinguish components of plant extracts with potential antioxidant or radical-scavenging properties.

Screening for Bioactive Compounds

An example of natural products isolation using the TLC bioautographic approach is a 2-methoxynaphthoquinone from Swertia calycina (Gentianaceae), a small plant found in Rwanda. This example illustrates well the combined use of TLC and HPLC in the search for new antifungal metabolites (Fig. 1). TLC bioautography of the dichloromethane extract of S.calycina showed a compound which strongly inhibited the growth of C. cucumerinum. HPLCUV and HPLC-MS analyses of the extract revealed the presence of three main compounds: a bitter principle, a xanthone and a naphthoquinone derivative with a MW of 188.

Comparison of on-line UV and MS data with a data bank allowed identification of the bitter principle as sweroside and the xanthone as decussatin. As these have no antifungal properties, the strong activity of the dichloromethane extract was attributed to the naphthoquinone, a class of compounds which is known to have strong antimicrobial properties. Targetted isolation afforded the active compound, identified as 2-methoxy-1,4-naphthoquinone. Interestingly, quinones were previously not known to occur in the Gentianaceae. The minimum quantities of 1 required to inhibit the growth of C. cucumerinum and C. albicans on TLC plates were 0.1 and 0.4 mg, respectively. By comparison, the reference substance propiconaole was active at 0.1 and 0.001 mg, respectively.

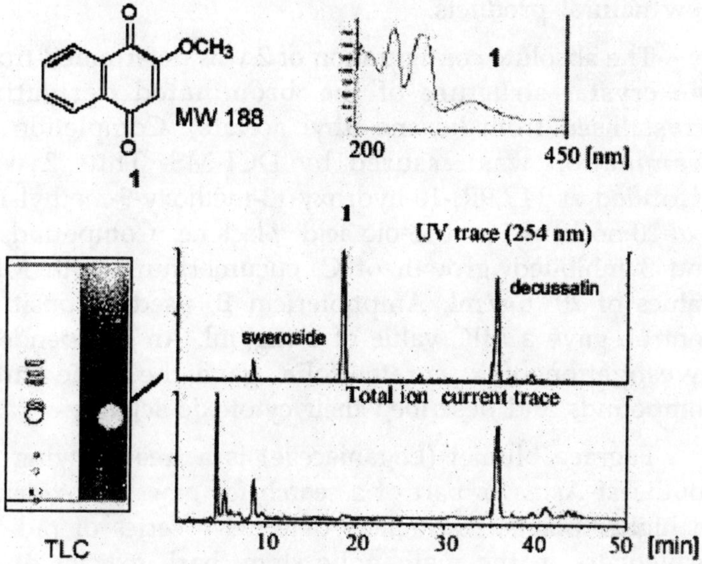

Figure 1: TLC bioautography (C. cucumerinum) and LC/UV/MS analysis of Swertia calycina (Gentianaceae) whole plant dichloromethane extract.

During the screening of plants for biological activities, a dichloromethane extract of Parinari capensis (Chrysobalanaceae) whole plant gave a positive response in the C.cucumerinum TLC bioassay. Analysis of this extract by LC/UV/MS showed the presence of 3 major peaks (2-4) in the HPLC chromatogram when detecting at 210 nm (Fig. 2). LC/MS was performed with a thermospray interface, which is well adapted for the ionisation of moderately polar molecules. The LC/TSP-MS of the peak 2 gave a protonated molecular ion $[M+H]^+$ at m/z 345.

Fractionation of the extract was performed by a combination of medium-pressure LC, silica gel CC and Sephadex LH-20 gel filtration to give three major constituents 2-4. Strucure elucidation by a combination of 1D- and 2D-NMR analysis showed the three compounds to be kaurenoid diterpenes, two of which, 2 and 4, were new natural products.

The absolute configuration of 2 was determined from the crystal structure of the brominated derivative (crystallised from hexane-ethyl acetate). Completion of bromination was assured by DCI-MS. Thus 2 was identified as (4R,9R)-10-hydroxy-13-methoxy-9-methyl-15-oxo-20-norkaur-16-en-18-oic acid γ-lactone. Compounds 2 and 3 inhibited growth of C. cucumerinum with MIC values of 20 μg/ml. Amphotericin B, used as positive control, gave a MIC value of 1 mg/ml. An independent investigation of P. curatellifolia gave the same three compounds and described their cytotoxic activities.

Fagraea blumei (Loganiaceae) is a tree growing in southeast Asia. As part of a search for new antioxidants in higher plants, researchers detected a series of radical scavengers in the methanolic stem bark extract of F. blumei. These compounds exhibited on TLC plates a strong yellow or blue fluorescence which prompted them to undertake their isolation. The stem bark was successively extracted with dichloromethane and methanol. The methanolic extract was then fractionated by Sephadex LH-20 followed by centrifugal partition chromatography, medium pressure liquid chromatography and high performance liquid chromatography on RP-18 to afford blumeosides AD.

Blumeosides are new iridoid glucosides containing either a hydroxy or a dihydroxy terephthalyl moiety. While iridoids and secoiridoids are widespread in Loganiaceae, terephthalic acid derivatives are rather uncommon in plants.

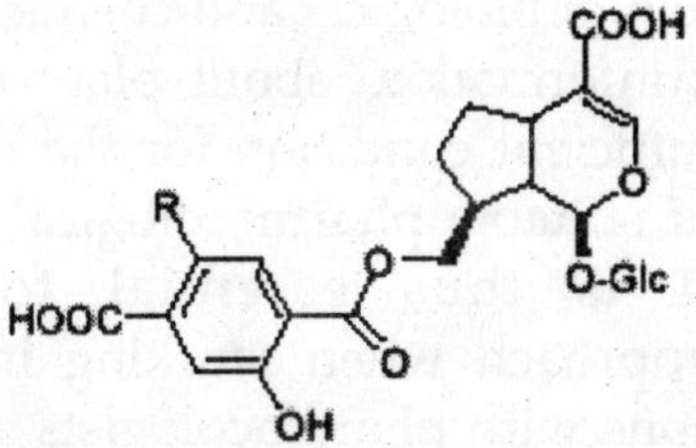

5 R = OH
7 R = H

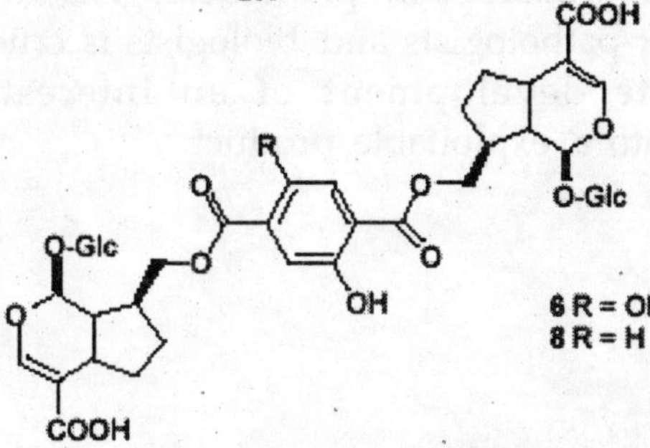

6 R = OH
8 R = H

Radical scavenging properties of blumeosides were evaluated against the DPPH radical. By using DPPH as a TLC spray reagent, 5 and 6 (10 μg) appeared as yellow spots against a purple background, while the same amount of 7 and 8 did not react with the radical. Compounds 5-8 were also tested against DPPH in a spectrophotometric assay. Quercetin and BHT were used as reference compounds. The activity of blumeoside A (5) remained lower than that of quercetin but was higher than that of BHT.

Compound 6 was less active than 5, while 7 and 8 did not reduce significantly the free radical. Interestingly the two compounds which contain a hydroquinonic moiety exhibited the strongest radical scavenging activity. The antioxidative activity of compounds 5-8 was also evaluated spectrophotometrically on the bleaching of the water soluble carotenoid crocin. Compounds 5-8 were all active in this chapter but their potency remained lower than that of rutin. Among the iridoids, 5 and 8 exhibited the strongest activity, comparable to that of gallic acid.

The combination of biological and chemical screening provides important information about plant constituents but will not be a sufficient condition for the discovery of potent new drugs if suitable pharmacological models are not available. It is thus essential to adopt a multidisciplinary approach when working in this field. Efficient collaborations with pharmacologists and medical doctors, plant pathologists and biologists is crucial to see the complete development of an interesting lead compound into a exploitable product.

7

Forest Botanicals as Pharmaceuticals

Forest botanicals are also used in the manufacture of a great many medicinal compounds and pharmaceuticals as well as nutritional supplement products. Medicinal compounds used for naturopathic remedies include a large number of herbs used to make teas, oils, and other products that are alleged to have curative or therapeutic effects on many common ailments. Some of these products may possess no real medicinal properties, yet have long-term established markets and represent a continuing economic opportunity.

Other botanicals do possess specific physical chemistries of interest to manufacturers of pharmaceutical drugs. While modern medical technology has enabled pharmaceutical manufacturers to synthesise many natural chemical compounds, there is renewed interest in exploring medicinal applications of a great many new plant chemicals.

In the future, it will likely become more important to make a distinction between medicinals and pharmaceuticals because the difference in economic opportunities represented by the two types of compounds will become increasingly great. Some experts feel that demand for botanical products that possess desired pharmaceutical chemistries will become much more important than demand for alleged medicinals in the not-too-distant future. In addition, many botanicals with medicinal uses are also used as foods, in cosmetics, in dyes, as dried florals, and for a variety of other uses (fungicides, insecticides, animal products, and aromatics).

A great many botanicals lend themselves to small farm production as crops and are therefore less likely to be good prospects for forest harvesting. For example, chamomile, peppermint, garlic, and raspberry have widely accepted medicinal qualities but are relatively easy to grow as crops so are not likely to become agroforestry alternatives for landowners.

The plants listed below do have commercial potential for wildcrafting as medicinals, pharmaceuticals, or foodrelated uses, based on those knowledgeable in the field. The life zone, description, history, chemistry, uses, harvesting, reforestation, marketing, and toxicity of most of these botanicals are detailed in Native Plants of Commercial Importance.

United States presently imports over 10 times the volume of herbs and spices that it exports, primarily because most spices and herbs require special dehydration to control the quality of the volatile oils, and the hand-drying of these crops is very laborintensive, which gives great advantage to developing countries with very cheap labour. Nonetheless, the market for native American herbs and spices that might be wildcrafted or "forest farmed" appears to be promising.

There is presently a large and growing demand from food manufacturers and spice companies for herbs and spices, and these markets should continue to grow for many years. Direct (retail) marketing and also bulk marketing are discussed in The Potential of Herbs as a

Cash Crop. Direct (retail) options for the wildcrafter or forest farmer include the roadside stand, U-pick operation, roadside market, farmers' market, "peddling," gift basket, and mail order. Also covered are direct sale to retailing outlets, local and small specialty manufacturers, and restaurants.

Herbs may have the best potential as cash crops in areas that are not suited to more familiar farm crops. Areas with limited water and relatively poor soil sometimes can produce as much income per acre with herbs as the most fertile areas with abundant water can produce income per acre with traditional farm crops. If leaseholder systems continue to evolve toward forest farming, small acreages of herbs may become a familiar sight in forests.

The market for the harvest and sale of wildcrafted fresh greens is more limited. For one reason, fresh wild greens are delicate, far more so than mushrooms, for example. They crush easily, just by their own weight, and they wilt easily. Just 2 hours in the hot sun will ruin them. One of the larger businesses in the Northwest in wild edibles had only very modest success with wild greens, even when it limited foragers to those plants that were safest to identify, such as miner's lettuce and sorrel.

Plant identification is more difficult than for other edibles (like morel mushrooms, for example). The harvester must have a very good knowledge of botany to be trained to forage for edible greens. Just one error with greens, such as mistakenly getting hemlock leaves into a batch of edible greens, would create enormous difficulty for the entire "wild edibles" industry. Nevertheless, wild harvested greens can be marketed. For example, a cooperative network of growers and harvesters in Michigan specialises in exotic produce items. Among the wild harvested spring greens and potherbs sold by mail order are miner's lettuce, wild leeks (ramps), fiddleheads, cattail shoots, cattail kittens, and stinging nettles.

All of these have potential for commercial cultivation or for management on forest lands as food products. Also marketed by the cooperative network are wild harvested fresh mushrooms and dried mushrooms; dried blueberries, cherries, cranberries, currants, and tomatoes; organic wild rice; and edible flowers, among other items.

There are two primary markets for fresh products-gourmet restaurants and their associated food service operations, and grocery stores. Grocery stores would be the more dependable market, since restaurants are an "iffy" market and sell wild edibles as a fad or novelty as much as anything else. However, the economy does have a great effect on people's eating habits, and caution is advised in beginning a business related to cooking greens. A major education effort might be necessary as a part of any marketing area. The secondary market is direct mail order to individuals.

Importance of Pharmaceutical

The continuing popularity of natural remedies and nutritional supplements and the growing interest in plantderived chemical compounds for pharmaceuticals are creating important new market opportunities for forest botanicals. Many medicinal plants sold as alternative health care products or nutritional supplements are readily marketable through herb and botanical buyers or, in some cases, directly to the retail market.

Furthermore, while sales of medicinal plants to mainstream pharmaceutical firms provide only a limited market presently, one need only consider the phenomenon of the anticancer substance taxol and its source, the Pacific yew tree, to realise how quickly that market can change with the discovery of an important new drug derived from chemical compounds found in plants.

In addition, specialists in native plant marketing emphasise that for almost all pharmaceutical products from botanicals, the European market is about 10 times as large as the U.S. market. For example, the European market for goldenseal and cascara sagrada bark (used for laxatives) is more than 20 times that in the United States. Ginseng provides perhaps the most familiar example of the potential market for a forest botanical used for medicinal purposes. Ginseng is used as a nutritional supplement and as an ingredient in skin cremes.

It is widely believed to improve circulation, increase vitality, and mitigate the effects of aging. Ginseng is widely consumed in oriental countries, and the United States exports significant amounts. In 1990, the United States exported over 1 million pounds of ginseng worth over $80 million. Another example of a major drug plant from the forest that is harvested for major export markets is cascara sagrada bark from the west coast.

Medicinal plants for the herbal and alternative health care markets are marketed primarily through small regional botanical or herb buying houses that process and package the plant parts for final processors or the retail market. The annual Whole Foods Source Directory lists a number of different wholesalers, retailers, and manufacturers for each herb and spice as well as sources for warehousing and transportation. These firms typically publish buying and selling catalogs that list the types and quantities of plant materials they purchase and sell.

Most large buyers of medicinal plants are located on the coasts. Marketing of medicinal plants is characterised by small start-up firms. The popularity of herbal and alternative health care products makes new product market entry relatively easy. Producers who have sufficient quantities of plant material that has been harvested correctly to produce a consistent, high-quality product may be able to produce a direct retail product with processing and packaging assistance.

Producers marketing medicinal plants need to familiarise themselves thoroughly with Federal and State regulations regarding health care products. In general, if the product is marketed only as a food substance/nutritional supplement, with no medical claims, then the product will not have to undergo the extensive testing and certification required of pharmaceutical drugs. Pharmaceutical firms that produce prescription and overthe-counter drugs are another market for certain medicinal plants.

While many biologically based drugs have been replaced with synthetic drugs, there are still drugs produced from cultivated or wild medicinal plants. For example, reserpine, used to reduce hypertension, is produced from Rauwolfia serpentine, and colchicine, which relieves gout, is produced from meadow saffron (Colchicum autumnale). Recent discoveries, such as the cancer-fighting potential of taxol, are creating renewed interest in exploring chemical composition of forest plants.

However, since pharmaceutical firms seek synthesised compounds if possible (for quality control purposes), the market for medicinal plants used in prescription and over-the-counter drugs is still very small. But if a plant compound cannot be artificially synthesised, then these firms will first seek cultivated plants grown under very uniform growing conditions and then wild plants if they cannot be field-grown.

The following rules of getting started have been suggested by those most familiar with the marketing of wild harvested botanicals:

— Don't talk to a buyer until you have something ready to sell. Most people make the mistake of trying to contact a large buyer to try to find out from them if it is worth their while to try to wildcraft a product and sell it. But most buyers are not interested in talking to anyone about that. They are only interested in buying. A broker, however, will work with a small harvester, grade the product, and give advice.

— Do a feasibility study that will produce a large enough volume of materials to actually sell, such as 2,000 pounds. Any company interested in buying in very small volumes (hundreds of pounds) probably is not a true reflection of the market anyway.

— Always send samples of your product, and be able to back these up with at least 2,000 pounds of materials to sell.

— If you are intending to make a career out of specialty forest products, find a buyer in your region and "get in line." Work at modest levels of production if necessary for several years while moving up the line.Consider these early years as schooling, and any financial setbacks as tuition and book fees. If you break even, consider it a pretty cheap education. If you try to crowd (that is, get to the top of a buyer's list), people who do not like your ethics are going to avoid doing business with you. Greedy people are generally not in the industry longer than about 2 years.

— Realise you must learn the craft and business slowly and from the ground up. Many people get into trouble trying to hire other people to do the actual harvesting, for example. But this is exactly what the entrepreneur needs to learn first for himself or herself. No one can start out from scratch and expect to immediately become a "wheeler dealer." Everyone needs to start out at the lowest rungs of the ladder, or they will miss some valuable lessons, and maybe lose the whole ball game.

There are various ways for harvesters to notify wholesalers that they have botanicals available for sale. A bulk sheet mailer is one way, accompanied by a sample. This may lead to a buyer offering to buy the product on the spot, perhaps for a minimum quantity of anywhere between 500 and 5,000 pounds. The 500-pound buyers are usually the regional wholesalers and cooperatives, including some of the chain food stores, small manufacturers or local marketers, and most buying clubs and cooperatives.

The standard method of purchase is either spot buying (on specials) or on contract, whereby the farmer/wildcrafter ships on a monthly or bimonthly basis. The 5,000-pound buyers may also be regional wholesalers, but ones who include processing as part of their services to manufacturers. Large manufacturers may use these wholesalers to process their products for interfacing such things as tea bagging machinery. They most often prefer to buy 5,000- to 10,000-pound quantities on a monthly or bimonthly basis.

The import/export houses are the large wholesales houses, often oriented toward trade agreements, and are involved in both the import and export of natural resources. Most are in cities with major ports. A typical wholesale house might buy more than 200 tons of a crop, although it might buy in smaller quantities when opening a new market. Ideally, the harvester would also secure a contract harvest for the next year.

Harvesting

It is generally felt that a minimum of a 2- to 4-acre stand of plants is necessary to harvest efficiently. The harvester should be prepared to spend 50 percent of time actually searching for the worthwhile patches. Only minimum harvests of 500 pounds dry weight are regarded as economically feasible.

Wildcrafters should take special care to get permission from landowners prior to any harvesting. To avoid problems (for example, claims of poaching), it is a good idea to also alert local authorities that you are in an area harvesting. Plants must be harvested from areas that have not been sprayed or otherwise contaminated by road dust, etc. Perhaps the most underutilised resource is the slash material left by loggers. By following logging crews, one can salvage whole plants, barks, roots, and leaves.

By working with logging crews, it is possible to increase the awareness of timber operators of the value of some of the "trash" species, and the salvage work can help clean up a cut area. Loggers can also alert wildcrafters to new areas where the plants being sought grow. Each product will require different processing and packaging procedures. Communication with a buyer is essential to ensuring that the product is harvested, processed, and packed correctly.

Drying and Storage

Drying is one of the most critical steps in the processing of crude botanicals. Removing moisture not only prevents molding but also inhibits the chemical reactions that otherwise would reduce the plant's end use. Each part of a plant-leaf, herb, root, bark, or flower-must be dried to the correct percentage of moisture required for both storage and transport. The drying process must also be done in such a way as to prevent either the loss of volatile oils (natural flavors) and/or the loss of cosmetic integrity (colour or appearance) of the product. This requires close monitoring of both airflow and temperature.

Siscussion of airflow, temperature, and vapor pressure considerations in drying herbs and species is contained in

Miller. Also discussed are sun-cure and shade-drying methods, a solar drying system, rack drying, a drying shed design, packaging and storage, tags and labels, and trucking. Recommendations are given for the temperature, method of drying, problems to avoid, storage method, and packaging method for about 100 herbs and spices.

If heat is not available, the crop should be covered with tarps to slow the change in temperature. At the same time, good air circulation is critical during storage to prevent spoilage. Bags will need to be off the floor (for example, on pallets) and away from walls. All products will lose weight as they lose moisture. Crops stored for longer than 6 months will need to be reweighted before shipping. Harvesters should adhere to good marketing principles and ship a little more product than they bill for.

Where processed herbs and spices are concerned, proximity to the market is not as important as with many other commodities. Once dried, botanicals are relatively easy and lightweight to store and transport. The high prices received for them generally make it economical to ship long distances. A 10-ton load of wheat may be worth $2,000 or less, but a similar load of herbs may be worth $10,000. Buyers of medicinal plants are located nationwide, and several new firms and grower cooperatives (primarily for herb production) recently have been established. Shipping can normally be handled by conventional package or contract shippers.

Where fresh greens are wildcrafted, distribution time to local or regional markets must be minimal. Fresh food of any type will probably require special containerised packaging, and delivery time will be critical. While such arrangements are possible, they will be more costly than for dried botanicals and should be justified by the sales.

Depending on the quantities, wild greens may be packaged using any of the usual food container options. Dried greens can be packaged in plastic bags. There are a variety of inexpensive wood and shook box containers to accommodate the usual "flat" and "basket" quantities. Long-distance shipping may require temperaturecontrolled containers.

Producers interested in manufacturing a final retail medicinal plant product should identify potential regional retailers. Natural medicinal plant products normally are retailed through health food or natural food stores in metropolitan areas. Drug stores and grocery stores are beginning to stock some medicinal plant products, such as herbal teas, but few are using small, locally produced products yet.

All forest products that are being collected on a commercial scale from public lands require permits. The permit process typically involves purchasing a local map, obtaining a legal description of the land and the owner(s) (such as a private timber company, national forest, or private individual), obtaining permission from the landowner, and obtaining a permit validation at the sheriff's office. It is important to carry the permit at all times during harvest operations.

Harvesting wild herbs for botanicals calls for hard work, since often the plants are widely scattered over large areas. Large-scale forage operations should be based on an aerial photograph to determine the potential size, quality, and the ease of access to the crop in question. A "motorcycle scout" may do an on-site evaluation. It is also essential to identify a good staging area where the crops will be dried and processed.

Of course, where edible materials are concerned, the single most important requirement is the training given the harvester. In the worst-case scenario, improper plant identification could result in inadvertent poisoning. Equally important is the forager's knowledge of the plants and their habitats. Like all plants, wild greens generally have seasons during which they are at their best for harvesting.

Good training of workers is also needed to ensure appropriate harvesting methods. Harvesting and processing of relatively small areas can usually be achieved by small teams. Most wildcrafters need to make a minimum of $75 a day to make the work worthwhile. They frequently need to advance money to access remote locations and to obtain the necessary brush permits. Harvesters must often live on forest floors or in other temporary housing.

Basic equipment for foraging would include implements for cutting and digging and containers in which to hold the plants as they are gathered, such as baskets or bags. Harvesters generally carry burlap or woven polypropylene sacks. A wire can be used to hold the sack open, and a shoulder strap will keep the wearer's hands free to work. Most foragers have developed "specialised" tools for particular applications. In general, the equipment is not expensive or difficult to find. It will depend on the species being harvested.

Typically, roots, bark, leaves, or flowers are collected. A variety of hand tools may be used by the harvester, such as shovels, rakes, axes, and chain saws. Bark is removed by hand stripping, using a sharp knife. Roots and rhizomes are dug with a shovel or an asparagus knife. Light machinery such as a plow, potato digger, or lifter may be used for more deeply rooted plants, and a shrubbery digger can be used on deeply rooted plants.

Occasionally, a come-along or gas-powered weed eater equipped with a saw blade may be needed, or even a specialised and prototype piece of light machinery. A small chipper is an important tool for bark and roots to break them into premilling forms and to make the crop easier to dry quickly. Much of this equipment may be available from used farm yard equipment dealers for relatively little money.

Occasionally, renting a piece of commercial equipment may be advised. Industrial sized vacuums fitted with a rake at the hose end can be used for harvesting flowers. A portable backpack-type vacuum/blower may be used to pull material into bags for drying. Commercial ventures will usually require a covered, heated building for drying: air, solar, and heat dryers may be needed. Crops that are to be dried in the sun will require tarps. In some cases, a baler and other farm equipment can be used in areas where there is easy access. A truck with high sidewalls and/or a trailer will be needed to move materials to the staging area.

If a purchase order has already been obtained, an operator will want to have a truck waiting at the staging area to receive the bagged or boxed material and ship it directly to a weigh station and on to the buyer. In such cases, a generator will be useful to provide lighting.

Conservation of Wild Plants

Even plants that are easily grown and locally abundant can be so severely overcollected that their populations are not sustainable. Many wildcrafted plants are now becoming harder to find. Any plan to pursue botanicals on a commercial basis must include a reforestation plan. Each botanical has its own needs for resource protection to ensure that it is not overharvested. The owner or manager of a given area must also be assured that the crop will be regenerated for the future. Many medicinal plants are fragile and some are rare.

Some species are also slow growing. There is also an unfortunate tendency to harvest endangered species of edible plants. Even though it is against the law to pick them, most people do not know what the endangered plants are in a region. If a particular rare plant becomes a "fad," for example, in the time it might take authorities to track down pickers, an entire community of plants could be lost. Hundreds of pounds can be removed in a few hours, roots and all.

Several healthy plants should always be left to spread and continue natural production. Plant physiology departments in local universities may have good suggestions on regeneration of specific species. Several organisations concerned with the conservation of native plants are beginning to take strong positions advocating that large suppliers of plant materials take action to ensure that only propagated and cultivated, not wild-harvested, materials are sold. Groups like the Nature Conservancy are strongly discouraging the buying and selling of wild-harvested native plant materials through the nursery trade. A trend to discourage (and, in fact, to blacklist) firms that sell certain wild-dug or harvested nursery stock has already become clearly established.

There are no doubt dozens of plant species whose commercial wild harvest can be accomplished on a sustainable basis. Most edible greens are cut, not dug up, and there is usually only one cutting per year of an individual plant. Nevertheless, it is reasonable to assume that strong forces will be brought to bear on wild medicinal plant harvesting if the industry does not take strong steps to ensure there is no reduction in the longterm viability of all native plant populations. It would be advisable to begin action on developing cultivated sources of woodland botanicals, perhaps through forest farming or leasing operations.

8

Medicinal Value of Phytoecdysteroids

When phytoecdysteroids were discovered in plants, they have been shown to stimulate the synthesis of proteins in animals and humans, and to have adaptogenic, antimutagenic, hypocholesterolemic, immunostimulating, nutritive, and tonic properties.

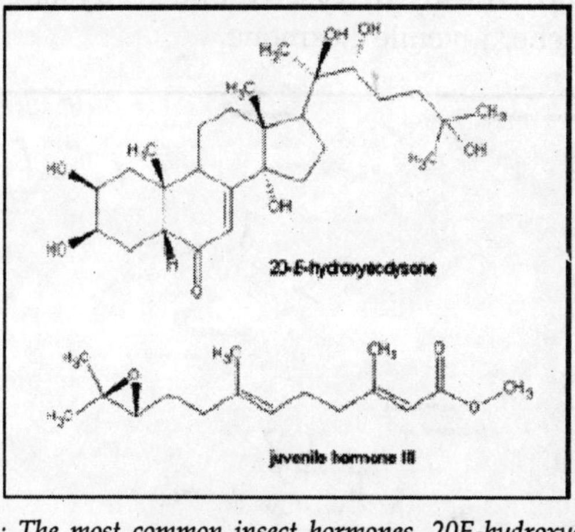

Figure 1: The most common insect hormones, 20E-hydroxyecdysone (ecdysone) and juvenile hormone.

Plants have survived assaults from organisms and environmental stress for millennia. They have done so by various mechanisms including physical barriers such as thorns and thick cuticles, and by synthesising an array of defense chemicals as well as other growth and defense mechanisms. Protective mechanisms used by animals and humans are often similar in strategy and complementary in the substances used for protection. Phytoecdysteroids are a class of chemicals that plants synthesise for defense against phytophagous (planteating) insects.

These compounds are exact replicas of ecdysteroids, hormones used by the arthropod (insect) and crustacean (crab/lobster) families in the molting process known as ecdysis. Insects that ingest phytoecdysteroids and have not adapted to this defense are subject to serious adverse effects, including reduced weight, molting disruption, and/or mortality.

Chemistry of Phytoecdysteroids

The two most common hormones found in insects are the ecdysteroid, 20E-hydroxyecdysone (ecdysone) and the sesquiterpene, juvenile hormone.

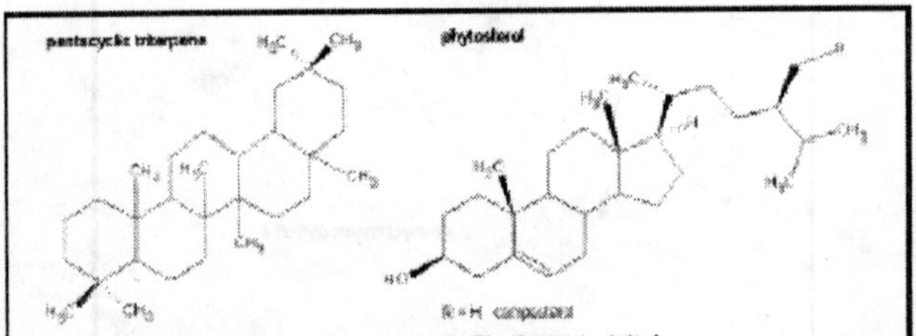

Figure 2: Molecular structure of triterpenoid saponins, phytosterols, and phytoecdysteroids.

They are usually accompanied by a number of other minor ecdysteroids. Chemically, phytoecdysteroids are classed as triterpenoids, the group of compounds that includes triterpene saponins, phytosterols, and phytoecdysteroids (Figure 2). Plants synthesise phytoecdysteroids from mevalonic acid in the mevalonate pathway of the plant cell using acetyl-CoA as a precursor (Figure 3).

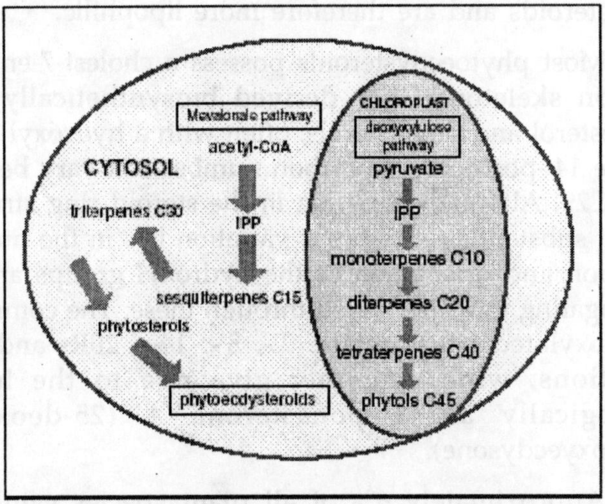

Figure 3: Biosynthetic pathway of phytoecdysteroids in the plant cell.

Animals and humans also synthesise some of the same products from the mevalonate pathway, such as ubiquinone and sterols. They cannot, however, synthesise ecdysteroids. Over 250 ecdysteroid analogs have been identified so far in plants, and it has been theorised that there are over 1,000 possible structures which might occur in nature. There is evidence that most plants retain the genetic capacity to produce ecdysteroids, but their expression is turned off. The question remains whether the capacity to synthesise ecdysteroids is genetically or environmentally induced.

Either way, it may be possible to alter the expression of genes as a way to increase the amount of phytoecdysteroids in plants to increase protection of crops and to provide raw material to produce dietary supplements. Ecdysteroids are polar steroids, almost sugar-like in their solubility properties. While mammalian steroid hormones have more variable structures, they universally lack the polyhydroxylated side chain characteristic of ecdysteroids and are therefore more lipophilic.

Most phytoecdysteroids possess a cholest-7-en-6-one carbon skeleton (C27), derived biosynthetically from cholesterol and phytosterols, often with a hydroxyl group in the 14‥-position. The carbon number can vary between C19-C29. Although variation in the steroid ring structure is not substantial, significant variation lies in the number, position and orientation of the hydroxyl groups and the conjugating moieties linked through these. The commonly hydroxylated sites are the 2'-, 3'-, 14‥-, 20R- and 22R-positions, which together give rise to the highly biologically active ponasterone A (25-deoxy-20-hydroxyecdysone).

Approximately 6% of all plant species synthesise phytoecdysteroids. Phytoecdysteroid levels in plants are usually found to be 0.1% or less of their dry weight and have been isolated from all parts of plants in much higher amounts than those present in arthropods. Low concentrations of various phytoecdysteroids deter some insects (2-25 ppm), while other insects are resistant to very high concentrations (400-1000 ppm).

It appears ecdysteroid concentrations are highest in tissues which are most important for the survival of the plant and that these levels change throughout plant development. The most common phytoecdysteroid found in plants is ecdysone. While most plant families have at least some species that accumulate ecdysteroids, less than

2% of the world's flora has been investigated for the presence of ecdysteroids.

Among plant species highest in phytoecdysteroids is spinach containing 50 ug/g fresh weight. Other examples are: ajugasterone in Ajuga L., Lamiaceae and Vitex L., Verbenaceae; leuzeasterone in Leuzea carthamoides (syn. Rhaponticum carthamoides (Willd.) Iljin, Asteraceae); 2-deoxy-20-hydroxyecdysone 3-glucoside and 3-epi-2-deoxy-20-hydroxyecdysone in Tinospora cordifolia (Willd.) Miers, Menispermaceae; ecdysterone and inokosterone in Achyranthes bidentata Blume, Amaranthaceae; polypodine B in Leuzea carthamoides; and ecdysterone, ajugasterone C, ajugasterone C-20, 22- monoacetonide in Rhaponticum uniflorum (L.) DC., Asteraceae.

Adaptogenic Activity

The term adaptogen, coined by Lazarev in 1958, has no correlation in modern pharmacology although scientific research on the anabolic and adaptogenic properties of plants has been published in the Russian literature since the mid-1960s. Ingestion of certain plant extracts could improve stress markers in laboratory animals.

An adaptogen should:

— be innocuous and cause minimal disturbance to the normal physiological function,

— have a nonspecific action; and,

— have a normalising action irrespective of the direction of the preceding pathological changes.

While the definition of an adaptogen refers specifically to these three criteria, other bioactive properties are nonetheless characteristic of adaptogens. These include anabolic, antioxidant, hepatoprotective, and hypoglycemic activity. Phytoecdysteroids have also been found to have similar bioactivities.

Some adaptogenic plant species have been tested and found positive for presence of phytoecdysteroids. These are: Achyranthes bidentata, Tinospora cordifolia, Pfaffia paniculata, Leuzea carthamoides, Rhaponticum uniflorum, and Serratula coronata. The three latter species belong to a larger group of genera encompassing the Cardueae tribe in the Asteraceae. The adaptogenic property of these three Cardueae species has been suggested to be due to phytoecdysteroids.

Many of the species in this tribe have not been tested for adaptogenic activity. Species in the Cardueae genera such as Atractylis L., Carduus L., Carthamus L., Centaurea L., Cnicus L., Cynara L., Saussurea DC., and Silybum Adans, have been used in both indigenous medical practices and in modern herbal medicine. Saussurea is one of the larger genera in Cardueae having at least 300 species widely distributed in Eurasia. Saussurea species are currently harvested from the wild for both medicinal and religious purposes in India.

Due to habitat specificity and its narrow range of distribution almost all the Saussurea species growing in the high altitude of the Himalayas need conservation. Some Saussurea species, in particular, Saussurea costus Lipsch. and Saussurea medusa Maxim., may be adaptogenic, as suggested by use in Tibetan and Chinese medicine for wasting of muscles and memory deficit. Carlina biebersteinii Bernh. ex Hornem as a species studied for adaptogenic properties. Carlina biebersteinii is placed in Carlininae, a subtribe of the Cardueae. The history of medicinal use of species in the Cardueae thus suggests that this tribe and closely related species may have adaptogenic activity.

Some species related to known adaptogens were found to contain phytoecdysteroids such as Tinospora capillipes Gagnep., Menispermaceae, Achyranthes fauriei

H. Lev. & Vaniot, and Achyranthes rubrofusca Wight, Amaranthaceae, and Lamium maculatum L., Lamiaceae. Atragene sibirica L., Ranunculaceae has been described as an adaptogen, but this species has not been tested for the presence of phytoecdysteroids. However, many genera of the Ranunculaceae contain phytoecdysteroids. The presence of phytoecdysteroids in the Ranunculaceae could possibly explain the mechanism of action of the nerve and mood properties of Anemone patens L.

It is notable that plant species in the ginseng (Araliaceae) family, many of which have adaptogenic properties, have not been tested for phytoecdysteroids. Since phytoecdysteroid compounds can produce an adaptogenic effect, it is therefore possible that some adaptogenic plant species contain phytoecdysteroids. If so, the mechanism of action for adaptogenic species may involve this class of plant compounds. Phytoecdysteroids may act synergistically with triterpene, phenylpropane and oxylipin compounds.

The design and bioactivity of phytoecdysteroids have likely been shaped by the genetic evolution of organisms interacting over millennia. Bioactive compounds once used by lower organisms as signals for food and danger may have evolved into bioregulating signals in higher organisms such as mammals.

Mammalian cells recognise phytoecdysteroids. There is evidence that phytoecdysteroids can induce RNA synthesis, accelerate translocation, and stabilise both proteins and phospholipids in the cell membrane. The enhancement of skeletal muscle growth by ecdysteroids is perhaps best evidenced by their use in inducible gene expression systems to culture skeletal and muscle cells.

The bioactivity of many plant compounds, including phytoecdysteroids, has been linked to nongenomic effects. These effects arise from hormone ligand binding to a nuclear receptor, resulting in a long series of subcellular processes that include mRNA production and modification, translation into proteins, protein translation and/or insertion into membranes. This process can take hours before a response is seen. Nongenomic effects result in the same response but do not involve direct ligand to receptor binding and the response is almost immediate.

Ecdysterone is thought to stabilise cell membranes resulting in modifications of membrane proteins, accumulation of ligands, and other membrane associated effects. Two mediators of the stress response, neurosteroids and aldosterone are believed to work via nongenomic effects.

The binding of phytoecdysteroids in arthropods mimics the dimerisation mechanism observed in steroid hormone receptors. In arthropods, ligand binding to the ecdysteroid receptor (EcR) promotes dimerisation with the ultraspiracle receptor (USP). This dimerisation enhances ecdysteroid binding to EcR. That is, EcR forms a heterodimer with USP. The ultraspiracle receptor belongs to the superfamily of nuclear receptors which are ligand-inducible transcription regulators.

The homologue of USP in animals and humans is the retinoid X receptor (RXR) and when expressed in these systems, EcR has been shown to partner with RXR. Experiments indicate that EcR and RXR proteins are capable of forming a hetero-complex, and that both proteins are required for binding to ecdysteroids. Both USP and RXR receptors heterodimerise with other receptors to form active receptor complexes. For RXR, agonistic ligands like the 9-cis retinoic acid are known to bind to RXR and modulate the activity of the RXR dimeric partner.

The ligand binding cavities of USP and RXR have one part in common, close to helices 3 and 5, but the cavity is wider for USP. The nuclear receptors for ecdysone, thyroid and retinoid X receptor are evolutionarily closely related, having descended from a common ancestor. A phylogeny of nuclear steroid receptors suggests the possibility that ecdysone supplements are recognised in humans via one of more of a broad family of recently identified receptors that can bind a broad variety of ligands.

The pregnane X receptor (PXR), human nuclear receptor (hPAR), and steroid xenobiotic receptor (SXR), and vitamin D receptor (VDR) because there is research relating antioxidant activity of ecdysteroid administration to vitamin D deficiency are in this family. Glucocorticoid and glucocorticoid metabolites act as agonists for this family of receptors. The effect of ecdysteroids on reproductive tissues of animals and humans has shown enhanced sexual activity.

Ecdysteroids have been found to have many pharmacological effects in animals and humans such as increasing acetylcholine esterase activity in the brain, reducing the hyperglycemic response to exogenous glucagon, and decreasing hepatic cholesterol by stimulating excretion of cholesterol in the bile. These effects have important meaning for pathologies related to dysfunctional stress adaptation, which has been hypothesised to be caused by excess or deficient release of stress mediators such as cortisol. It is possible that the metabolism of ecdysteroids in animals and humans may produce metabolites that are structurally similar to endogenous steroids.

Side effects of synthetic anabolic steroids include acne, increased facial and body hair, impotence, prostate enlargement, gynecomastia, high blood pressure, liver failure, and neurological problems such as aggressive moods, delusions and paranoia. Yet, ecdysteroids have not shown any side effects in humans. Toxicity studies, concluding that ecdysteroids have no toxic response in animals.

Phytoecdysteroids do not appear to activate mammalian steroid hormone receptors, even at very high concentrations. Rats and birds feed on seeds containing amounts as much as 20 grams of 20-hydroxyecdysone per kilogram without any apparent problems. The hormonal actions of ecdysteroids seem to be limited to arthropods.

Commercial Preparations

The history of ecdysteroid supplements began forty years ago when Burdette discovered that ecdysterone could enhance the rate of protein synthesis in mammalian tissue. Anabolic effects from ecdysterone were found in mice in 1969 by Hikino et al, and separately by Otaka, et al. Syrov attributed the anabolic effects of Pfaffia paniculata extracts to ecdysterone in 1984. Since then, Russian and Chinese Olympic athletes have been suspected of using ecdysteroid supplements.

Today, more than 140 dietary supplements containing ecdysone are available on the Internet and elsewhere such as: Syntrabol®, Ecdysten®, Ecdybol®, and MethoxyFactor®. As an example, each 200 mg capsule of Syntrabol® contains isinokosterone (20-hydroxyecdysterone). These ergogenic supplements are believed to produce anabolic and growth-promoting effects, and are primarily marketed to weight lifters and sports enthusiasts as pseudo-steroidal muscle enhancers.

Plants that contain high amounts of phytoecdysteroids are cultivated in Europe as a source of these compounds for the dietary supplement market. These plant species are primarily represented by Leuzea carthamoides, Rhaponticum uniflorum, and Serratula coronata. Other preparations based on purified ecdysteroids or on ecdysteroid-containing plant powders/

extracts are sourced from the following plants: Cyanotis somaliensis (Commelinaceae), Achyranthes aspera, Cyanthula officinalis (Amaranthaceae), Leuzea carthamoides (Asteraceae), Pfaffia paniculata, P. iresinoides (Amaranthaceae), Polypodium vulgare, P. aurea, P. glycyrrhiza (Pteridophyta), and Ajuga turkestanica (Lamiaceae).

Silkworms (Bombyx mori) contain ecdysteroids and have been shown to enhance the rate of protein synthesis in mammals. The medicinal fungi called dong chong xia cao (Cordyceps sinensis (Berk.) Saccardo Clavicipitaceae) is used to increase stamina and for impotence (e.g., adaptogenic properties). Cordyceps is in the same family as ergot that attacks and parasitises insects. In this case, the host is the larvae of Hepialus armoricanus Oberthur or Holotrichia koraiensis Murayana, Hepialidae.

The stalked fruiting bodies of the fungi attached to the larva is the traditional form of dong chong xia cao. Today, Cordyceps sinensis is often mass-produced on grain, not on a larval host. In a recent comparison of bioactive ingredients in various Cordyceps products, ecdysteroids were not even mentioned. Whether ecdysteroids are a part of the bioactivity of Cordyceps products is not known.

Nor is it known whether Cordyceps grown on grain contains phytoecdysteroids, or whether the fungi itself produces ecdysteroids. Phytoecdysteroid compounds may be found in fungi. Fungi are no longer classed in the plant kingdom; rather, the closest relatives of fungi are animals. Ecdysteroids in mammals can be traced to dietary vegetables and fruits or to human parasites such as worms. In any case, the larvae may be crucial to the bioactivity of the traditional form of Cordyceps.

9

Herb-drug Interactions

Herbal medicines include dietary supplements that contain herbs, either singly or in mixtures. Also called botanicals, herbal medicines are plants or plant parts used for their scent, flavour, and/or therapeutic properties. Food and Drug Administration (FDA) regulations regarding accuracy of active ingredients content or efficacy and safety of active ingredients.

Health care in older adults focuses on chronic disease: Older adults typically manifest one chronic disease for each decade past age 50 and most chronic diseases are treated with multiple drug therapy. This means the average older adult takes 5 prescriptions each day. The addition of herbal medicines to a program of multiple drug therapy holds the potential for herb-drug interactions.

Herbal medicine has been an essential component of oriental medicine (OM), which has existed for over two thousand years. Herbal prescriptions comprise the vast majority of OM practice in China and Southeast Asia. Scientific verification and applications beyond traditional prescriptions are beginning to be explored in the West. While literature emphasises recent development in this area, it is worthy to acknowledge that herbal interactions were documented in ancient traditional TCM texts, by traditional theories. For example, in all formulae, warm herbs are balanced by cool herbs and vice versa. TCM herbalists have to carefully prescribe formulae based on disease manifestation and the patient's energy 'Qi'. Therefore, cold or hot drugs are rarely recommended for extended use-it is believed that they can deplete the body's energy 'Qi'.

In Western medicine, laxatives and steroids are typical examples of cold and hot drugs. In addition to utilising the herbs' energetic property TCM practitioners also rely on the tastes of an herb as part of a therapeutic guide. For example, sweet herbs like licorice (glyccerhiza) are thought to be neutral and nourishing so it is often used in TCM herbal formulae to ameliorate side effects of other ingredients. Traditional herbal texts recognised a number of herb-herb interactions as summarised below:

Incompatible combinations: This includes three herbs (aconite, licorice, and veratrum) with 6 other herbs. Their combinations would lead to herb-to-herb interactions and/ or toxicity.

R. Glycerrhiza (Gan Cao)	Incompatible combinations	R. Euphorbiae Kansui (Gan sui), R.Euphorbiae seu Knoxiae (Da ji), Fos Geukwa (Yuan Hua), andHerba sargassum (Hat zao)
Rhizoma Aconite (Wu tou)		Bulbus fritillariae cirrhosac (Chuan bet mu), bulbus fritillariae thundergii (Zhe bet mu), Fructus trichosanthis (Gua leu),
Rhizoma pinelliac (Banxia),		R. Ampelopsis (Bat lian) and Rhizoma bletillae (Bat ji).
Rhizoma et Radix veratri (Li lu)		R. ginseng (Ren shen), R. Glehniae (Bet sha shen),

R. adenophorae (Nan shi shen), R. scrophulariae (Xuan she), R. paeoniae alba (Bat shao), R. paeoniac Rubra (Chi shao), and Herba asari (Xi xin).

Herbs with teratogenic (birth defects) effects:

Hirudo seu whitmania	Shui zhi
Moschus	She xiang
Mulabris	Ban mao
Radix euphorbiae	Da ji
Radix phytolaccae	Shang lu
Rhizoma sparganii	San leng
Rhizoma zedoariae	E Zhu
Semen crotonis	Ba dou
Semen pharbitidis	Qian niu zi
Tabanus	Meng chong

Herbs with potential for toxic effects: These herbs are very strong Qi and Blood movers and can certainly cause side effects if used inappropriately. They should also be avoided during pregnancy.

Semen persicae	Tao ren
Flos carthami	Hong hua
Rhizoma and Radix Rhei	Da huang
Fructus aurantii	Zi shi
Radix aconite	Fu zhi
Rhizoma zingiberis	Gan jiang
Cortex cinnamomi	Rou gui

Oriental herbal medical principles are fascinating. In general TCM herbal formulation often consists of 4-12 ingredients. Each herb plays an important role in the delivery and action of the formula. For example, certain ingredients assist in delivering the main herb to the organ or meridian while other ingredients act to reduce the side effects or to augment the desire effect. Oriental herbal medicine utilises plants, minerals, insects, and animal products. Rarely find herbs being prescribed as a single agent.

However, consuming herbal medicine has not been without risks. Some Chinese herbs have been reported to contain heavy metals and/or adulterated with western drugs. For example, PC-SPES was recalled in California because it may have been contaminated with warfarin, alprazolam, and diethylstilbesterol. Recent surveys have shown that trends for complementary and alternative (CAM) usage have increased steadily among adults over the past 50 years.

About 60 million Americans (1 in 5) use CAM therapy, and this trend is expected to significantly increase if insurance coverage for CAM increases in the future. It was estimated that 20% of patients regularly taking prescription drugs were also taking herbal or nutritional supplements, suggesting that about 15 million Americans are at potential risk for herb-drug interactions. Also, about a third of patients reported they seek CAM therapies for health promotion and disease prevention.

One review 2/3 of the 108 case reports was classified as 'unable to be evaluated', which meant they lack critical information to explain other possibilities. For example, many the case reports focused solely on the agents involved and failed to include relevant information such as: patient history; concurrent diseases, conditions, or medication associated with adverse event; concomitant medications; description of interaction; alternative explanations; chronology, and time sequence of drug administration etc.

One of the challenges in integrative medicine at the presence is that most supplements available over-the counter are not standardised. Purity and potency standards are only available for a small selection of herbs. To further complicate this matter, patients may take supplements from different manufacturers. Likewise similarities in names and appearance have caused some Chinese herbal products to contain misidentified plants.

Pharmaceutical drugs and a significant level of heavy metals were also found in some herbal patents. Without a standard for purity and potency, the possibilities for interactions increase greatly for drug-herb, herb-herb, or reactions to contaminants. Besides posing risks of toxicity for patients, it is also difficult to verify reports on herb-drug adverse reactions due to numerous unknown variables. The greatest potential for adverse effects between herb-drug combinations occurs when the followings are combined:

— *Sympathomimic (anti-seizure), and Cariovascular drugs*: Ephedra (Ma huang) contains ephedrine, and pseudoephedrine that interferes with this class of drugs.

— *Diuretic drugs*: A variety of herbs can increase or decrease this effect. The most commonly used oriental herbs for their diuretic effects include:, Polypori Umbellati (Zhu ling), Semen plantaginis (Che qian zi), and Alismatis orientalis (Ze xie), Akebia trifoliata (Mu Tong),.

— *Anti-diabetic drugs*: Anemarrhena asphodeloidis (Zhi mu), Gypsum fibrosum (Shi gao), Scrophularia ningpoensis (Xuan shen), Atractylodes (Cang Zhu), Dioscorea oppositae (Shan yao), and Astragalus membranacei (Huang qi).

— *Anti-coagulating drugs*: Because Coumadin (Warfarin) interacts with a wide range of herbs, it is best to avoid combining Coumadin with all herbs unless the patient has guidance from an experienced health professional. TCM herbs with the greatest potential for interfering with anti-coagulants includes: Salviae miltiorrhizae (Dan shen), Angelica sinensis (Dang gui), Ligustici chuanxiong (Chuan xiong), Persicae (Tao ren), Carthamus tinctorii (Hong hua), and Hirudo seu whitmania (Shut zhi). Likewise, patients should also monitor their green vegetables intakes when they are on anti-coagulant therapy.

In addition, it is possible to predict when herb/drugs interact by knowing their pharmacokinetic properties, and their pharmacodynamic behaviours. Pharmacokinetic properties entail changes in absorption, metabolism, and elimination of the drugs/herbs whereas pharmacodynamic behaviours refer to how the herb/drug interacts inside the body (synergistic or antagonistic). In general, herb/drug that alters the stomach pH (anti-acids), or intestinal motility (laxatives) will have an effect on absorption.

Drug/herb metabolism occurs principally in the liver. The duration (life-span) of an herb or drug in the body depends on whether the liver's metabolism is induced or inhibited. An herb lasts longer in the body if its metabolism is inhibited by another drug; likewise, it is excreted faster if one's liver metabolism is induced. Further, drug/herb elimination primarily occurs at the kidneys and is affected by the individual's kidneys function or by drugs' toxic side effects. Lastly, the extent to which an herb-drug interacts depends on the individual's health condition, age, body weight, metabolic rate, and dosage.

Patients should not try to mix drugs that have a narrow therapeutic range (digitalis, theophylline, lithium, and warfarin) with potassium lowering herbs (licorice, and aloe), herbal stimulants (ephedra, caffeine, guarana, green tea), and antiplatelet herbs (Ginkgo, bilberry leaf, ginger, black cohosh, and Chamomile). Just as important, if patients insist on integrating herbal medicine they must be taking their medication and herbs consistently in order to avoid severe under or overdose.

In addition to herb-drug interactions, food can and do also interact with medication. Traditional Chinese medicine views food the same way it views medicine. For example, all foods and drinks are classified by their energetic properties such as hot, warm, neutral, cool, and cold (Yin and Yang). Further, foods are also graded by their tonic potential versus their draining effects on the body such as excessive heat, cold, damp, or dry. For example, rice is considered a tonic whereas cream is considered cold and damp.

Thus, TCM thinks about food as medicine and their potential for benefits as well as interactions with herbal therapy. When a patient with excessive heat, cooling herbs are prescribed and instructed to avoid dry or hot food i.e. chips, deep-fried food, or spicy food. Instead, the patient is advised to eat mung bean or mung bean sprouts.

Working with patients who use complementary and alternative medicine (CAM) and conventional medicine: With no clear guidelines for integrating CAM and conventional medicine, it is important for clinicians to foster an open dialogue with their patients. Eisenberg and colleagues reported that about 60% of the people surveyed did not discuss their CAM use with their primary care physicians. This lack of communication is expected to be more prevalent among immigrant communities due to language and cultural barriers. For example, many patients do not want to appear disobedient toward their providers by admitting that they are seeking other treatments, or think their providers care or need to know about their traditional practices.

Additionally, providers should be aware of reasons why their patients seek out CAM therapies. For example, 1) conventional therapies no longer provide relief or are producing unwanted side effects; and 2) no specific conventional therapy exist or the treatment plans are contrary to patient's belief. Sometimes, a misunderstanding of the instruction of how to take the medicine, urgency of their conditions, or difficulties in filling the prescriptions can pose barriers for proper health care among immigrant communities.

Further, since CAM therapies have been an integral part of Southeast Asian's health promotion and health maintenance practice, they do not generally associate potential for toxicity when combining CAM therapies with western drugs.

Suggestions for Exploring CAM Therapies

Suggestions with vietnamese patients: Acknowledge that certain traditional health practices are common in their communities. For example, in Southeast Asia, 'coining' and 'cupping' are often used at home for minor aches, pain and colds. These techniques often leave bruise-like appearances on the skin. Herbal tonics and dietary therapies are also commonly used for health maintenance.

Some therapies clearly offer relieves, others are harmful especially when combined with western medication. The effects of combining both traditional and conventional therapies may take weeks or months to be apparent. Certain combinations can be detrimental. Integrative medicine is a young practice, still needing a safe practice guideline, and resources for clinicians and patients alike. When working with patients utilising CAM and western medicine, a step-bystep strategy is recommended. This includes:

— Asking patients to identify the principle complaint and maintaining a symptom diary;

— Discussing patient's expectations and preferences, and reviewing safety and efficacy issues;

— Identifying a suitable licensed provider;

— Establishing a treatment strategy with CAM provider and requesting documentation; and

— Scheduling follow-up visit to review treatment plan.

Popular Herb Remedies

Herbal supplements are widely available in supermarkets, mail order, and other retail outlets. In fact, only a small percentage of herbals (4.5%) are actually sold in pharmacies. Nonetheless, the tremendous sales growth and popularity of herbals requires that pharmacy technicians expand and their knowledge regarding the appropriate use of, and adverse reactions and drug interactions with herbal preparations. Pharmacy technicians are often the point of initial contact by patients and consumers seeking information concerning natural products. Both pharmacists and technicians feel inadequately equipped to provide a cogent response due to a paucity of peer-reviewed drug information.

Herbs are Natural

Herbs are natural so they must be pure: When evaluating herbal supplements one must realise that, unlike proprietary medications, the purity and potency of herbs are not regulated by the FDA. Herbal medicines may contain contaminants (i.e. allergens, pollens, spores, pesticides, other plant species, bacteria, and fungi). In addition, their potency is dependent on many factors such as the climate and soil conditions where they are grown, as well as when they are harvested, and how long they are permitted to stand. Even some prescription drugs (i.e. phenylbutazone, aminopyrine, prednisone, testosterone and diazepam) and heavy metals (arsenic, mercury, lead and cadmium) have been found as unlabelled ingredients in herbal preparations and resulted in poisoning.

Pharmacy technicians, working under the supervision of registered pharmacists, should direct consumers to products that are manufactured by companies that adhere to Good Manufacturing Practices (GMP) that can provide a certificate of analysis upon request. To achieve a positive response to an herbal preparation one should select a standardised product that contains the same or very similar amount of active ingredient(s) used in clinical trials that may have been conducted. Consumers should be educated to purchase only standardised products that include the percentage of active ingredient(s) per dosage unit and not to be misled by labels that "standardise" to the weight of the unit.

Herbs are as Effective and have Less Side Effects

Herbs are as effective and have less side effects than conventional medications: Product labelling of herbs is governed by the Dietary Supplement Health and Education Act of 1994. Because libelling of herbs is designed to promote product use and not necessarily inform the consumer, pharmacy technicians can assist in the selection of appropriate herbals and to screen for possible interactions with conventional therapies.

Pharmacists and technicians, as well as physicians, dieticians, and other health care providers must become knowledgeable about herbal supplements and prospectively seek information regarding their patients' use of unconventional medicines to avoid adverse consequences. Consumers need to be reminded that herbs are composed of chemicals that may, in some cases be toxic, especially if large quantities are ingested.

Many consumers do not realise that herbal products are treated by the FDA as dietary supplements, thus manufacturers are not required to demonstrate a herb's safety or efficacy prior to marketing. Because herbal therapies generally cannot be patented, it is unlikely that manufacturers will invest the $230 million, and the 8-10 years required for FDA approval. Before the FDA can require a product be removed from the market, the agency must prove that the product is unsafe or ineffective. It has been suggested that manufacturers of herbal products supply data to support any claims made in advertising.

The FDA only permits claims of the supplement's effect on structure or function of the human body (e.g. "supports the immune system"), and manufacturers must include the following statement in their labelling: "This product is not intended to diagnose, treat, cure, or prevent any disease." The FDA does identify about 250 herbs as "generally recognised as safe" based on long-term use without reports of significant side effects. Pharmacy technicians should report adverse reactions involving herbal products to the pharmacist for referral to the FDA's Med Watch programme.

The majority of research on herbal preparations has been performed in Germany where "reasonable proof" must be shown prior to marketing. The German Health Commission reviewed and published nearly 300 monographs, 200 of which were found to have a reasonable risk/benefit ratio. The monographs, however, do not include the scientific basis for their findings. Unfortunately, most studies are of limited clinical utility since some were conducted in animals, or performed in humans for a short period of time, or were small open-label trials subject to bias and methodological errors.

Similarly, much of the information regarding adverse effects of herbs is based on isolated or anecdotal case reports.

Herbs are Less Expensive

Herbs are less expensive than OTC and prescription drugs: As with other alternative therapies, herbal products are typically not covered under most insurance plans, thus the consumer pays out of pocket for these products. Monthly costs of brand name herbal products are typically more than generic versions of proprietary medications, but are generally less than brand name prescription products. For example, in France it was estimated that the annual cost to their social security system was 15% less per patient if the physician practiced homeopathy (which may influence further coverage in other health systems). However, these savings were a result of fewer diagnostic tests and a lower cost of homeopathic medicines as compared to conventional therapies in France.

Herbs can be Taken Safely

Herbs can be taken safely without consulting a physician or a pharmacist: Medically- unsupervised use of herbs and other natural dietary supplements is imprudent. Some products have adverse effects and may interact with other medications. Furthermore, many conditions that patients attempt to self-diagnose and/or self-treat may be serious, requiring a careful history and examination by a physician. For example, unsupervised use of saw palmetto for urinary symptoms may delay a diagnosis of prostate cancer.

Similarly, patients with symptoms such as chronic insomnia, anxiety and depressed mood, should be referred for medical management. Patients with cardiovascular disease, such as hypertension, heart failure, and hyperlipidemia, should be under a physician's care and appropriate prescription drugs prescribed. Some general guidelines for using herbal substances for consumers

— Avoid use in children under 2 years of age

— Avoid use in pregnancy or lactation

— Review potential herb-drug interactions prior to initiation with your physician or pharmacist

— Select only standardised herbal products from manufacturers utilising good manufacturing practices

— Review the potential side effects and contraindications prior to use

— Inform your physician and pharmacist with regards to the herbal

Popular Herbal Alternatives

Immune Modulators

— *Echinacea* (Echinacea purpurea, Echinacea angustifolia, and Echinacea pallida).

  — *Common use*: Prevention and treatment of colds and wound healing.

  — *Precautions*: Long-term use may lead to immune suppression

  — *Dose*: Capsule: 500mg TID day followed by 250mg QID standardised to 4% echinacosides (E. angustifolia) or 4% sesquiterpene esters (E. purpurea) per dose

Studies have supported its use for upper respiratory tract infections, urogenital infections, and wounds. The effects of echinacea were dose-dependent when studying its effects on upper respiratory tract infections. Animal studies have revealed probable mechanisms of Echinacea-induced immune enhancement, such as increasing the number of circulating white blood cells, stimulating cytokine production and triggering the alternate compliment pathway.

The most common side effect is unpleasant taste and symptoms of immunostimulation have occurred with intravenous use (shivering, fever and muscle weakness). Its use is not recommended in patients with progressive and autoimmune disorders including AIDS, tuberculosis, multiple sclerosis, collagen disorders and diabetes mellitus. Because the flower is related to ragweed, cross allergenicity may occur in those individuals allergic to ragweed.

In addition, electrolyte balance has been reported, although in 1991 it was reported that no serious side effects had been noted in over 2.5 million prescriptions per year in Germany. Hepatotoxic effects have been associated with persistent use, thus it should not be administered with other known hepatotoxins (anabolic steroids, amiodorone, methotrexate, or ketoconazole). Prophylactic use is suggested at three weeks on medication and one week off and use for acute infections is not recommended beyond 10 days.

Antihyperlipidemics

— *Garlic (Allium sativum)*:

— *Common use*: Lipid-lowering, antithrombotic, antihypertensive

— *Dose*: 400mg 2-3 times/day (equivalent to 1200mg fresh garlic) 10mg alliin standardised to equal 4mg total allicin potential

While garlic has been used throughout centuries for its flavoring properties, researchers studied it for its antiseptic qualities and anti-cancer effects; it is most popular for its effect as a lipid- lowering agent. Allicin and alliin, the suggested active ingredients, are destroyed by heat, acid and crushing so efficacy is enhanced by using the enteric coated tablets or consuming raw cloves.

However, that even standardised products have been shown to lack the necessary amount of allicin to be effective. There have been numerous studies with conflicting results regarding its ability to lower lipids. Positive findings in three trials exhibited a lowering of cholesterol from 6.1-11.5% primarily due to the lowering of low-density lipoprotein.

More recent studies have yielded conflicting results. A 12-week study using garlic powder in ambulatory patients resulted in a 14% reduction of serum cholesterol. Garlic's mild antihypertensive effects have been documented in some studies, showing either a modest decline (-5% to -7%) or no change. A meta-analysis of eight trials revealed three studies with significant reduction in systolic blood pressure and four with reductions in diastolic blood pressure in patients with mild hypertension.

Garlic has also been shown to inhibit platelet aggregation in vitro and should be used with great caution in individuals with bleeding disorders. While a spontaneous epidural hematoma did occur in one case report, it appears to be isolated. Garlic can, however increase the international normalisation ratios (INR) in patients receiving warfarin so closer monitoring seems prudent in these patients. The FDA considers garlic safe and the most prominent side effect is malodorous breath and skin that may be reduced when using enteric coated tablets. Use should be cautioned in individuals already receiving antihypertensives, or those prone to orthostasis.

Cardiovascular & Cerebrovascular

— *Ginkgo Biloba*

— *Common Use*: Intracerebral and peripheral vascular insufficiency (for memory and claudication)

— *Dose*: 40-80mg three times daily standardised to 24-27% ginkgo flavone glycosides and 6-7% triterpines per dose

While the mechanism of Ginkgo is not full understood, it is thought that the flavonoids, terpenoids and organic acids found in Ginkgo act as free radical scavengers. Free radicals have been implicated as a cause of Alzheimer's disease, for example. These constituents have also been shown to inhibit platelet activation factor (reducing thrombosis), dilate arteries and capillaries and block the release of chemotactic factors and inflammatory mediators. It has been used for centuries to treat various brain disorders.

Ginkgo is considered relatively safe. The leaves have been associated with mild GI side effects and headache. Ginkgo, a known neurotoxin, is found in the leaves and seeds and for this reason Ginkgo is not recommended in patients with seizure disorders. The ingestion of the seeds, may result in fatal neurologic and allergic reactions and therefore not used for medical purposes. Ginkgo ingestion has been associated with a spontaneous hyphema (blood in the anterior chamber of the eye) in an elderly man and spontaneous subdural hematomas attributed to ginkgolide.

Ginkgolide B is a potent inhibitor of platelet activating factor necessary for normal platelet aggregation. As a result, one should avoid administering Ginkgo in patients using anticoagulants, antiplatelet therapy or with active bleeding such as peptic ulcer disease.

— *Hawthorn* (Crataegus oxyacantha L., C laevigata, and C mo nogyna)

  — *Common Use*: Congestive heart failure, hypertension

— *Dose*: 250mg 1-3 times a day standardised to contain at least 2% vitexin and/or 20% procyanidins per dose.

The biflavanoids in Hawthorn was found to dilate both peripheral and coronary blood vessels which results in decreased peripheral vascular resistance and improved coronary blood flow. Improvement in coronary blood flow in vitro was shown to be 20-140% following administration of approximately 1mg of the dried extract. Hawthorn is used for congestive heart failure (CHF), angina and peripheral vascular disease; it also exhibits some angiotensinconverting enzyme inhibition.

The proanthrocyanidins are said to exert a spasmolytic effect and to reverse the atherosclerotic process where as the flavanoid component is used to affect the collagen in blood vessels to reduce capillary fragility. Chinese animal studies have resulted in improvements in triglycerides, cholesterol and blood sugar. While side effects seen with low dose Hawthorn are minimal, caution should be exercised when used with other antihypertensive agents, as well as with patients on digoxin or other cardiac glycosides. It is sometimes used with digoxin to enable a reduction in the digoxin dose as well as decreasing the toxic effects of cardiac glycosides. As a result from its antihypertensive effects, Hawthorn may cause drowsiness and dizziness; patients should be warned about the operation of machinery until they are familiar with their response.

Cns: Neuropsychiatric and Analgesia

— *St. John's Wort* (Hypericum perforatum)

— *Common Use*: Depression

— *Precautions*: Photosensitivity

— *Dose*: 300mg three times a day standardised to 0.3-0.5%hypericin and/or 3-5% hyperforin per dose

This yellow flowering plant named for St. John the Baptist contains 10 constituents of which hypericin is believed to be the most active ingredient. It has a high affinity for γ-aminobuteric acid which when stimulated produces an antidepressant effect. Hypericin has also been shown to activate dopamine receptors and inhibit serotonin receptor expression. In vitro it has been shown to block reuptake of serotonin and norepinephrine. These mechanisms explain the lag time associated with effectiveness of the herb.

While in vitro studies demonstrated monoamine oxidase activity, wide use without restrictions of tyramine-containing foods suggests that MAO inhibition is minimal in vivo. Numerous studies have been conducted on the effectiveness of St. John's wort in depression and it is now prescribed four times as often as fluoxetine. A meta-analysis concluded that it was more effective than placebo in treated mild to moderate depression. When compared to low dose tricyclic antidepressants, it has a comparable effect with significantly fewer side effects.

Evidence also supports its effect as an anti-inflammatory agent and anti- infective agent. It has been used to treat muscle soreness, neuralgia, and to accelerate wo und healing. The antiviral activity of St. John's wort has also been identified at higher doses. Based on its pharmacology, St. John's wort should not be administered with other serotonin uptake inhibitors as symptoms of serotonin syndrome (headache, sweating, dizziness and agitation) have been observed. It is contraindicated in pregnancy since it has exhibited uterotonic activity.

It has been associated with photosensitivity, thus, patients should be cautioned to wear sunscreen and adequate clothing when exposed to the sun. It can alter digoxin levels when taken together and may induce the CYP450-3A4 enzyme system resulting in a significant decrease in indinavir concentrations. There have been two recent cases of heart transplant rejection associated with the use of St. John's wort that resulted from a reduction of cyclosporine plasma concentrations.

— *Valerian* (Valeriana officinalis)

   — *Common Use*: Anxiolytic, sleep-aid, antispasmotic

   — *Precautions*: Rare palpitations

   — *Dose*: 200mg 1-4 times a day standardised to 0.8-1% valerenic acids per dose 200-400mg at bedtime for insomnia

The root of this plant has been used for its calming effect for centuries. It was used in World War I for the treatment of "shell shock." In 1998 it was the tenth most popular herb in the US. Valerian species are highly variable in their constituents and should not be substituted for one another. The active ingredients appear to be valepotriates (thought to be responsible for the sedative effects) and valeric acid which bind to the same receptors as benzodiazepines and mediate the release of g-aminobuteric acid.

The antispasmotic effects are thought to result from mediation of the influx of intracellular calcium. These compounds have also exhibited anticonvulsive and hypotensive actions. Randomised placebo-controlled trials have validated that Valerian is effective in improving the quality of sleep, decreasing sleep latency (the time to get to sleep), with no hangover effect in the morning. Habituation and addiction have not been reported. Valerian has been used as a flavoring agent in food.

Mild side effects have included paradoxical stimulation (restlessness and palpitations) especially with long-term use. Valerian should not be used in pregnancy as in vitro studies demonstrate cytotoxic and mutogenic effects. Valerian may have an additive effect with other CNS depressants and patients should be cautioned regarding the operation of machinery when initiating therapy until they are accustomed to the effects. Other side effects seen in clinical trials included headaches, excitability and uneasiness.

— *Ginseng* (Panex ginseng, P. quinquefolius)
  - — *Common Use*: Performance enhancer and aphrodisiac
  - — *Precautions*: May increase heart rate and blood pressure
  - — *Dose*: 100-600mg/day in divided doses standardised to a minimum of 5% ginsenosides per dose

The term ginseng means "man-root" and is believed by the ancient Chinese to benefit all aspects of the human body. Derived from the root of the plant, the ginsenosides are a compilation of over 20 saponin triterpenes found in ginseng and thought to be the active ingredients. Siberian Ginseng is from Eleutherococcus senticosos that has different properties than ginseng from the Panax family. Siberian ginseng is associated with falsely elevated digoxin levels due to an interaction with the assay.

The active ingredients in ginseng may work by stimulating the secretion of ACTH, resulting in increased production of cortisol (in non-diabetic patients). Diabetic patients exhibit a decrease in cortisol production. The herb may also play a role in stimulating the production of adrenal hormone precursors. This herb is considered by many to enhance physical (including sexual) and mental performance as well as resistance to stress. Because these benefits are so subjective controlled clinical trials are difficult to interpret.

Ginseng may increase serum testosterone, dihydroxytestosterone, follitropin dihydroxytestosterone, follitropin and lutropin as well as sperm count and motility. Ginseng is on the FDA's list of herbs "generally recognised as safe" and has been associated with few serious side effects. The one fatality attributed to it was with a product that had ephedra as a contaminant. Because it can have a mild stimulant effect, use with other stimulants in patients with cardiovascular disease should be cautioned. It has also been associated with reversible mastalgia and post-menopausal bleeding, although this appears to be a rare side effect.

The immunostimulating effects have been studied and some have speculated that the herb facilitates the body's ability to adapt to post-surgical stress and chemotherapy. It has also been shown to increase cell- mediated and killer cell activity in mice. A type of ginseng abuse syndrome has been described.90 It is characterised by diarrhea, hypertension, nervousness, dermatologic eruptions, and insomnia, and may be exhibited after high doses or protracted periods of use. Because ginseng has been associated with reducing glucose levels, its use is cautioned in diabetics or patients prone to hypoglycemia.

Ginseng has been associated with reduction in the INR of a warfarin-treated patient stabilised for the previous nine months at an INR ranging from 3.0-4.0. The patient's INR dropped to 1.5 two weeks after initiating ginseng and returned to therapeutic range 2 weeks following discontinuation. Ginseng has also been associated with altered hemostasis and is therefore contraindicated in active bleeding and cautioned for use in patients receiving anticoagulant and/or antiplatelet medications.

— *Feverfew* (Tanacetum parthenium)

— *Common Use*: Migraine prophylaxis

— *Precautions*: Rebound headaches may occur upon withdrawal, frequently associated with oral ulceration; cross allergenicity with ragweed

— *Dose*: 100-250mg per day standardised to 0.2% parthenolide (migraine prophylaxis) 250mg TID for anti- inflammatory effects

Feverfew is a daisy- commonly found like flower. Its leaves are used to prevent migraines and treat inflammatory conditions such as arthritis. While doubleblind, placebo-controlled trials have not proven beneficial effects on arthritis, significant reduction in both frequency (mean 24%) and severity of migraines has been demonstrated, although the duration of individual attacks was not altered. This migraine study also demonstrated side effects to be less than that of placebo.

Feverfew is available in capsule form as an over the counter medicine. Feverfew suppresses prostaglandin production without inhibiting cyclooxygenase. Nonsteroidal anti- inflammatory agents may reduce the effectiveness of feverfew. It has also been shown to have comparable response rates to beta blockers and valproic acid but the high rate of aphthous ulcers and GI irritation limit its utility. Feverfew can alter platelet activity and has been used historically to induce menstrual bleeding so it should not be used in pregnancy, patients receiving anticoagulant therapy or patients with active bleeding (e.g. peptic ulcer disease).

Caution is warranted in patients receiving other antiplatelet medications; feverfew-containing products should be discontinued prior to surgical procedures. The mechanism of action of parthenolide, which is believed to be the active ingredient, is down regulation of the cerebral vascular response to biogenic amines which may explain why it is effective in preventing, but not aborting, migraine headaches. Patients trying feverfew should be counseled to allow at least a month to determining its efficacy. There is also evidence that constituents in feverfew are involved in the inhibition of phagocytosis, platelet aggregation, and secretion of inflammatory mediators (leukotrienes, prostaglandins, and thromboxanes), but further studies are needed to prove efficacy as an anti-inflammatory agent.

Other adverse effects include "post feve rfew syndrome" which may occur upon discontinuation of the herb. Symptoms include nervousness, insomnia, tiredness, joint stiffness, and pain. Because the flower is related to ragweed, cross allergenicity may occur in those individuals allergic to ragweed.

— *Chamomile* (Matricaria recutita)
  - — *Common Name*: German chamomile
  - — *Common Use*: Sedative, spasmolytic, anti-inflammatory, wound healing
  - — *Precaution*: Cross allergy with ragweed
  - — *Dose*: Oral 400-1600mg/day in divided doses standardised to 1.2% apigenin per dose.
  - — *Tea*: 1 heaping teaspoonful of dried flowers steeped in hot water for 10 minutes up to 3 times a day

Although few human studies have been performed with chamomile, it is cultivated worldwide for use as a sedative, spasmolytic, anti-inflammatory, and vulnerary (wound healing) agent. The active component apigenin has been shown to bind the same receptors as benzodiazepines to exert an anxiolytic and mild sedative effect in mice.

Apigenin has also been shown to reversibly inhibit irritant induced skin inflammation in animals as well as exert antispasmotic effects in the intestines. It also contains coumarin that contributes to its antispasmotic activity. No coagulation disorders have been reported to date but close monitoring of patients on anticoagulants is advised. In vitro it has been shown to be bactericidal to some staphylococcus and Candida species.

Chamomile is commonly used as a tea or applied topically as a compress. It is considered safe by the FDA but should be used with caution in individuals with an allergy to ragweed as cross-allergenicity may occur. Symptoms include abdominal cramping, tongue thickness, tight sensation in throat, angioedema of lips and eyes, diffuse pruritis, urticaria, and pharyngeal edema. Because of its sedative effects, caution should be used when taking it in conjunction with medications with sedative side effects or with alcohol.

— *Ginger* (Zingiber officinale)

— *Common Use*: Antiemetic for motion sickness

— *Dose*: 250mg TID standardised to 4% volatile oils or 5% 6-gingerol & 6-shogaol per dose. (250mg is about equal to ¼ tsp. powdered root)

Ginger is cultivated in Asia, Africa and the Caribbean and has been used for centuries as a flavoring agent and for its antiemetic properties. The root contains a volatile oil containing shogaol and gingerol. Gingerol has been shown in animals to exhibit analgesic, sedative, antipyretic antibacterial and reduced GI motility effects. Human studies have shown a significant reduction in nausea in hyperemesis gravidarum in doses of 250mg QID and perioperative nausea and vomiting in doses of 1Gm prior to surgery.

A study comparing ginger to 100mg dimenhydrinate and placebo showed that ginger was superior to both when patients were subjected to a revolving chair designed to produce motion sickness. Ginger is on the FDA's "generally recognised as safe and effective" list and has few side effects. Ginger has exhibited potent inhibition of thromboxane synthetase that resulted in prolonged bleeding. It therefore should be avoided in pregnancy, especially near term, as well as in combination with anticoagulants. It can also cause mild GI upset.

— *SAMe* (S-adenosyl methionine)

— *Common Use*: Depression, fibromyalgia

— *Other uses*: Cardiovascular disease, hepatitis, arthritis

— *Dose*: 400-1600mg/day

Although S-adenosyl methionine (SAMe) is not an herb. SAMe was first discovered in Italy. It gained widespread use in Europe, and it became the fourth most popular supplement in drugstore chains and retail outlets. It is not available in the diet in adequate amounts and must be internally biosynthesised via the combination of methionine and adenosine triphosphate (ATP). SAMe's role in the body is to donate methyl groups in the synthesis of nucleic acids, proteins, phospholipids, catecholamines and other neurotransmitters.

The oral form has a poor bioavailability (<1%), although blood levels ma y not correlate well with clinical response. Once the methyl groups have been donated, SAMe converts to homocysteine. A potential concern however is that elevated homocysteine levels has been correlated with the development of cardiovascular disease. Although at present it is unknown how use of SAMe affects homocysteine levels, or whether this is of any clinical significance. Intravenous SAMe may improve membrane fluidity via its role in phospholipid production; this may facilitate neurotransmission. SAMe's methyl donation also results in formation of other essential amino acids including cysteine, glutathione and taurine.

Glutathione is used in the body as an antioxidant. SAMe is also involved in the formation of polyamines:

spermidine, puescine and spermine that are essential for cell growth and differentiation, gene expression, protein hosphorolation, neuron regeneration and DNA repair. When compared to placebo, intravenous administration of SAMe resulted in a 97% increase in the major metabolite of serotonin (5-HIAA) in the cerebral spinal fluid. Limitations of available human trials of SAMe include intravenous administration versus oral, short study period, small sample size, lack of randomisation, and lack of placebo control.

Kagan performed a double-blind, placebo controlled trial comparing oral SAMe to placebo in 18 patients. Significant improvements were seen in the treated group, however the sample size and length of the study (21 days) were limitations. Carrieri conducted a double-blind, cross-over study with 21 Parkinson's patients with depression (mean age 69). Wash out periods were used prior to each arm of the study. Significant improvements were seen, but results could only be generalised to Parkinson's patients and the study size and length (30 days) were limitations. SAMe has not yet been compared to the serotonin reuptake inhibitors in human trials.

Minor side effects that have been seen with SAMe include nausea, dry mouth and restlessness. Reports indicate it can block platelet aggregation in vitro and should therefore be monitored closely in patients using anticoagulants and avoided in patients with active bleeding disorders. Administration of SAMe may trigger a manic or hypomanic episode (manifested by pressured speech and grandiose thinking). It should be administered with vitamins B6, B12 and folic acid to enhance production of methionine as a by-product and to avoid homocysteine accumulation.

The mechanism of action suggests that SAMe may interact with MAO inhibitors, although no case studies were found in a literature search. SAMe may increase the risk of serotonin syndrome (tremor, shivering, hyperreflexia, myoclonus, and ataxia).

Genitourinary

— *Saw Palmetto* (Serenoa repens)

  — *Common Use*: Benign prostatic hypertrophy (BPH) and prostatitis

  — *Dose*: 160mg twice daily standardised to 80-90% fatty acids and sterols per dose

The extract for Saw Palmetto comes from the fruit of the palm tree and is used as a first line agent to treat BPH in much of Europe. Saw Palmetto Extract (SPE) is thought to inhibit the 5α-reductase and thus block the conversion of testosterone to dihydrotestosterone, which is responsible for stimulating growth of the prostate gland. It also blocks the uptake of both hormones by the prostate. It also exhibits some anti-inflammatory effects, presumably by inhibiting cyclooxygenase pathways.

Numerous double-blind, placebo-controlled trials have been conducted with Saw Palmetto. While results were significantly positive in seven out of eight of these, results from the two that were randomised conflict. The study concluding that the effects produced by the herb were no greater than placebo randomised 70 patients for one month. The larger randomised study (176 patients) treated participants for two months. Significant improvements were noted in urinary flow, reduction of nocturia, and reduction in residual urine.

Saw Palmetto was also compared to finasteride over a six month period in a randomised study. Results were significant in that the study yielded similar improvements in the prostate symptom score, peak urinary flow rate and quality of life, but without the side effects exhibited by finasteride (impotence, decreased libido and altered PSA). While these results are promising, α-1 antagonists (doxazosin, terazosin) are considered more effective than either Saw Palmetto or finasteride, but may offer advantages when patients cannot tolerate the side effects of α-1 antagonists. Side effects are uncommon with Saw Palmetto and include headache and GI upset. It should be used cautiously when used with other a-adrenergic blockers due to its activity in vitro to inhibit α-1-adrenoceptors.

— *Black Cohosh* (Cimicifuga racemosa)

 — *Common Use*: Treatment of menopausal symptoms

 — *Precautions*: Use with caution in patients intolerant to salicylates. Avoid in salicylate allergy

 — *Dose*: 20-40mg twice daily standardised to 1mg triterpene glycosides

Black cohosh is a plant native to Eastern North America. It contains a group of chemicals referred to as phytoestrogens because they mimic the effects of estrogens. For this reason it was a common remedy used by Native Americans for the treatment of painful menses (known as squawroot). The active constituents include formononetin and 27-deoxyactein, compounds that have estrogen binding activity.

Isoferulic is also found in Black Cohosh and exhibits anti- inflammatory and antispasmotic effects. Salicylic acid is a minor constituent but most likely contributes to the anti-inflammatory and analgesic properties. Its anti-inflammatory effects have propelled its use for rheumatic complaints as well as for premeopausal symptoms (hot flashes, depression, insomnia, and anxiety).

Black cohosh may cause a variety of mild side effects including nausea in 7% of patients and headache. It can cause hypotension in higher doses and is likely to exert inhibition of platelet aggregation due to its salicylate content. It should be avoided in patients allergic or intolerant to aspirin, and patients with active bleeding. It should not be used in lactating or pregnant women since it has been shown to stimulate contractions in animals. It is contraindicated in women with a history of estrogen-dependent tumors or endometrial cancer.

Black cohosh should be used with caution for patients already receiving hormone replacement therapy. The German Commission E Monograph suggests limiting its use to 6 months as no long-term trials have been conducted. Although estrogens are still the cornerstone of menopausal therapy due to their cardioprotection and prevention of osteoporosis, black cohosh offers an alternative for symptoms of menopause for women that refuse estrogen, or cannot tolerate estrogenrelated side effects.

Yohimbe (Pausinystalia yohimbe)

Yohimbine is found in nature from the bark of the Pausinystalia yohimbe tree and is used for impotence. Yohimbine is the active constituent and acts by blocking α-2 adenoreceptors centrally. As a result, there is an increase in release of norepinephrine and increases in cholinergic activity. Heightened cholinergic activity is associated physiologically with penile erection. Yohimbine also inhibits monamine oxidase that is responsible for the breakdown of norepinephrine and serotonin without increasing testosterone levels.

A meta-analysis of seven double-blind, placebo-controlled trials that investigated monotherapy with yohimbine in erectile dysfunction has been published. Study sizes varied from 11-100 men with various causes of erectile dysfunction in which dosages ranged from 15-

30mg daily. Studies found yohimbine to be more effective than placebo in five of the seven studies, although the primary endpoints were subjective improvements in sexual function. Side effect ranged from 10-30% and included hypertension, rash, anxiety, dizziness, increased urinary frequency, GI disturbances, and lethargy. Eight of the patients withdrew due to the seriousness of the side effects. Other side effects that could be expected due to its central activity include agitation, tremor, insomnia, sweating, tachycardia, nausea and vomiting.

Once case of a lupus- like syndrome occurred in a 45 year-old man after ingesting 60mg in one day. Yohimbine has been associated with agranulocytosis after prolonged use, but this appears to have been an idiosyncratic response to prolonged therapy. It has also been linked to an allergic reaction that resulted in a lupus- like response and renal failure. Overdoses of 20-30mg/day have resulted in excessive salivation, piloerection, mydriasis, changes in blood pressure and death.

Yohimbine is not recommended in individuals with hypertension and liver disease, and should be avoided in schizophrenics as it may exacerbate acute psychotic episodes. It is contraindicated in pregnancy and renal disease, as well as patients with a history of gastric or duodenal ulcer and cardiac disease. Yohimbine should not be taken with tyramine-containing foods (certain cheeses, chocolate, wine, aged meats), or with tyrosine or phenylalanine due to its MAO-I activity and the potential for hypertensive episodes. Clonidine may be used to reverse some of the adverse effects of yohimbine.

Both the German Commission E and the American Urological Association do not recommend the use of yohimbine. The FDA does not recommend the use of yohimbine for erectile dysfunction but has approved it as a prescription mydriatic. Although its use has been banned since 1989 as an aphrodisiac due to lack of safety and efficacy, it is still purchased on the internet; its should be discouraged.

Licorice Root (Glycyrrhiza Glabra)

Licorice is widely known as a flavoring agent but has historically been used as an antitussive, treatment of adrenal insufficiency and a variety of GI disorders. Most licorice candy is artificially flavored and does not contain natural licorice root. Active constituents include glycyrrhizin, liquiritin, glabrol and glabridin. The glycyrrhizic acid is converted in the intestine to glycyrretic acid that is responsible for many of the side effects. Glycyrrhetinic acid derivatives may be found as a flavoring agent in che wing tobacco.

Electrolyte alterations have been seen following excessive use. Glycyrrhiza has an aldosterone- like effect; thus excessive licorice use may result in pseudohyper-aldosteronism. The glycyrrhetinic acid prevents the conversion of cortisol to its inactive form. The excess cortisol in the kidney achieves access to the mineralocorticoid receptors and mimics aldosterone. This is characterised by sodium retention and resulting peripheral edema, and hypertension.

Hypokalemia and resulting lethargy, paresthesias, muscle cramps, headaches, and tetany may also be seen. This is generally seen after chronic ingestion. Licorice has also been shown to exhibit anti-inflammatory effects. In human neutrophils it inhibits the formation of leukotrienes and platelet activating factor, among other inflammatory mediators. Licorice has been shown to stimulate tracheal mucosa and increases the rate of mucous secretion which is the basis the mechanism for its expectorant effect. Licorice has also been associated with inhibition of platelet aggregation and should therefore be avoided in patients with bleeding and/or hemostatic disorders. It should be used with caution in patients receiving anticoagulants or drugs with antiplatelet activity.

A recent negative finding regarding licorice demonstrates that it may be associated with decreased testosterone and libido in young men. The apparent mechanism involves the inhibition of 17-β hydroxysteroid dehydrogenase and 17,20-lyase, enzymes whic h are involved in the conversion of 17-hydroxyprogesterone to androstenedione. Androstenedione is normally converted to testosterone. Testosterone levels, which decreased secondary to licorice use subsequently rebounded 4 days after licorice was discontinued.

Licorice is contraindicated in hypertension, diabetes mellitus, cholestatic lever disorders, cirrhosis, hypokalemia, adrenal insufficiency, seizure disorder, pregnancy and lactation.

Kava Kava (Piper methysticum)

Kava Kava is a plant native to the South Pacific used as a sedative and anxiolytic. One of the unique claims made about this herb is that its anxiolytic properties are purportedly exerted while devoid of deficits in memory or motor impairment. It appears to act on the amygdalacomplex in the limbic system, as opposed to the benzodiazepine receptors like valerian root and traditional anxiolytic medications. Extracts of kava have also been used to treat attention deficit disorder.

Kava is known to be a dopamine antagonist and should not be used by patients. Combinations with other anxiolytic and sedative medications and/or alcohol should be avoided due to its pharmacologic effect. Common side effects include transient nausea and vomiting, and photosensitivity. It has also been associated with extrapyramidal side effects in doses of 100-450mg/day.

These include both oral and lingual dyskinesia, torticolis, painful twisting movements of the trunk and exacerbation of Parkinson's disease.

While the German E commission found kava to be safe and effective in the treatment of anxiety, there is still a need for additional controlled trials with larger numbers of participants. The American Herbal Products Association's Kava Committee has recommended that manufacturers should label their products so that daily consumption does not exceed 300mg of the kava lactones. It seems prudent to withhold recommending use of kava until more studies confirm its safety and efficacy.

Ephedra (Ephedra sinica, Ma Huang)

Ephedra has been popular in the US and use as a bronchodilator and decongestant. Ephedra is composed of the alkaloids ephedrine and pseudoephedrine, the later is available as an over the counter decongestant (e.g. Sudafed^R). Ephedra causes vasoconstriction and cardiac stimulation though its agonistic properties on both α and $\beta 1$ adrenergic receptors. By stimulating $\beta 2$ receptors it causes bronchial smooth muscle relaxation and bronchodilation, a beneficial effect in asthmatic patients.

Use of ephedra, and ephedrine-containing products can result in an increase in both systolic and diastolic blood pressure and therefore should be avoided by anyone with cardiovascular disease (e.g. hypertension, angina, history of myocardial infarction), as well as in thyroid disease, diabetes, and prostate abnormalities. It should not be administered with other sympathomimetics including pseudoephedrine and phenylpropanolamine, or caffeine. Ma Huang, also referred to as "herbal fen-phen", is promoted as a weight loss agent.

Ephedra is a constituent of the weight loss product Metabolife. Ephedrine is thought to exert its anorexiant effect via adrenergic pathways to the hypothalamus and possibly by increasing the metabolic rate. When caffeine is added, the metabolic rate increases two-fold but it also further stimulates the cardiovascular system. The combination of ephedra and St. John's wort is referred to as "herbal Prozac." The FDA has cautioned consumers not to consume the ephedrine-containing herbal preparations known and marketed as "herbal ecstasy" which manufacturers claim will heighten ones "sexual awareness".

Ephedra is a common additive ingredient in herbal preparations. Over 100 products have been identified in over 800 reports of adverse reactions in which herbal preparations contained, or were thought to contain, ephedra. Side effects are consistent with sympathomimetic agents and include insomnia, nervousness, tremor, headache, hypertension, seizures, arrhythmias, heart attack, stroke and even death. Many of the reports occurred in patients under the age of 40 as ephedra preparations have been marked for weight loss and for enhancing athletic performance. It should not be used in patients with a history of hypertension or other cardiovascular disease. Renal stones have developed in patients taking ephedra. It is also contraindicated for patients taking MAO inhibitors.

Sassafras (Sassafras albidium)

Sassafras is a species of trees common to North America. The main constituent, safrole, comes from the root. It was used for numerous purposes including scent in perfumes and soaps, thickener for soup, flavoring agent in a variety of foods, topically as an antiinflammatory, and as an antifungal. However, there are no therapeutic benefits associated with the ingestion of sassafras or its constituents.

Safrole was banned by the FDA as a food additive because of its carcinogenic potential. It also acts as a neurotoxin, and has been shown to cause hepatic tumors in animals. A dose of 0.66mg safrole is considered hazardous to humans and a cup of tea may have as much as 200mg. Other toxic effects include vomiting, stupor, hallucinations, liver cancer, diaphoresis, and abortion.

Pokeroot (Phytolacca americana, P. decandra, P. rigida)

Pokeroot is a perennial plant that is native to North America and grows in damp woods and fields. It is also known as Poke greens, American nightshade, pokeberry, red ink plant and a number of other names. It has a red tinted stem and develop purple berries that ripen in July. It has been used for arthritis and as an emetic. It has also been used to treat edema, skin cancer, dysmenorrhea ringworm, scabies, tonsillitis and syphilis. The triterpene saponins are the toxic plant components.

Pokeweed mitogen (PWM) is a protein found in the plant that has the ability to cause various blood cell abnormalities (alterations in T-cells and B-cells). There is no medicinal value to the plant. Berries are edible when cooked but ingestion of poisonous parts of the plant may result in severe stomach cramps, nausea, diarrhea, vomiting, labored breathing, hypotension, convulsions and even death. Drinking brewed tea can also result in serious outcomes as well as those who ingest improperly cooked Pokeroot shoots.

Comfrey (Symphytum officinale L., S. asperum Lepechin).

Comfrey root, also known as knitbone, bruisewort, blackwort, and slippery root, has been used as an herbal remedy in America for the treatment of burns, sprains, swelling, bruises, gastric ulcers, hemorrhoids, bronchial congestion and inflammation. Allentoin is a component of comfrey and enhances cell proliferation, which may be the mechanism for its topical use as an anti-inflammatory agent. The allentoin is 100 times more concentrated in the roots than in the leaves.

In an animal study, rats fed comfrey root or leaves developed hepatocellular adenomas within 180 days of initiation of treatment. Urinary bladder tumors were also inducible at low levels. This is most likely due to the alkaloid echimidine. When rats were fed the alkaloid, a dose-dependent hepatocellular necrosis resulted. It may cause elevations in liver function tests, veno-occlusive disease (Budd-Chairi syndrome) and subsequent hepatic necrosis. Animals that ingest comfrey can pass the alkaloids to humans in their milk. There are however, some commercial sources of comfrey without these toxic alkaloids available.

10

Bioactive Compounds in Legume Natural Products

In the face of the vast number of natural products collectively produced by plants, the study of specific pathways had been viewed as somewhat esoteric, and attempts to obtain a more global understanding of natural product biosynthesis seemed beyond easy grasp. Those views have been changing in recent years due to the realisation of the importance of natural products for plant, animal, and human health, and the impact of genomics technologies on all areas of biology. At least 25% of the genome of Arabidopsis encodes enzymes of metabolism, and the number may be similar or even higher in legumes, several of which now have extensive genomics resources.

Whole genome-level DNA sequence information, coupled with improved methods for profiling natural products, now make possible combined genetic and biochemical approaches for addressing natural product function, deciphering biosynthetic pathways, and engineering novel pathways in transgenic plants.

Within the approximately 650 genera and more than 18,000 species of legumes, quinolizidine (characteristic of Lupinus species; Fig. 1), dipiperidine, pyrrolizidine, -carboline, phenylethylamine, and indole alkaloids have been reported. The Tyr-derived Erythrina alkaloids appear to be found only in the large genus Erythrina. NPAAs are also common within the Leguminosae, with canavanine, pipecolic acid, and djencolic acid derivatives the most important groups. NPAAs are often highly toxic, and are responsible for several serious human toxicoses, among the best known of which is lathyrism, a nonprogressive motor neuron disease associated with high consumption of grasspeas.

As early as the 5th century BC, writers described the irreversible weakness in the legs of the inhabitants of ancient cities during times of war and starvation, when they were forced to eat a diet containing a high proportion of pulses. Grasspeas, which are ideally suited to arid regions such as Ethiopia and the Indian subcontinent, contain high levels of ODPA (Fig. 1) in their seeds, and this compound is responsible for the neurological symptoms and also for deleterious effects on bone formation, particularly in children. Although low-ODPA lines of grasspea have been developed through traditional breeding and selection that appear suitable as supplementary material for animal feeds, removal of the neurotoxin from the seed by transgenic approaches is yet to be reported. More work is needed on the molecular biology of the biosynthetic pathways leading to the many nitrogen-containing natural products of the Leguminosae.

In figure 1, the compounds are seed coat proanthocyanidin from alfalfa (Medicago sativa, 1); formononetin malonyl glucoside, a constitutive isoflavone conjugate from roots of alfalfa and barrel medic (Medicago truncatula, 2); genistein, an isoflavone from seeds of soybean (Glycine max, 3); avicin D, a complex triterpene saponin from seed pods of Acacia victoriae (4); isoliquritigenin, a chalcone from roots of licorice (Glycyrrhiza galbra; 5); glycyrrhizin, a triterpene saponin

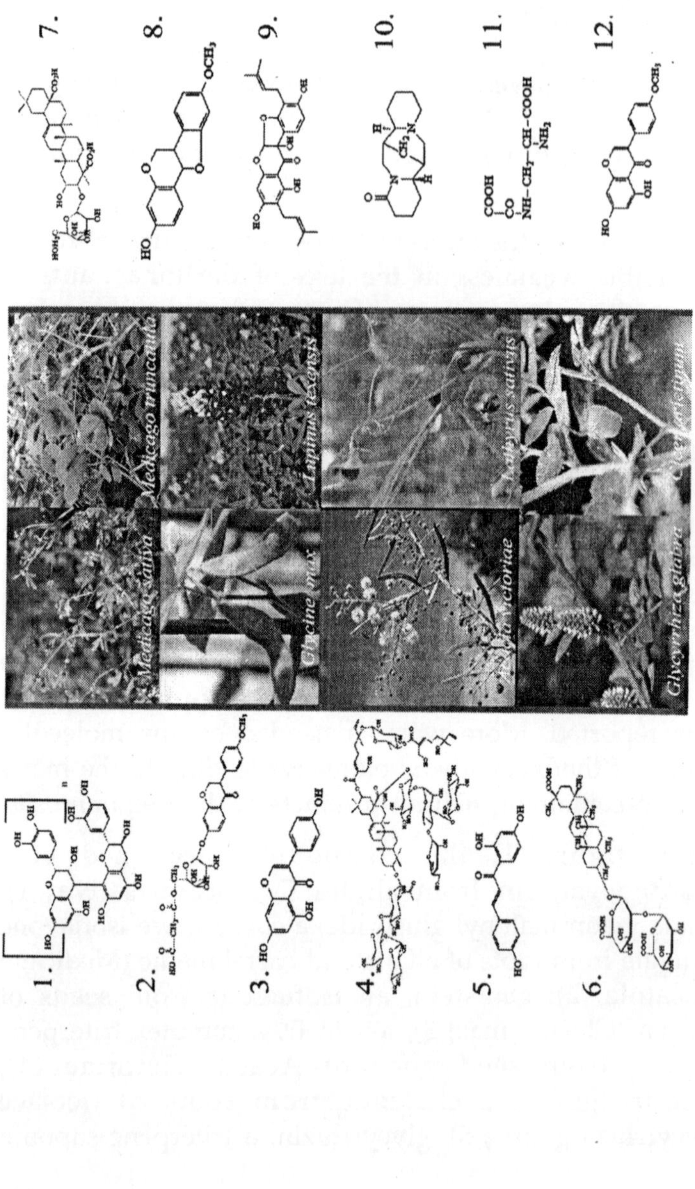

Figure 1: A small fraction of the biochemical diversity of legumes is shown in this selection of natural products from eight species.

from roots of licorice (6); medicagenic acid glucoside, a triterpene saponin from roots of alfalfa and barrel medic (7); medicarpin, a pterocarpan phytoalexin from fungally infected barrel medic and alfalfa (8); a prenylated isoflavone (lupinol A) from roots of Lupinus species (9); lupanine, a quinolizidine alkaloid from roots of Lupinus species (10); 3-N-oxalyl-L-2,3-diaminopropanoic acid (ODPA) from seed of grasspea (Lathyrus sativus, 11); and biochanin A, an isoflavone from seeds of chickpea (Cicer arietinum, 12).

Flavonoids are found throughout the plant kingdom, whereas isoflavonoids are more restricted. Isoflavonoids are particularly prevalent in the Papilonoideae subfamily of the Leguminosae, in which they are widely distributed and function as preformed or inducible antimicrobial or anti-insect compounds, as inducers of the nodulation genes of symbiotic Rhizobium bacteria, or as allelopathic agents. Pterocarpan-type phytoalexins such as medicarpin and constitutive isoflavone malonyl glycosides (Fig. 1) are typical of the isoflavonoids from these species.

A large body of literature has reported temporal and spatial correlations between phytoalexin accumulation and disease resistance in legumes, but a role for isoflavonoids in disease resistance has only recently been confirmed by genetic approaches. Isoflavonoids are formed from flavanones (ubiquitously present in plants) by an unusual aryl migration reaction catalysed by the cytochrome P450 enzyme CYP93C1 (2-hydroxyisoflavanone synthase, commonly termed isoflavone synthase [IFS]). It would appear that the IFS gene has arisen independently during evolution in taxonomically distinct families, because, in addition to their general occurrence in papilonoid legumes, isoflavonoids have also been reported in a few members of other families, including the Rosaceae, Chenopodiaceae, Apocynaceae, and Pinaceae.

Isoflavones exhibit estrogenic, antiangiogenic, antioxidant, and anticancer activities, and are now popular as dietary supplements. Genistein (Fig. 1) has been the subject of over 3,600 published studies (listed in Biological Abstracts) in the last 10 years. Major sources of isoflavones for humans are seed products of soybean (daidzein and genistein) and chickpea (biochanin A, Fig. 1), and the health-promoting activity of high-soy diets is believed to reside in their isoflavone components. Epidemiological studies suggest a link between consumption of soy isoflavones and reduced risks of breast and prostate cancers in humans.

Isoflavones may possess other health-promoting activities, including chemoprevention of osteoporosis, and prevention of other postmenopausal disorders and cardiovascular disease. A recent study indicated that a high-soy diet may even help improve cognitive function in students presented with a variety of complex mental tasks. Plants containing certain prenylated isoflavones have been used by the Zulus of South Africa for the treatment of impotency, and they appear to be active in improving erectile dysfunction. Is it possible to introduce genistein or other isoflavones into vegetables, grains, and fruits for dietary disease prevention?

Soybean IFS has been expressed in Arabidopsis, corn (Zea mays), and tobacco (Nicotiana tabacum). However, in all cases, only small amounts of genistein glycoconjugates were formed. Limiting factors for obtaining significant isoflavone accumulation in a heterologous target plant include limitation of IFS activity itself, limitation of precursor pools, and, most importantly, competition between IFS and other enzymes, such as flavanone 3-hydroxylase, that use the same substrate. This competition may be indicative of metabolic channeling at the branch points for the formation of the various classes of flavonoids. Armed with this knowledge, it should now be possible to optimise isoflavonoid biosynthesis in nonlegumes to expand the delivery of dietary isoflavones and to develop new sources for the more complex bioactive isoflavonoids.

Important areas for future research on isoflavonoids include understanding flux control between isoflavonoid biosynthesis and competing pathways, deciphering the physical basis for association of biosynthetic enzymes in metabolic channels, and validating the various health-promoting effects ascribed to dietary provision of isoflavones. The latter point is of great importance if transgenic foods with value added health benefits are ever to make it to the market place.

All known classes of terpenoids have been reported within the Leguminosae. Particularly interesting are the triterpene saponins, whose biological activities can positively and negatively impact plant traits. Some saponins display allelopathic, antimicrobial, and anti-insect activity, but they can also be toxic to monogastric animals, act as antipalatability factors, or reduce forage digestibility in ruminants. Monogastric animals often avoid consuming foods that contain saponins, and, therefore, development of saponin-free alfalfa is an agronomic target. Saponins also have useful pharmacological activities.

Many are anticholesterolemic or can act as adjuvants. The roots of the licorice plant (Glycyrrhiza glabra) are one of the oldest known botanicals in Chinese medicine. Health beneficial activities include anti-inflammation, antiulcer, antiallergy, and anticarcinogenesis, and the triterpene saponin glycyrrhizin (Fig. 1) may account for many of these properties, although licorice also contains bioactive chalcones (Fig. 1), isoflavans, diketones, and hydroxyphenols.

Desert shrubs of the genus Acacia contain complex triterpene saponins, known as avicins, within the developing seedpods, where they presumably protect the seeds from predation. These compounds, which consist of an acacic acid triterpene skeleton conjugated to eight sugars and two linear monoterpenes (Fig. 1), are now under development as anticancer agents in view of their ability to induce cell cycle arrest in mammalian cells. Their mode of action in target cells appears to involve induction of apoptosis by mitochondrial perturbation. Most of the steps in the biosynthesis of triterpene saponins remain uncharacterised at the molecular level.

The model legume barrel medic contains a complex mixture of saponins, including glycosides of medicagenic acid (Fig. 1), some of which have also previously been found in soybean. The first committed step in their biosynthesis is catalysed by a specific oxidosqualene cyclase, -amyrin synthase. -Amyrin synthase has been functionally characterised from several plants, including pea and barrel medic, and is closely related to plant cycloartenol synthase involved in sterol biosynthesis. The steps between -amyrin and the various saponin aglycones produced in Medicago and soybean involve a series of oxidative reactions that, by analogy to similar reactions in brassinosteroid biosynthesis, probably are catalysed by cytochrome P450 enzymes.

The aglycones are subsequently converted to the saponins by the action of a series of glycosyltransferases (GTs). To date, only a single GT involved in saponin biosynthesis in soybean has been characterised biochemically. This pathway is a prime candidate for functional genomics approaches. Important areas for future research on triterpene saponins for legume improvement and commercial exploitation include obtaining a basic understanding of their biosynthesis from initial cyclization to final conjugation, discovering regulatory genes for coordinated up-regulation of triterpene pathways, and using transgenic approaches to learn more about triterpene function as a basis for genetic modification studies.

Condensed tannins (CTs, also known as proanthocyanidins) are polymers or oligomers of flavan-3-ol units derived from the flavonoid pathway. They are common components of seed coats throughout the plant kingdom. CTs are found in many legumes with a tree-like habit, and occur in the leaves of some forage legumes such as bird's foot trefoil (Lotus corniculatus) and sanfoin (Onobrychis viciifolia). Their structures can be quite variable, among the commonest being a series of four to eight linked (-)-epicatechin units terminating in a catechin unit (Fig. 1), as found in the alfalfa seed coat.

CTs most likely play a protective function within the plant, but are now attracting attention because of their widespread effects on human health and ruminant nutrition. They are powerful antioxidants with beneficial effects on cardiac health and immunity. CTs from fruits such as cranberry (Vaccinum macrocarpon) protect against urinary tract infections, and the CTs and their precursors (catechins and epicatechins) are important for determining flavor and astringency in wines and tea, while at the same time conferring potential health beneficial effects to these beverages. Chocolate contains CTs, and the health-promoting effects of this important (for some!) dietary component is now being publicised by the industry.

The most important agronomic trait involving CTs is their ability to prevent the "bloating" characteristics of forage legumes such as alfalfa and white clover (Trifolium repens) that lack CTs in the consumed aerial portions. CTs bind to dietary proteins in the rumen and thereby slow down their rate of degradation, preventing bloat and improving the animal's nitrogen nutrition by increasing the amount of dietary protein exiting the rumen. This can lead to increased body weight and wool production. In addition to reducing bacterial degradation of proteins in the rumen, CTs can also slow down protein degradation during ensiling of forage legumes, thereby improving the nitrogen nutritional value of the feed.

Although the flavonoid pathway has been extensively studied by chemists, biochemists, and geneticists for over 60 years, the enzymatic formation of the 2,3-cis-flavan-3-ol [(-)-epicatechin] unit that forms the major portion of most CTs has, until recently, remained a mystery. Mutations in the BANYULS (BAN, named after the colour of a French red wine) gene in Arabidopsis result in a transparent testa (tt), associated with a lack of CTs and precocious accumulation of anthocyanins in the seed coat. On the basis of this phenotype and the amino acid sequence similarity of BAN to a reductase of flavonoid biosynthesis (dihydroflavonol reductase), it was suggested that BAN encodes leucoanthocyanidin reductase, a yet poorly characterised enzyme proposed to convert flavan-3,4-diols to 2,3-trans-flavan-3-ols such as (+)-catechin, the "starter unit" for CT condensation.

It has now been shown that the BAN genes from Arabidopsis and barrel medic encode a new enzyme, anthocyanidin reductase, that converts cyanidin to 2,3-cis-(-)-epicatechin. Therefore, anthocyanins are not, as previously believed, only end products of flavonoid metabolism. Although BAN expression in barrel medic is primarily limited to young seed coats, transgenic expression of barrel medic BAN in tobacco leads to accumulation of CTs throughout the pigmented portions of the petals, with concomitant reduction in anthocyanin levels. These results suggest that it should soon be possible to engineer CT accumulation in forage legumes for protection of animals against pasture bloat.

Lignin is a phenylpropanoid polymer found in all higher plants, and an important factor affecting cell wall digestibility in forage legumes. Lignin levels increase with progressive maturity in stems of many forage legumes, including alfalfa. In addition, the lignin composition often changes with advanced maturity toward a progressively higher syringyl to guaiacyl (S/G) ratio, reflecting an increased degree of methylation of the lignin. Some studies have linked decreased forage digestibility to increased S/G ratio as a function of increased plant maturity, whereas others have questioned the effect of lignin composition on digestibility.

Genetic manipulation of lignin levels in forage legumes has, to date, targeted just three of the 10 or more enzymes involved in the formation of the guaiacyl and syringyl lignin monomers (monolignols). Antisense reduction of caffeic acid 3-O-methyltransferase (COMT) to less than 5% of wild-type values in the tropical pasture legume Stylosanthes humilis resulted in no apparent reduction in overall lignin levels but in a strong reduction in S lignin. In vitro digestibility of stem material in rumen fluid was increased by up to 10% in the transgenic plants exhibiting strongest COMT down-regulation.

Up to 30% decreases in Klason lignin levels, near elimination of S lignin, and appearance of novel benzodioxane units in the lignin fraction, were observed in transgenic alfalfa in which COMT down-regulation was targeted using the vascular tissue-specific bean PAL2 promoter. Forage material from COMT down-regulated alfalfa plants had significantly increased neutral detergent fiber, acid detergent fiber, and in vitro true digestibility. In-rumen digestibility was increased by up to 4% in a series of replicated analyses in fistulated steers.

Near elimination of caffeoyl coenzyme A 3-O-methyltransferase (CCoAOMT) activity in transgenic alfalfa reduced G lignin by up to 50% in some lines, but had no effect on S lignin. CCoAOMT-down-regulated plants had a significant decrease in overall lignin content and increased neutral detergent fiber, acid detergent fiber, and in vitro true digestibility. In-rumen digestibility of CCoAOMT-down-regulated alfalfa forage was increased by up to 6%. Antisense down-regulation of cinnamyl alcohol dehydrogenase in transgenic alfalfa to approximately 30% of wild-type level led to a red colouration of the stem and a reduction in lignin S/G ratio primarily due to a decrease in S units.

The most strongly down-regulated plants exhibited increased in situ digestibility of dry matter in cannulated sheep. Taken together, the above studies indicate the success of transgenic approaches for improvement of forage quality in alfalfa, and new cultivars incorporating these traits may soon reach the market. Major areas for future research on lignins and proanthocyanidins for forage legume improvement include development of improved analytical methods for determining the content and composition of polymeric phenylpropanoids and flavonoids, understanding the exact relationships between lignin and proanthocyanidin content and composition and forage quality, developing better and more predictable approaches for engineering the lignin polymer, and understanding all the factors necessary for synthesis and assembly of proanthocyanidins in leaf tissues.

The success of large-scale genome and expressed sequence tag (EST) sequencing projects has greatly expanded the scale on which natural product biosynthesis and biological systems in general can be addressed. Extensive DNA sequence resources are currently available for soybean and barrel medic Bioactive Natural Compounds for the Treatment of Gastrointestinal Disorders. The sequences of many genes encoding enzymes of natural product biosynthesis are already present in these databases. The question is how to identify them. One answer is to apply functional genomic approaches that encompass global assessment of the transcriptome and the metabolome.

The comprehensive profiling of large numbers of metabolites can be used to assess gene function and to query holistic responses of biological systems to external stimuli. This approach is the key means to qualitatively and quantitatively defining the chemical phenotype (chemotype) of a genetically or environmentally perturbed biological system. The current and prevailing opinion is that no single technique will provide a comprehensive assessment of the chemically complex metabolome, particularly when considering the chemical diversity of natural products; thus, multiple tools must be used. These include thin-layer chromatography, infrared spectroscopy, NMR, gas chromatography/mass spectrometry (GC/MS), liquid chromatography with UV or MS detection, liquid chromatography/MS/MS, capillary electrophoresis, and capillary electrophoresis/MS.

The best methods for chemical profiling of flavonoids and isoflavonoids use HPLC for separation coupled to UV absorption and/or mass selective detection. The need to profile intact glycosidic conjugates, the relatively high Mr of the conjugates, and the multiplicity of polar hydroxyl groups obviate against the use of GC separation because of the need for extensive derivatisation and the limited m/z range of most commercial GC/MS instruments. In addition to a plethora of reports on the extraction and identification of individual compounds, specific protocols for the routine profiling of the flavonoid and isoflavonoid complements of various legume species, including red clover (Trifolium pratense), soybean, and lupin, a rich source of prenylated isoflavonoids (Fig. 1).

Saponins contain poor chromophores; thus, the preferred method for profiling the triterpene glycoside complement of legumes such as alfalfa and barrel medic is reversed-phase HPLC coupled with electrospray-ionization MS. Using this technique, it has been demonstrated that the model legume barrel medic contains a more complex mixture of triterpenes than found in the closely related and previously well-studied species alfalfa. Five different -amyrin-derived triterpene aglycones, soyasapogenol B, soyasapogenol E, medicagenic acid, hederagenin, and bayogenin were found to be the core of the 27 barrel medic saponins identified.

Analysis of lignin presents far greater technical challenges than for most other natural products because it is a complex insoluble heteropolymer. The reader is referred elsewhere for a description of the problems and some current approaches. Profiling of proanthocyanidin polymers is likewise challenging, and most studies rely on simple chemical extraction and colourimetric determination, protocols that do not provide structural information. Structures have been determined for several legume proanthocyanidins, but the methods fall far short of high throughput profiling and new approaches are needed. The following example outlines the utility of genomics coupled to metabolomics in deciphering a biosynthetic pathway, the formation of the -amyrin-derived triterpenes in barrel medic, for which the exact route of biosynthesis is experimentally undetermined.

In-depth targeted metabolite profiling with the approaches outlined above is first used to determine the exact complement of the metabolites of interest and their potential precursors. The best approach compares tissues that make the compound(s) in question with those that do not. Therefore, the biological system can be a particular species, set of ecotypes, or group of species. Alternatively, an inducible system such as elicited roots or cell cultures can be studied. In the case of the triterpenes, elicitation of cell suspension cultures with methyl jasmonate results in a striking induction of the compounds and, presumably, their biosynthetic enzymes.

Based on the metabolite profiles and perhaps already existing knowledge, a tentative pathway can be proposed; this consists essentially of P450- and GT-catalysed reactions in the case of triterpene saponins. If not already available, cDNA libraries are then made from tissues of the plant in which the particular chemistry is active, and high-throughput EST sequencing performed. In barrel medic, there are more than 250 expressed cytochrome P450s and nearly 300 expressed GTs, based on EST counting in the more than 30 cDNA libraries sequenced to date. Bioinformatic approaches such as use of self-organising maps for in silico expression analysis of EST libraries, coupled with DNA array analysis of transcripts from at least two cell or tissue types (chemical producers and nonproducers), can then provide a shortcut to candidate gene identification from among, in this particular case, the approximately 600 candidate P450s and GTs.

The number of candidates revealed in this way is small enough for direct expression studies in a heterologous system such as Escherichia coli or yeast. When dealing with complex pathways for which intermediates are unavailable, parallel approaches such as stable or transient down-regulation of candidate genes coupled with metabolite profiling may also have to be used. Although a bewildering array of plant natural products exists in nature, most are constructed using a relatively small number of enzyme types, e.g. polyketide synthase, terpene cyclase, reductase, acyltransferase, O-methyltransferase, etc.

A better understanding of the relationship between amino acid sequence and catalytic activity is the key to a better prediction of function for enzymes of natural product biosynthesis based on primary DNA sequence information. This requires knowledge of structure-function relationships among the various classes of enzymes involved in natural product biosynthesis. This knowledge is just beginning to appear. For example, the three-dimensional structures of a number of natural product pathway enzymes from alfalfa, including three O-methyltransferases of flavonoid, isoflavonoid, and lignin biosynthesis, have recently been solved by x-ray crystallography.

Information of this type not only increases predictive ability for functional genomics, but also facilitates structure-directed modification of catalytic activity for the generation of novel natural products through in vivo transgenic approaches or, ultimately, in vitro combinatorial biochemistry. Functional and structural genomics, coupled with increases in the resolving power of metabolomics, are poised to make a huge impact on our understanding of plant natural product biosynthesis, and, therefore, on our ability to harness nature's wonderful chemical diversity for the benefit of humankind. These approaches take advantage of the rapidly decreasing costs of DNA sequencing to generate databases for natural product gene discovery.

Legumes will be at the forefront of these endeavors because these species combine emerging genomic accessibility with chemistry that is of relevance for plant, human, and animal health. Genomics will also provide new approaches for discovering the transcriptional regulators that control expression of natural product biosynthetic enzymes. Whereas many will probably fall into the known classes of transcription factors currently known to regulate phenylpropanoid and terpenoid biosynthesis, new types of factors may perhaps exist in legumes. Metabolic engineering by ectopic expression of transcription factors holds great promise for exploiting legumes as factories for production of bioactive secondary metabolites.

11

Production of Secondary Metabolites from Medicinal Plants

Discoveries of cell cultures capable of producing specific medicinal compounds at a rate similar or superior to that of intact plants have accelerated in the last few years. New physiologically active substances of medicinal interest have been found by bioassay. It has been demonstrated that the biosynthetic activity of cultured cells can be enhanced by regulating environmental factors, as well as by artificial selection or the induction of variant clones. Some of the medicinal compounds localised in morphologically specialised tissues or organs of native plants have been produced in culture systems not only by inducing specific organised cultures, but also by undifferentiated cell cultures.

The possible use of plant cell cultures for the specific biotransformations of natural compounds has been demonstrated. The major advantages of a cell culture system over the conventional cultivation of whole plants are:

— Useful compounds can be produced under controlled conditions independent of climatic changes or soil conditions;

- — Cultured cells would be free of microbes and insects;
- — The cells of any plants, tropical or alpine, could easily be multiplied to yield their specific metabolites;
- — Automated control of cell growth and rational regulation of metabolite processes would reduce of labour costs and improve productivity;
- — Organic substances are extractable from callus cultures.

In order to obtain high yields suitable for commercial exploitation, efforts have focused on isolating the biosynthetic activities of cultured cells, achieved by optimising the cultural conditions, selecting high-producing strains, and employing precursor feeding, transformation methods, and immobilisation techniques. Transgenic hairy root cultures have revolutionised the role of plant tissue culture in secondary metabolite production. They are unique in their genetic and biosynthetic stability, faster in growth, and more easily maintained. Using this methodology a wide range of chemical compounds have been synthesised.

Advances in tissue culture, combined with improvement in genetic engineering, specifically transformation technology, has opened new avenues for high volume production of pharmaceuticals, nutraceuticals, and other beneficial substances. Recent advances in the molecular biology, enzymology, and fermentation technology of plant cell cultures suggest that these systems will become a viable source of important secondary metabolites. Genome manipulation is resulting in relatively large amounts of desired compounds produced by plants infected with an engineered virus, whereas transgenic plants can maintain constant levels of production of proteins without additional intervention.

Large-scale plant tissue culture is found to be an attractive alternative approach to traditional methods of plantation as it offers a controlled supply of biochemicals independent of plant availability. Current developments in tissue culture technology indicate that transcription factors are efficient new molecular tools for plant metabolic engineering to increase the production of valuable compounds. In vitro cell culture offers an intrinsic advantage for foreign protein synthesis in certain situations since they can be designed to produce therapeutic proteins, including monoclonal antibodies, antigenic proteins that act as immunogenes, human serum albumin, interferon, immuno-contraceptive protein, ribosome unactivator trichosantin, antihypersensitive drug angiotensin, leu-enkephalin neuropeptide, and human haemoglobin.

The appeal of using natural products for medicinal purposes is increasing, and metabolic engineering can alter the production of pharmaceuticals and help to design new therapies. At present, researchers aim to produce substances with antitumour, antiviral, hypoglycaemic, anti-inflammatcry, antiparasite, antimicrobial, tranquiliser and immunomodulating activities through tissue culture technology. Exploration of the biosynthetic capabilities of various cell cultures has been carried out by a group of plant scientists and microbiologists in several countries during the last decade. In the last few years promising findings have been reported for a variety of medicinally valuable substances, some of which may be produced on an industrial scale in the near future.

Role of Tissue Cultures in the Production of Pharmaceutical Products

Advances in the area of cell cultures for the production of medicinal compounds has made possible the production of a wide variety of pharmaceuticals like alkaloids, terpenoids, steroids, saponins, phenolics, flavanoids, and amino acids. Successful attempts to produce some of these valuable pharmaceuticals in relatively large quantities by cell cultures are illustrated.

Taxol

Taxol (plaxitaxol), a complex diterpene alkaloid found in the bark of the Taxus tree, is one of the most promising anticancer agents known due to its unique mode of action on the micro tubular cell system. At present, production of taxol by various Taxus species cells in cultures has been one of the most extensively explored areas of plant cell cultures in recent years owing to the enormous commercial value of taxol, the scarcity of the Taxus tree, and the costly synthetic process.

In 1989, Christan et. al. reported for the first time the production of taxol (placlitaxel) by Taxus cell cultures. Fett-Neto et al. have studied the effect of nutrients and other factors on paclitaxel production by T. cuspidata cell cultures. Srinivasan et al. have studied the kinetics of biomass accumulation and paclitaxel production by T. baccata cell suspension cultures. Paclitaxel was found to accumulate at high yields (1.5 mg/l) exclusively in the second phase of growth. Kim et al. established a similar level of paclitaxel from T. brevifolia cell suspension cultures following 10 days in culture with optimised medium containing 6% fructose.

Ketchum and Gibson reported that addition of carbohydrate during the growth cycle increased the production rate of paclitaxel, which accumulated in the culture medium. In addition to paclitaxel, several other taxoids have been identified in both cell and culture medium of Taxus cultures. Parc et al. reported production of taxoids by callus cultures from selected Taxus genotypes. In order to increase the taxoid production in these cultures, the addition of different amino acids to the culture medium were studied, and phenylalanine was found to assist in maximum taxol production in T. cuspidata cultures.

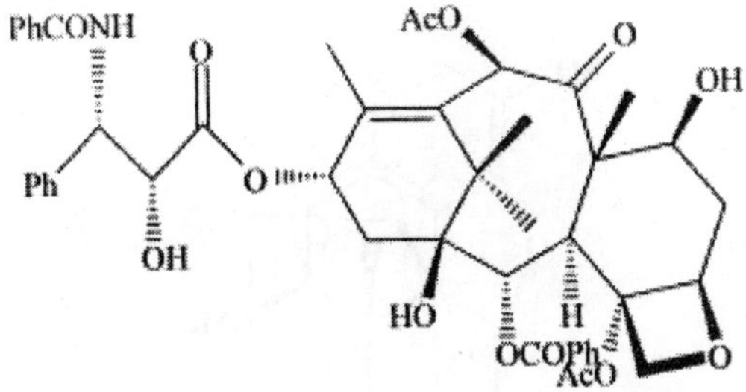

Taxol

The influence of biotic and abiotic elicitors was also studied to improve the production and accumulation of taxol through tissue cultures. The production of taxol from nodule cultures containing cohesive multicultural units displaying a high degree of differentiation has been achieved from cultured needles of seven Taxus cultivars. Factors influencing stability and recovery of paclitaxel from suspension cultures and the media have been studied in detail by Nguyen et al. The effects of rare earth elements and gas concentrations on taxol production have been reported.

Morphine and Codeine

Latex from the opium poppy, Papaver somniferum, is a commercial source of the analgesics, morphine and codeine. Callus and suspension cultures of P. somniferum are being investigated as an alternative means for production of these compounds. Production of morphine and codeine in morphologically undifferentiated cultures has been reported. Removal of exogenous hormones from large-scale culture systems could be implemented using a two-stage process strategy. Without exogenous hormones, maximum codeine and morphine concentrations were 3.0

mg/g dry weight and 2.5 mg/g dry weight, respectively, up to three times higher than in cultures supplied with hormones.

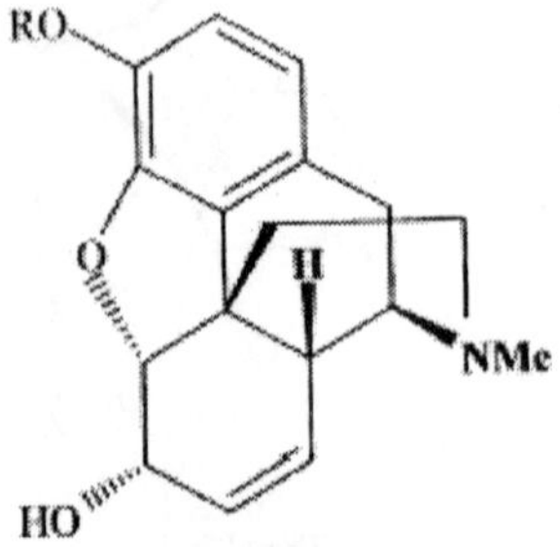

R=H: Morphine, R=Me Codeine

Biotransformation of codeinone to codeine with immobilised cells of P. somniferum has been reported by Furuya et al. The conversion yield was 70.4%, and about 88% of the codeine converted was excreted into the medium.

Ginsenosides

The root of Panax ginseng C.A. Mayer, so-called ginseng, has been widely used as a tonic and highly priced medicine since ancient times. Ginseng has been recognised as a miraculous promoter of health and longevity. The primary bioactive constituents of ginseng were identified as ginsenosides, a group of triterpenoid saponins. Among them, ginsenoside Rg1 is one of the major active molecules from Panax ginseng. Chang and Hsing obtained repeatable precocious flowering in the embryos derived from mature ginseng root callus cultured on a chemically defined medium. Also, plant regeneration through somatic embryogenesis in root-derived callus of ginseng has been reported.

In recent years ginseng cell culture has been explored as a potentially more efficient method of producing ginsenosides. The effect of medium components like carbon, nitrogen, and phosphate concentrations and plant growth hormones were thoroughly studied to increase the production of ginsenosides. Influence of potassium ion was also studied. Large-scale suspension culture of ginseng cells was first reported by Yasuda et al. Later on an industrial-scale culture process was initiated by Nitto Denko Corporation in the 1980s using 2000 and 20000-1 stirred tank fermentors to achieve productivities of 500-700 mg/l per day. This process is considered an important landmark in the commercialisation of plant tissue and cell culture on a large scale.

In addition to this, Agrobacterium tumefaciens infected root cultures were introduced, productivity of which was found to exceed the callus of normal roots threefold. Other types of tissue cultures, such as embryogenic tissues and hairy roots transformed by Agrobacteria have been examined. Yu et al. reported ginsenoside production using elicitor treatment. These developments indicate that ginseng cell culture process is still an attractive area for commercial development around the world and it possesses great potential for mass industrialisation.

Concentration of plant growth regulators in the medium influences the cell growth and ginsenoside production in the suspension cultures. Recent studies have shown that addition of methyl jasmonate or dihydromethyl jasmonate to suspension cultures increases the production of ginsenosides. Also, jasmonic acid improves the accumulation of gensinosides in the root cultures of ginseng.

L-DOPA

L-3,4-dihydroxyphenylalanine, is an important intermediate of secondary metabolism in higher plants and

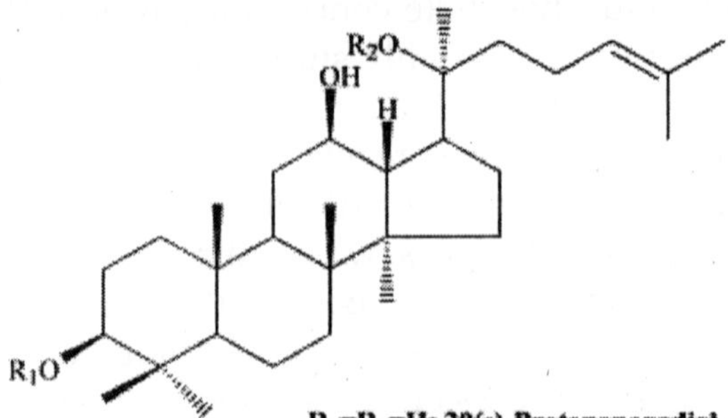

R_1=R_2=H: 20(s)-Protopanaxadiol

Ra: R_1= glucose-6-1-glucose-6-1-glucose
R_2= glucose-3-1-glucose-3-1-glucose

Rb$_1$: R_1= glucose-2-1-glucose
R_2= glucose-6-1-glucose

Rb$_2$: R_1= glucose-2-1-glucose
R_2= glucose-6-1-arabinose(pyr)

Rb$_3$: R_1= glucose-2-1-glucose
R_2= glucose-6-1-xylose

Rc: R_1= glucose-2-1-glucose
R_2= glucose-6-1-arabinose(fur)

Rd: R_1= glucose-2-1-glucose
R_2= glucose

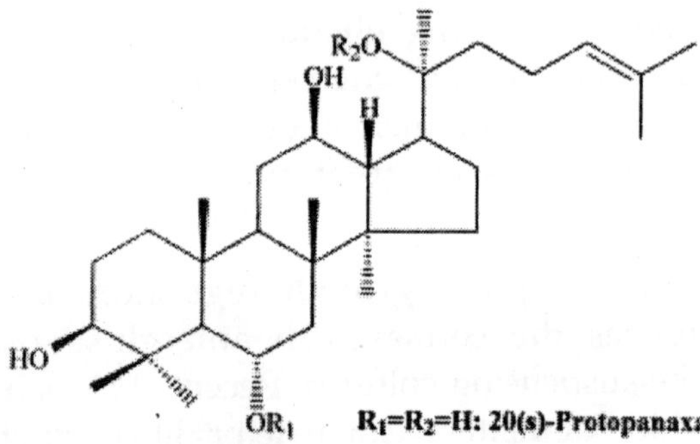

R_1=R_2=H: 20(s)-Protopanaxatriol

Re: R_1= glucose-2-1-rhamnose
R_2= glucose

Rf: R_1= glucose-2-1-glucose
R_2= H

Rg$_1$: R_1= glucose
R_2= glucose

Rg$_2$: R_1= glucose-2-1-glucose
R_2= H

Structures of Ginsenosides

is known as a precursor of alkaloids, betalain, and melanine, isolated from Vinca faba, Mucuna, Baptisia and Lupinus. It is also a precursor of catecholamines in animals and is being used as a potent drug for a progressive disabling disorder associated with a deficiency of dopamine in the brain.

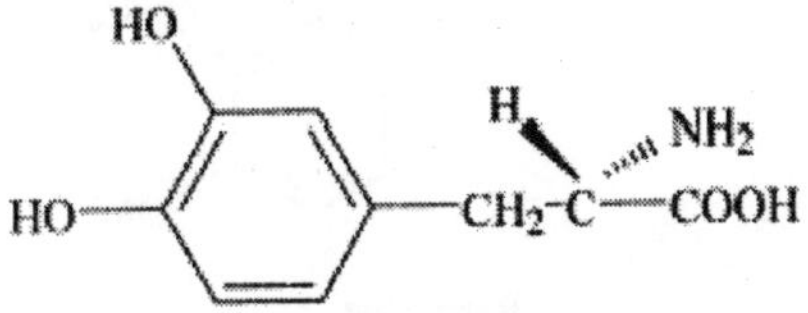

L-DOPA

The widespread application of this therapy created a demand for large quantities of L-DOPA at an economical price level, and this led to the introduction of cell cultures as an alternative means for enriched production. Brain found that the callus tissue of Mucuna pruriense accumulated 25 mg/l DOPA in the medium containing relatively high concentrations of 2,4-D. Teramoto and Komamine induced callus tissues of Mucuna hassjoo, M. Pruriense, and M. deeringiana and optimised the culture conditions. The highest concentration of DOPA was obtained when M. hassjoo cells were cultivated in MS medium with 0.025 mg/l 2.4 -D and 10 mg/l kinetin. The level of DOPA in the cells was about 80 mmol/g-f.w.

Berberine

Berberine is an isoquinoline alkaloid found in the roots of Coptis japonica and cortex of Phellondendron amurense. This antibacterial alkaloid has been identified from a number of cell cultures, notably those of Coptis japonica, Thalictrum spp., and Berberis spp. The productivity of berberine was increased in cell cultures by optimising the nutrients in the growth medium and the levels of phytohormones. By selecting high yielding cell lines, Mitsui group produced berberine on a large scale with a productivity of 1.4 g/l over 2 weeks.

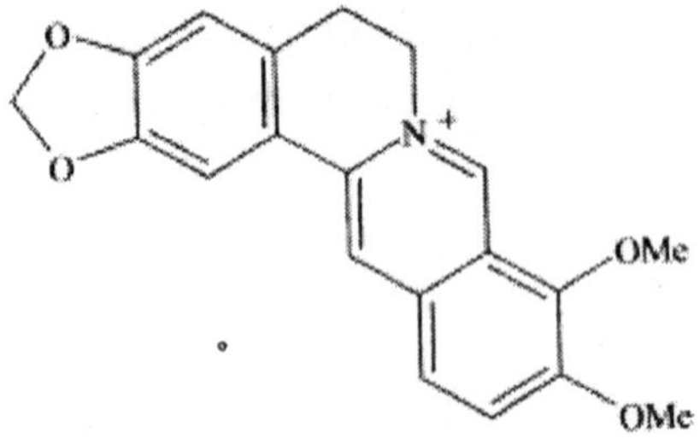

Berberine

Other methods for increasing yields include elicitation of cultures with a yeast polysaccharide elicitor, which has been successful with a relatively low producing T. rugosum culture. The influence of spermidine on berberine production in Thalictrum minus cell cultures has been reported.

Diosgenin

Diosgenin is a precursor for the chemical synthesis of steroidal drugs and is tremendously important to the pharmaceutical industry. In 1983, Tal et al. reported on the use of cell cultures of Dioscorea deltoidea for production of diosgenin. They found that carbon and nitrogen levels greatly influenced diosgenin accumulation in one cell line. Another researchers established Dioscorea immobilised cell cultures, in which reticulated polyurethane foam was shown to stimulate diosgenin production, increasing the cellular concentration by 40% and total yield by 25%. Tal et al. have been able to obtain diosgenin levels as high as 8% in batch-grown D. deltoidea cell suspensions. However, the daily productivity was only 7.3 mg/l. Several other groups have also attempted cell cultures for diosgenin production.

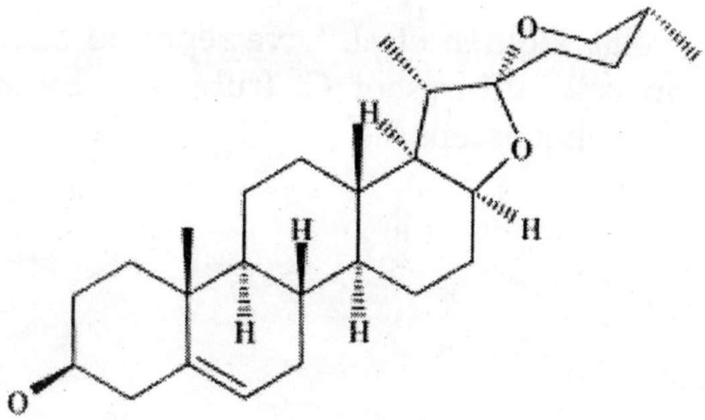

Diosgenin

Kaul et al. studied the influence of various factors on diosgenin production by Dioscorea deltoidea callus and suspension cultures The search for high-producing cell lines coupled to recent developments in immobilised cultures and the use of extraction procedures, which convert furostanol saponins to spirostanes such as diosgenin, should prove useful in increasing productivity in the years to come.

Capsaicin

Capsaicin, an alkaloid, is used mainly as a pungent food additive in formulated foods. It is obtained from fruits of green pepper. Capsaicin is also used in pharmaceutical preparations as a digestive stimulant and for rheumatic disorders. Suspension cultures of Capsicum frutescens produce low levels of capsaicin, but immobilising the cells in reticulated polyurethane foam can increase production approximately 100-fold.

Further improvements in productivity can be brought about by supplying precursors such as isocapric acid. Lindsey reported that treatments which suppress cell growth and primary metabolism seem to improve capsaicin synthesis. A biotechnological process has been developed for the production of capsaicin from C.

frutescens cells. Holden et al. have reported elicitation of capsaicin in cell cultures of C. frutescens by spores of Gliccladium deliquescens.

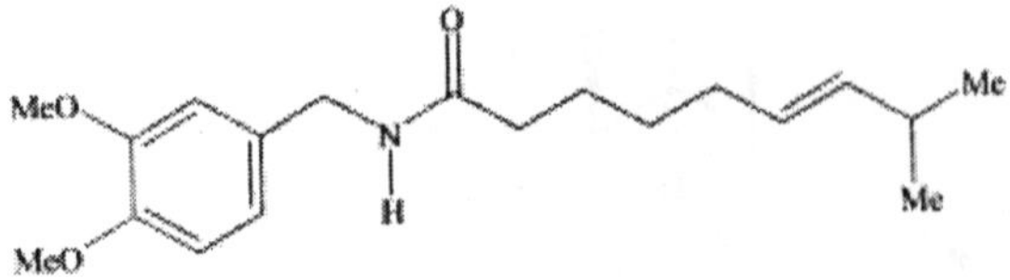

Capsaicin

Researchers were thoroughly studied the effects of nutritional stress on capsaicin production in immobilised cell cultures of Capsicum annum. Biotransformation of externally fed protocatechuic aldehyde and caffeic acid to capsaicin in freely suspended cells and immobilised cells cultures of Capsicum frutescens has also been reported.

Camptothecin

Camptothecin, a potent antitumour alkaloid was isolated from Camptotheca acuminata. Sakato and Misawa induced C. acuminata callus on MS medium containing 0.2 mg/l 2,4-D and 1 mg/l kinetin and developed liquid cultures in the presence of gibberellin, L-tryptophan, and conditioned medium, which yielded camptothecin at about 0.0025% on a dry weight basis. When the cultures were grown on MS medium containing 4 mg/l NAA, accumulation of camptothecin reached 0.998 mg/l. 10-Hydroxycamptothecin, a promising derivative of camptothecin is in a clinical trials.

Vinblastine and Vincristine

The dimeric indole alkaloids vincristine and vinblastine have become valuable drugs in cancer chemotherapy due to their potent antitumour activity against various leukemias and solid tumours. These compounds are extracted commercially from large quantities of Catharanthus roseus. Since the intact plant contains low concentrations (0.0005%), plant cell cultures have been employed as an alternative to produce large amounts of these alkaloids.

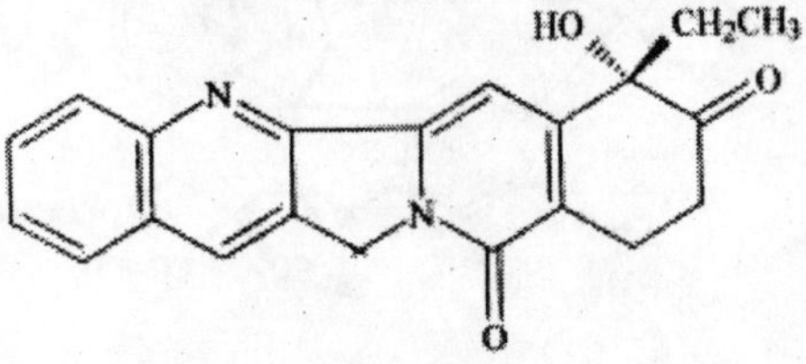

Camptothecin

Vinblastine is composed of catharanthine and vindoline. Since vindoline is more abundant than catharanthin in intact plants, it is less expensive. Misawa et al. established an economically feasible process consisting of production of catharanthine by plant cell fermentation and a simple chemical or an enzymatic coupling. The significant influence of various compounds, like vanadyl sulphate, abscisic acid, and sodium chloride on catharanthin production have been described by Smith et al. Endo et al. attempted synthesis of anhydrovinblastine (AVLB from catharanthine and vindoline through enzymic coupling followed by sodium borohydride reduction).

A crude preparation of 70% ammonium sulphate precipitated protein from the cultured cells of C. roseus was used as an enzyme source. The reaction mixture contained catharanthine, vindoline, Tris buffer, Ph 7.0, and the crude enzyme; the mixture was incubated at 300°C and for 3 h. The products of the reaction were various dimeric alkaloids including vinamidine, 3(R)-hydroxyvinamidine, and 3, 4-anhydrovinblastine. Dimerisation using ferric ion catalyst in the absence of enzyme resulted in anhydrovinblastine and vinblastine in 52.8% and 12.3% yields, respectively. The yield of vinblastine via chemical coupling was improved in the presence of ferric chloride, oxalate, maleate, and sodium borohydride.

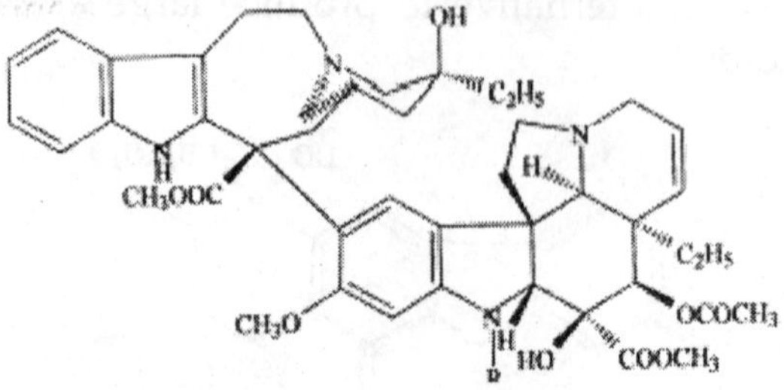

R=CH_3: Vinblastine, R=CHO: Vincristine

Influence of various parameters like stress, addition of bioregulators, elicitors and synthetic precursors on indole alkaloids production were studied in detail by Zhao et al. Also, metabolic ratelimitations through precursor feeding and effect of elicitor dosage on biosynthesis of indole alkaloids in Catharanthus roseus hairy root cultures have been reported.

Tanshinones

Tanshinones are a group of quinoid diterpenoids believed to be active principles of Danshen, a well known traditional Chinese medicine. Tanshinone I and cryptotanshinone prevent complications of myocardial ischemia; tanshinone II A has undergone successful clinical trials for the treatment of angina pectoris in China. Plant cell and organ culture technology provide an alternative means of producing these active ingredients.

Researchers established a cell line containing abundant amounts of cryptotanshinone from S. miltiorrhiza. Adventitious root cultures of S. miltiorrhiza and the culture conditions for high yield production of tanshinones in the adventitious roots were reported.

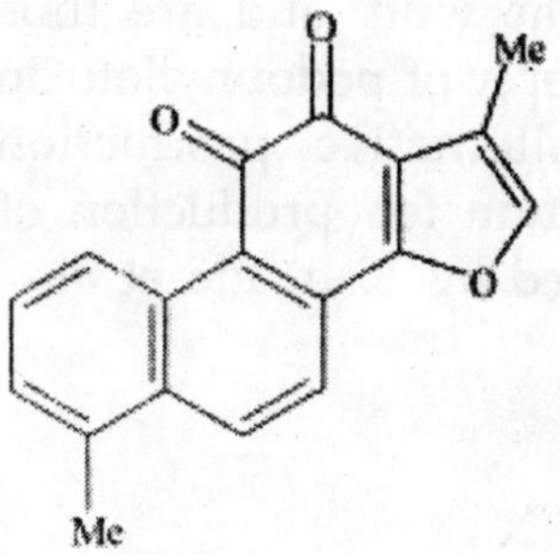

Tanshinone I

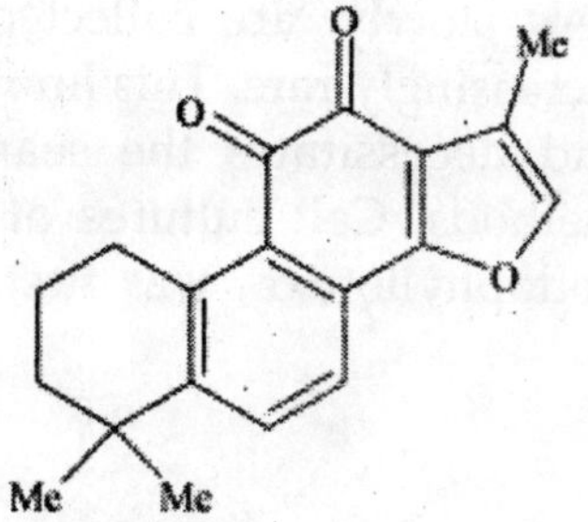

Tanshinone II

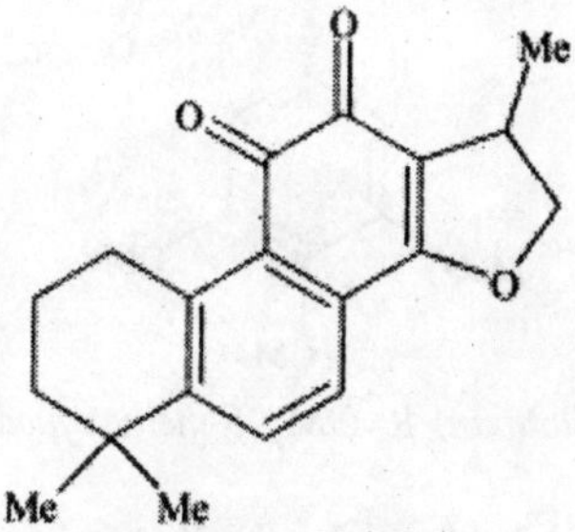

Cryptotanshinone

Diterpenoid production in Ti-transformed root or hairy root cultures of S. miltiorrhiza has also been established. In these cultures, although relatively high tanshinone production was achieved, the morphological characteristics of the hairy roots require special bioreactors for the cultivation, which has hindered the scale-up of such processes.

Podophyllotoxin

Podophyllotoxin is an antitumour aryltetralin lignan found

in Podophyllum peltatum and Podophyllum hexandrum. It also serves as a starting material for the preparation of its semisynthetic derivatives, etoposide and teniposide, widely used in tumour therapy. These plants, which grow very slowly, are collected from the wild and are thus increasingly rare. This limits the supply of podophyllotoxin and necessitates the search for alternative production methods. Cell cultures of P. peltatum for production of podophyllotoxin was first attempted by Kadkade et al.

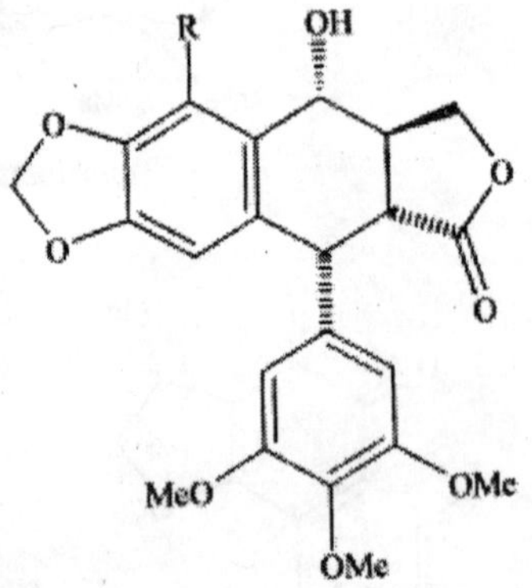

R=H: Podophyllotoxin, R=OM_e: 5-methoxypodophyllotoxin

To increase the yield of podophyllotoxin, used a complex of a precursor, coniferyl alcohol, and b-cyclodextrin to P. hexandrum cell suspension cultures. The addition of 3 mM coniferyl alcohol complex yielded 0.013% podophyllotoxin on a dry weight basis, but the cultures without the precursor produced only 0.0035%. Smollny et al. reported that callus tissues and suspension culture cells of Lilium album produced 0.3% podophyllotoxin. Several other tissue culture approaches have been studied to increase the yields. Since 5-methoxypodophyllotoxin, an analogue of podophyllotoxin, has strong cytostatic activity, many researchers have tried to improve its yield through tissue cultures.

12

Herbal Pharmacokinetics

Herbal pharmacokinetics can provide valuable information to aid practitioners in prescribing herbs safely and effectively. It may also enable useful predictions to be made, for example regarding possible interactions between herbal remedies and conventional pharmaceuticals. For a given dose of any herbal medicine, its physiological effect (or that of its constituents) will be governed by the effective tissue concentration of the remedy which in turn is determined by pharmacokinetic parameters - the absorption, distribution, metabolism and excretion of its various components.

Drug-drug interactions constitute the bulk of the conventional pharmacokinetic literature, but currently herb-drug interactions are taking center stage, both in the popular media and in terms of increasing physician awareness of the widespread and often undisclosed use of herbal medicines by their patients, and the potential for significant pharmacokinetic interaction between herbs and prescription pharmaceuticals. Useful data about actual and potential interactions between pharmaceutical drugs comes from various sources, including clinical trials, preclinical trials investigating adverse effects, post licensing drug monitoring, controlled trials on healthy subjects required for drug licensing, in vitro or in vivo studies on animal or human cell lines or tissues, and Adverse Drug Reports (ADR's).

There are two important systems involved in pharmacokinetic drug interactions - the well known Cytochrome P450 (CYP450) enzyme system and the more recently understood P-glycoprotein (P-gp) efflux pump. These are described below;

CYP450

The Cytochrome P-450 (CYP450) system is a family of heme based enzymes located in the smooth endoplasmic reticulum, particularly concentrated in hepatocytes and mucosal enterocytes but also found in the kidneys, skin and lung tissues of humans. Also known as the mixed function oxidases, it is one of the most important systems for biotransformation of drugs. The CYP450 families of enzymes are responsible for Phase I of xenobiotic metabolism, catalysing predominantly oxidation, reduction and hydrolysis reactions which render lipophilic compounds more polar, prior to the Phase II processes of thiol conjugation, glucuronidation, sulfation or acetylation which enable the metabolites to be excreted by the kidneys.

The CYP450 system is a large field of ongoing research, with annual symposia devoted exclusively to the subject. Of the twelve known families of CYP450 isozymes representatives of only three families are significant in humans; the most important are 1A2 found in the liver; the diverse CYP2 group including 2C19, 2C9, 2D6, and 2E1 which are all involved to some degree in drug transformation, especially 2C9. CYP3A4 is the major human enzyme involved in drug biotransformation and is found extensively in hepatocytes and in small intestinal enterocytes, two sites where it plays a key role in modulating the bioavailability of orally administered pharmaceuticals.

The interaction of a given compound with the CYP450 system will determine its fate and possible effects in the body; the majority of intermediate metabolites are less toxic than their parent compounds but it is also possible for intermediates to be highly toxic, carcinogenic or mutagenic. For herbalists, the best known example of this process is of course the formation of hepatotoxic pyrrole metabolites from certain pyrrolizidine alkaloids present in Symphytum spp. and other genera. Xenobiotics, drugs, and a variety of naturally occurring dietary or herbal constituents can interact in several ways with the CYP450 system:

— A compound may be a substrate of, ie metabolised by, one or several CYP isoforms. If the main isoform is saturated, it becomes a substrate for the secondary enzyme(s).

— A compound can be an inducer of a CYP isoform, either of the one it is a substrate for, or may induce several different enzymes at the same time. The process of induction increases the rate of metabolism of substrates of that enzyme.

— A compound may also be an inhibitor of CYP450 enzymes. There are several mechanisms of inhibition, and a compound may inhibit several isoforms including others than those for which it is a substrate.

These are the actions that underlie the pharmacokinetic variations in drug metabolism, and that cause interactions between two or more drugs, or between drugs and nutrients, or drugs and herbs. Induction is a slow process, dependent on the rate of synthesis of new enzyme and usually noticeable after only a few days, and maximal after two weeks. Inhibition is more rapid, and can become maximal within the first 24 hours of exposure to the inhibitor - but likewise may reverse more rapidly.

There are many non drug inducers and inhibitors of CYP450, among the best known being grapefruit juice which inhibits CYP3A4, and vegetables such as Brussel sprouts and broccoli whose glucosilinate compounds induce CYP1A2. This enzyme metabolises many carcinogens, including tobacco related compounds and char grilled meat, and induction of 1A2 underlies the cancer preventative reputation of the Brassicaceae. Lists of substrates, inducers and inhibitors of the different enzymes are being regularly updated by new research, and there are several internet sites where the latest information is available. For clinicians, there is one aspect of the research which is of great importance in evaluating potential for interactions - the subject of individual variation in CYP450 expression.

There is a wide range of variation in expression of CYP450 enzymes. This accounts for much of the inter-individual variability in responses to drugs, as well as in the occurrence and severity of adverse effects and drug interactions. The underlying factors affecting individual variation in CYP450 expression are age; genetics including gender and race; disease, including both general infection as well as specific hepatic conditions. Beyond these factors, there is recognised a spectrum of phenotypic variation ranging from "poor metabolisers" to "extensive metabolisers" between whom there can be 10 to 20 fold differences in the a rate of drug metabolism.

These factors inevitably complicate any simple extrapolation from in vitro findings. In addition, difficulty of interpretation is compounded by the functional status of other, co-dependent or coregulating factors and pathways in an individual. For example, Phase I metabolites must be cleared by Phase II metabolism. Phase 2 enzymes such as glutathione-S-transferase, or N-acetyl transferase are also subject to polymorphism, and the phase II pathways are subject to rate limiting kinetics by the availability of conjugates such glutathione, its precursors (e.g. cysteine) and cofactors (e.g. selenium), and in turn the overall redox status of the individual...and so on. This all adds to the extraordinary complexity of the whole picture.

Ironically, there is here an obvious clinical point, often lost in the polemics of the mainstream debate about potential interactions; namely that the majority of natural healthcare practitioners, including medical herbalists, tend to evaluate individual hepatic detoxification status before devising therapeutic interventions involving modification of diet, consumption of nutritional supplements or herbal medicines precisely because they understand the inherent degree of variability of this system as well as its central importance in healthy function.

Restoring, supporting and optimising hepatic detoxification functionality is a time honored and foundational component of herbal therapeutics. Conversely, most physicians tend to prescribe pharmaceuticals in terms of generic doses, and rarely making adjustment for hepatic detoxification functionality which is not a part of their routine initial assessment of a patient.

Hypericum and CYP450 Modulation

Preliminary conclusions from the few studies that have directly investigated St John's Wort (SJW) extract interactions with the CYP450 system, suggest that St John's Wort may under some circumstances modulate CYP450 isoforms, particularly 3A4. Reviewing the studies does not currently enable firm conclusions to be drawn. Experimental and isolated constituent evidence is limited. Moore has found evidence that hyperforin and St John's Wort extracts induce CYP3A4 in hepatocyte cells via the pregnane X nuclear receptor, (this controls CYP3A4 expression), while Li showed that quercitin, another St

John's Wort constituent, inhibited 3A4 metabolism of acetaminophen by human hepatic microsomes.

Another recent in vitro study with an array of recombinant human CYP450 enzymes using substrate assay methods employed for pharmaceutical drug screening investigations of possible pharmacokinetic interactions examined crude extract of St John's Wort and isolated constituents for inhibitory activity. Crude plant extract (derived from encapsulated commercial product) showed inhibtion of five isozymes: 1A2, 2C9, 2C19, 2D6, and 3A4, with 2D6 being the most sensitive with 50% inhibition at a concentration of 9.1mM. Several isolated constituents were found to be capable of competitively inhibiting CYP activities, with the biflavone I3,II8-biapigenin being the most potent inhibitor (toward CYP3A4 at an IC50 =0.082mM).

However this biflavone is only present in the plant in small quantities(< 0.5%), while the marker compounds hyperforin and hypericin which demonstrated 50% inhibition at concentrations below 10mM for CYP 2C9, CYP2D6 and CYP 3A4 are present in significantly greater (< 5.0%) amounts. Another recent study of several plant extracts and pure compounds found that both St John's Wort extracts and pure hypericin caused in vitro inhibition of CYP3A4. One positive human study was conducted on 13 healthy volunteers given 300mg standardised extract St John's Wort TID for 14 days.

24 hr urinary excretion ratios of 6-betahydroxycortisol/ cortisol were used as an index of CYP3A4 activity. A significant increase, from zero up to around 2.5x over base was found in urinary ratios in 12 subjects, suggestive of 3A4 induction. However, another study using dextramethorphan and alprazolam probes to determine the effect of St John's Wort extracts (330mg standardised extract TID) on 3A4 and 2D6 in seven healthy

volunteers concluded that no significant differences in urinary levels were found with coadministration of St John's Wort with the probes, leading the authors to conclude "These results suggest that St. John's wort, when taken at recommended doses for depression, is unlikely to inhibit CYP 2D6 or CYP 3A4 activity."

A poster study using similar probe methodology to examine 3A4 and 2D6 in sixteen healthy volunteers divided into extensive and poor metabolisers was conducted by Ereshefsky and colleagues as part of a larger series of investigations into inducers and inhibitors of these isoforms. St John's Wort was administered for 8 days at 300mg TID and according to the urinary metabolite ratio measurements no significant changes were found after St John's Wort administration. The same research group also studied the effect of Hypericum extracts on CYP1A2 and the Phase 2 enzyme Nacetyltransferase (NAT2) using caffeine probe methodology in sixteen subjects. Five "slow acetylators" were excluded, and results, this time with plasma as well as urine samples, from the eleven "fast acetylators" suggested the conclusion of " a low potential for Hypericum interactions at CYP1A2 and NAT2 metabolic pathways".

Reviewing these studies for direct evidence of Hypericum interaction with CYP 450, the data is inconclusive. Isolated constituent studies suggest the possibility of both inhibition and induction of 3A4, with recent in vitro studies favouring an inhibition ; this is apparently in conflict with clinical data. Different experimental studies have used different methodologies for assessing CYP450 modulation. Recently, one investigator has found that fluorometric assays of CYP450 activity (such as used in the Budzinsky study above) are inherently susceptible to producing variable results depending on the assay substrate used, sometimes by an order of magnitude.

Of human studies on 3A4, results are also conflicting, with one study supporting induction, and one suggesting a mild inhibition. Again methodological problems are evident. In particular, several investigators have questioned the reliability of urinary 6-betahydroxycortisol/cortisol ratios as a reliable index of CYP3A4 activity, noting significant variations of circadian and menstrual rhythm in reported values. There is negative evidence for interaction with CYP2D6 and limited evidence for potential interaction with 1A2. The number of subjects was small in all these studies, and further investigations are clearly needed. Methodological factors may explain to some degree both the varying results and the conflict between experimental and clinical data.

P-glycoprotein (P-gp) and Multidrug Resistance Protein (MDRP)

P-glycoprotein (P-gp) is an ATP-dependent pump that effluxes substrates out of cells. P-gp is an inducible membrane transport protein that was initially discovered by cancer researchers studying multidrug-resistance whereby cells resistant to one class of cytotoxic agents such as the vinca alkaloids showed cross-resistance to structurally unrelated compounds such as the epipodophyllotoxins. This resistance is related to an overexpression of P-gp, or a family of related proteins, known as multidrug resistance proteins (MDRP, MDRP1, MDRP2). While it is well established that P-gp and related transporter molecules can efflux xenobiotics out of tumor cells, the precise role of this family of transporters in normal cellular function is not yet understood, and it is possible that they may play a major part in cell differentiation, proliferation and survival.

P-pg is found in normal human renal, intestinal and biliary epithelia, the adrenal gland, testis and pregnant uterus where it is a barrier to xenobiotic accumulation and a determinant of oral bioavailability of drugs. P-gp is also found in both the choroid plexus and cerebral endothelium where it contributes to the blood-brain barrier, and the blood-cerebrospinalfluid barrier which limit the accumulation of drugs in the brain. P-gp is also expressed in lymphocytes and has been shown to modulate the transport of cytokines IL-4, Il-6 and IFN-gamma by activated T cells.

Pg-p is known to be a determinant of drug-drug interactions such as the non-competitive interaction between digoxin and verapamil which is due to inhibition of renal P-gp by decreasing tubular excretion of digoxin. Recent research shows that P-gp can also be affected by a range of naturally occurring compounds found in foods and herbal medicines.

P-glycoprotein (P-gp) Modulation by Natural Substances

P-gp expression can be modulated by numerous natural substances, some of which, like grapefruit juice, also can modulate CYP450, although this appears to be serendipitous connection rather than intrinsic coregulation. In enterocytes, P-gp may also increase pre-systemic metabolism of drugs by the removal of CYP450 generated metabolites from the intracellular compartment. Reactive oxygen species (ROS) downregulate the expression of P-gp whilst several naturally occurring compounds, modulate P-gp.

Rosemary (Rosmarinus officinalis) extracts inhibit P-gp as evidenced by vinblastine uptake in MCF7 cells. Flavonoids may induce or inhibit P-gp, for example tangeretin inhibits P-gp whereas quercitin and kaempferol are inducers. Inhibition takes place both by direct binding to the P-gp sites and by inhibition of the protein kinase C (PKC) which drives the P-gp efflux pump by phosphorylation. These natural agents could have a possible therapeutic role to play in reversing barriers to drug availability in tumor multidrug resistance. By the same token, they have the potential to cause pharmacokinetic interactions.

Hypericum and P-glycoprotein Modulation

Currently there is no direct evidence for the influence of Hypericum extracts or isolated compounds upon P-gp activity or expression. However the preclinical study by Johne and colleagues on the digoxin -SJW interaction implicates P-gp modulation since Digoxin is is a known substrate of P-gp transport. Similarly, recent reports of SJW-cyclosporine interactions imply P-gp activation, because although cyclosporine is a substrate of 3A4, it is also a known inhibitor of P-gp, and the Hypericum extracts may have reversed this inhibition hence reducing oral bioavailability.

While the emerging information about the molecular biology of transporter proteins may be arcane to some herbalists, discoveries of plant synergy in this field will not surprise most plant experts. Stermitz studied the antimicrobial activity of berberine containing plants (B. fremontii, B. aquifolia and B. repens) against the human pathogen Staphylococcus aureus. This antimicrobial activity depends on the synergistic disabling of an MDR efflux pump in the bacterium by another compound present in the plant identified as 5′-HMC (5′methoxyhydnocarpin).

Isolated berberine alkaloids only accumulate strongly in the bacterium in the presence of 5′HMC, which on its own has no antimicrobial effect. Finally, it should be remembered that in vitro or animal experiments may have little or no bearing on human clinical situations. For example, tangeretin synergizes with tamoxifen in vitro MCF7 cancer cell lines, but in vivo rodent studies show the converse, that tangeretin appears to inhibit the effect of tamoxifen.

Hypericum - Drug Interactions

Cyclosporine

Ruschitzka and colleagues in Switzerland discussed acute rejection of cardiac grafts in two male patients. In both cases, immunosuppression was maintained with a standard triple therapy of azothiaprine, cyclosporine and corticosteroids. Both were admitted three weeks after beginning standardised SJW at 300mg TID. The first patient had self-prescribed SJW while the second had been prescribed SJW by a psychiatrist for anxiety and depression. In both cases, acute signs of rejection were apparent on endomyocardial biopsy, although apart from fatigue the patients were asymptomatic with normal lab values except for the low cyclosporine levels. SJW was suspected and stopped in both cases.

Aggressive immunosuppressive intervention was required to restabilise the first patient, the second stabilised after cessation of the SJW. In both cases, cessation of SJW led to increase in cyclosporine levels. A recent German report on 30 renal graft patients correlated a fall in cyclosporine levels with concomitant SJW administration, and an increase in levels after cessation of the herb. Another case of a renal graft patient registering a drop in cyclosporine levels during co-administration of Hypericum extract has also been recently reported.

Cyclosporine has long been known to be a substrate of 3A4, but this does not mean that 3A4 induction by SJW is responsible for the cyclosporine interaction. Indeed much of the variation in oral cyclosporine bioavailability previously ascribed to 3A4 variability is in fact now known to caused by P-gp affecting the rate of intestinal absorption. It is possible that SJW reversed the inhibitory effectof cyclosporine on P-gp, leading to decreased intestinal absorption at the enterocyte. In any event, the potential SJW interaction with cyclosporine is extremely serious and especially since graft rejection can proceed insidiously, coadministration of the two agents should be avoided.

HIV protease inhibitors

Indinavir (Crixivan®) is a common HIV Protease inhibitor. Piscitelli and colleagues performed a preclinical study on the effects of SJW on plasma levels of indinavir in healthy, non-HIV subjects. The study group was small (n=8) and a baseline steady state with 3 x 800mg doses of indinavir. over 24 hours was established. After 8 hr fasting they received a fourth dose of 800mg which was used to plot the AUC indinavir kinetics (=90% after 5 hours). The same dosing regime was repeated after fourteen days of standardised SJW extract consumption at 300mgs TID. There was a very large reduction in the indinavir AUC, averaging 57%, after the SJW therapy.

The mechanism of this interaction is unclear. Indinavir is metabolised by, and an inhibitor of 3A4. There is a potential for interaction between SJW and indinavir, and by extrapolation, with other protease inhibitors (ritonavir, amprenavir,nelfinavir, saquinavir). It is also the case that HIV patients are a group likely to be taking a number of medications concurrently, including the azole antifungals, and NNRTI's (non nucleoside reverse transcriptase inhibitors) which are well known CYP450 interactors. The same group is also likely to be taking SJW for various reasons, and extreme vigilance is recommended during SJW and drug administration in this sensitive group.

Whilst evidence for pharmacokinetic interactions with other drugs is currently not available, some tentative extrapolations from known data are possible. For example, several anticonvulsants are powerful CYP inducers, and are also substrates for a variety of different CYP450 isoforms including 2C9, 2C19, and 3A4. Benzodiazepines are metabolised by 3A4 and have widespread interactions with 3A4 modulators.

Pharmacodynamic Interactions

The pharmacodynamic study of St. John's Wort is ongoing, and the current consensus is that its actions cannot be reduced to a single constituent nor to a simple equivalent of a pharmaceutical agent such as SSRI or MAOI activity, although St John's Wort extracts do display multiple if moderate activities across a range of neurotransmitters and receptors. There is currently a tendency for "overreporting" of possible SJW interactions in the mainstream literature without careful evaluation and assessment of the quality of evidence.

The suggestions of "serotonin syndrome" during concomitant administration of SSRI drugs such as fluoxetine with SJW made by Lantz are typical, all five reported cases occurring in one geriatric ward of one hospital during sertraline and SJW co-administration. The reported ADR's of nausea, restlessness, irritability and anxiety subsided on cessation of SJW. Enthusiastic reports of mania ascribed to SJW consumption or interactions with anti-depressants are appearing with greater frequency: none of them allay the need for well constructed studies to establish some solid data in this complex field.

In the light of recent data concerning St John's Wort interactions, regulatory authorities have responded with differing degrees of caution and issued advisories for physicians and healthcare practitioners. The FDA advisory from the CDER (center for Drug Evaluation and Research) refers principally to the indinavir study, and suggests that caution be used to prevent problems due to CYP450 induction by SJW. The British Committee for Safety on Medicines issued a more thorough advisory, which made extrapolations to suggest theoretical interactions of SJW for example with triptans (migraine medications).

Many OTC and prescription pharmaceuticals have the potential to cause serious ADR's and interactions; traditionally risk-benefit ratio calculations, physician advice and proper product warning on labels are used to obviate the worst of these effects.

13

Risks of Plant-derived Vaccines

New technologies would produce vaccines for diseases that were not yet controllable by vaccination, and improve existing vaccines by reducing cost, removing the use of needles during immunisation and by providing specific technologies for heat stabile, oral, multi-component vaccines that required reduced or one-time administration. In the same year, the first plant made vaccines (PMVs) were described by Curtiss & Cardineau.

The expression of the Streptococcus mutans surface protein A was achieved in transgenic tobacco, followed by oral immunisation of mice with the plant material. The transgenic tobacco successfully induced antibody responses with indication that serum from immunised mice reacted with intact S. mutans. The Curtiss research group also created transgenic alfalfa for expression of the enterotoxigenic E. coli heat labile enterotoxin B-subunit (LT-B), and successfully induced both mucosal and serum antibody responses.

Since these first demonstrations, the list of antigens expressed by plants has grown to include antigens from viral, bacterial, mycoplasma, enteric pathogens, nonenteric pathogens, and self-antigens. To increase expression level, stability and ease of harvest, synthetic genes have been constructed and expression has been targeted to specific tissues. Variability of antigen expression in plant tissues has been circumvented by batch processing and investigations have determined the eficacy of plant-made antigens to induce immune responses as well as the immune response type, location, and duration.

Oral and nasal vaccination have shown the ability to induce mucosal and systemic TH2 immune responses, oral delivery of a plant-derived vaccine has induced a TH1 response and passive immunity has been passed to the offspring. The effectiveness of PMVs was demonstrated during the 1990's in animal antigenicity trials and animal challenge trials. Six human clinical trials have been conducted to date. When PMVs were first described in the general media and scientific literature, the technology was dubbed 'edible vaccines'.

Researchers proposed application through local field production and consumption as a routine food source, conjuring images of the world's poorest populations consuming vaccines through fresh produce derived from their local farmers, or even their own garden. The advantages of edible plants—as opposed to non-food crops—and their preferred use by most groups working in this field, frequently led to public misconception as to how these materials would be delivered in a practical sense. Through further development of the technology, researchers and regulators asserted that in order to control the level of exposure, restrictions on delivery would be needed and the paradigm of edible vaccines evolved to eating engineered fruit or vegetables prescribed by a health care worker.

The paradigm was inevitably forced to further evolve to meet standard requirements for pharmaceuticals, to obviate dose variability and a lack of framework for quality assurance. Edible vaccines are now more appropriately referred to as PMVs or a similar derivative, where a plant product derived from batch processed, freeze-dried (or similar processing method), plant tissues will be prescribed by a health care worker. The final product may not be recognisable as a plant material, but rather packaged as a pill or capsule. This current paradigm stipulates that PMVs are not food materials and will need to meet regulations which are still evolving within national regulatory authorities such as the United States Food and Drug Administration (FDA) and the United States Department of Agriculture (USDA).

The USDA regulates production and distribution of transgenic plants in the US and is primarily concerned with genetic containment and reducing the risk of gene transfer. In reviewing production methods, the USDA considers the nature of the project including the proximity to related crops and thus probability of cross pollination, and the genetic nature of the transgenic plant (chloroplast or nuclear transformation, controlling sequences, etc.). The USDA also considers risk management strategies that may already be in place such as containment of the project either through physical (greenhouse), geographical (location) or reproductive measures (sterility or seedless varieties).

Additional risk management practices are enforced by the USDA and these may include process methods for maintaining segregation from food or feed sources; procedural items such as security, transport and destruction methods, and other general preventative measures which can be employed depending on the plant species (e.g. detasseling transgenic corn). All biopharmaceutical plants are initially produced in a contained environment such as a greenhouse or growth chamber, as a core risk management strategy until the plant can be fully characterised and a risk assessment performed as part of the regulatory process for progression to the field.

Due to the infancy of PMV technology, especially for application in humans, most of the current public debate is focused on these USDA regulatory policies and whether they are able to protect against even the remotest of environmental risks and contamination of crops used to feed humans or animals. The FDA regulates the testing, manufacturing and sale of pharmaceutical products in the US. In all cases the use of a PMV, as with other vaccines, is likely to be highly regulated with a defined dose and a deliberate course of administration.

Although plant-based technology has presented significant perceived advantages for cost and utility of vaccine production, it is yet to be demonstrated in commercial practice. Commercial potential of this technology is dependent on showing broad protective immunity in humans, demonstrating a viable manufacturing process, and forecasting accurate cost of production. Many of the uncertainties associated with this technology cannot be either validated or disproved until a first product emerges.

The two major milestones in moving this technology forward are the successful development of a model product and demonstration of protection in humans. The achievement of these milestones will stimulate maturation of the regulatory framework in which risk assessment, management, and communication standards can be defined. The initial paradigm of vaccine distribution through food or local garden production does not address product quality, control of exposure, or potential environmental risks.

Risk Assessment

Risk can be defined as the probability that a substance or

situation will produce harm under specified conditions. Risk is a function of the probability that an adverse event will occur, and the consequences of that adverse event. Predicting the probability and severity of potential consequences can only be accurate by identifying and evaluating the cause and effect factors that are at play, singularly and in combination.

Assessment of risk requires objective evaluation of the probability of each potential hazard or threat, with clear presentation and consideration of all uncertainties and assumptions. Risk is important to all persons (stakeholders) who either individually or collectively may be influenced by a specific activity. Risk occurs on a variety of scales from individual risk, through community risk, to global or biosphere significance.

Risk is something that can never be completely eliminated and will arise from every action we do. For example, although the risk of a specific technology or device may suggest that it is too dangerous to proceed, the result of arresting that technology may impact another community by failing to provide new benefits to the community or failing to alleviate risks that already exist or may later arise. Therefore there is some degree of risk in taking an action, and in not taking an action.

By utilising formal risk analysis for a technology or defined action we gain better understanding of the severity and probability of associated risks, and guidance for informed decision-making. Because risk is best analysed when the greatest number of different perspectives can be described—both qualitatively and quantitatively—and considered within an organised framework, formal risk analysis should represent all stakeholders in some capacity. Stakeholders must provide the necessary input, objective information, and subjective perspective on behalf of society for accurate judgment to occur.

Stakeholders include those who stand to gain from a particular action, and those who stand to be disadvantaged. Risk analysis should integrate a comparison of competing risks and benefits, which will differ in probability and severity, in an attempt to conclude the solution that is most advantageous to society. Because of these competing demands, risk assessment should be coordinated by an entity that can impartially conduct a weight-of-evidence approach to decision making.

This is usually a government or quasi-government group that is ultimately responsible to the larger community as a whole—and must consider the value of the manufacturer within that environment for their effect in the economic prosperity and technology advances, which aid that community. The process of formal risk analysis requires the integration of a science based framework with the social, cultural, and economic impacts that may result through implementation of that technology.

Although no PMVs have progressed beyond preliminary clinical trials, and there has been no demonstration of complete manufacturing and regulatory strategies, researchers in this field remain broadly optimistic that products will emerge to the benefit of society. As the technology matures, increasing focus will be placed on the regulatory framework that controls and approves these materials.

The potential for delivery within the food tissue, and the extent to which human handling of the raw product may be required during production and harvesting phases. Even though food-grade systems such as eggs and yeast are already used to produce vaccines, the highly controlled production environment for those products is substantially different to how those systems are managed in the agricultural sector, and the antigens are extracted from the production system. With exception for cell culture production systems, most PMVs currently under development will utilise production and harvesting procedures, which are very similar to those used in the agricultural sector for food and feed production.

The duplication in production methods at the raw material stage, and the ability to utilise nonspecialist production facilities (i.e. a plot of land compared to a secured clean room) provides more robust opportunities for inadvertent contamination and exposure scenarios compared to the production of the same antigens in eggs or yeast. Six main risks have been identified as potential concerns because of the unique characteristics and production methods for PMVs:

— *Allergenicity*: The transgenic product may be subjected to different post-translational processes in plants compared to the natural pathogen, which could induce new allergenic responses in the vaccine recipient when ingested. Also, the use of oral adjuvants to broadly stimulate mucosal linings may induce hypersensitive responses to other food proteins.

— *Detrimental effects to the environment*: Natural loss and degradation of cellular components including DNA and protein—within the environmental system, or ingestion by non-target species may have unknown allergenicity or toxicity implications.

— *Oral tolerance*: If the antigen is delivered too frequently or at repeated low doses, the mucosal immune system becomes desensitised to the vaccine and susceptibility to the disease might no longer be mitigated by vaccination.

— *Gene transfer*: Migration of the antigen to the conventional food supply through genetic hybridization or product contamination could lead to oral tolerance. Incorporation of selectable marker genes that confer resistance to antibiotics or herbicides may reduce the effect of certain medical or agricultural treatments, which utilise the same compounds.

— *Inconsistent dosage*: An insufficient amount of antigen would not produce the immune response needed to provide protection against disease. Incorrect frequency or dosage could lead to tolerance and render the vaccine ineffective in some recipients.

— *Worker exposure*: Touching or inhaling of plant vaccine materials during production may lead to oral tolerance or allergenicity.

The probability and severity of each risk will need to be determined on a case-by-case basis for each potential PMV product, and will differ significantly depending on the antigen and the plant species which is used.

Factors for PMV Risk Management

The Cartagena Protocol on Biosafety was recently adopted by many countries in an attempt to standardise risk management for products such as PMVs. It is heavily dependant on the definition and use of the Precautionary Principle. This principle is one of risk management rather than risk assessment per se, and is used most frequently for 'cases such as the introduction of entirely new products and technologies'. The variety of possible definitions and subjective application of the Precautionary Principle provide significant doubt for how PMVs might be regulated in many countries, particularly developing countries.

Conversely, the existing premarket review and approval processes in the US are well established and expected to adapt to new technologies for transgenic plant products. The USDA recently announced its intention to reassess the regulatory control of transgenic plants (USDA-

APHIS, 2004). This will include a new, tiered approach to risk analysis according to the transgenic system, and a detailed environmental impact study to better estimate the effect of transgenic plants on the environment.

Within the proposed tiered system of risk analysis, there will be increased demand for risk assessment on transgenic proteins that are produced in food systems (as opposed to nonfood systems), including much closer evaluation specifically for plant made pharmaceuticals. No parallel initiative has yet been announced by the FDA. The process for gaining pharmaceutical product approval is such that extensive risk assessment—such as toxicity studies, pharmacokinetics, and efficacy studies—must ordinarily be completed in the course of product development before application for licensure.

Regulatory approval by the FDA incorporates risk management procedures within formalised production criteria such as Good Laboratory Practices (GLP) and Good Manufacturing Practices (GMP). Through these mechanisms, it is expected that FDA will engage in further determination of regulatory policy in this area as product development continues and as a case-by-case response to manufacturers. Formal assessment of risk should be determined by an entity that can represent the greater population at risk and provide judgment based on the weight of evidence for both risks and benefits.

For PMVs in the US it is clear that both USDA and FDA will need to be involved in such a process because of the overlap between agriculture, the environment, and security and confidence of our food and drug supply. There is a complex group of stakeholders who need to participate in providing the variety of risk perspectives that are involved. A recent report suggested five initial questions, which could be used as the basis for the problem formulation stage of risk assessment for PMVs.

By examining each question we can begin to identify who needs to be involved in providing the quantitative and qualitative input to risk assessment.

What is the stressor or activity causing harm?: In simple terms, we are asking what the transgenic material is and what its specific components are. The complete answer must describe the production characteristics and the functional components of the product. Production characteristics include describing the host plant system, how and where it is grown (i.e. field or greenhouse), what are the transgenic elements, and how and when are they expressed in the plant.

Functional components require description of the characterised transgene products, what is their known function—and nonintended functions if any are known—and what different forms of the material will exist. These aspects are integrated in the Investigational New Drug (IND) and New Drug Application (NDA) processes required by the FDA, and hence are provided by the manufacturer within the existing framework. The manufacturer is the only entity that knows these intricate details and therefore has perhaps the greatest role in the early stages of risk assessment.

What are the potential ecological effects?: Production characteristics are intricately connected to estimating potential ecological risks. We are specifically interested in identifying the methods for DNA or protein transfer to the environment and quantifying the probability of such transfer. This analysis is clearly species-dependant and heavily influenced by the surrounding environment. Field studies are being conducted on a range of genetically modified crops to gather this information. Conclusion regarding the potential for transgene escape should also consider the geographic isolation or physical containment that might be used in the manufacturing process.

Horizontal gene transfer (HGT) and vertical gene transfer (VGT) are common concerns for production of transgenic plants outside a controlled laboratory.

The risk of transferring antigen transgenes to the environment relates to tolerance as an overriding concern. If antigens were unknowingly produced in food crops and consumed on a wide scale, the risk of tolerance is likely to be much greater and probably undetected. It must be considered, however, that persistence of the gene in the environment is low in probability because it offers no known selective advantage to the plant. One exception to this probability is if the gene is randomly integrated at a locus which provides some other selective advantage to the plant, and therefore is retained as a bystander to some other phenotypic feature.

Although the primary function of PMVs is to produce an antigen, most current design strategies also incorporate a second transgene which confers resistance to either herbicides or antibiotics for initial transgenic event selection. Inheritance of the selectable marker, either antibiotic or herbicide, may have more significant effects. Herbicide resistance could offer selective advantage to the recipient plant. Antibiotic resistance could prove problematic for disease control in animals and humans depending on the marker that is used.

The antibiotic marker for Kanamycin resistance has been approved by the FDA for use as an aid in food production; however it has not been approved in parallel by the USDA for similar uses in veterinary biologics or animal feed. Related to the risk of transgene escape, is the concern that release of the DNA or antigen to the environment in raw form may have detrimental effects. Contact by insects, release of decomposing matter to the environment, or release of 'contaminated' water to the environment are all feasible mechanisms for DNA or antigen escape to the environment.

The proposed risks of this release are either DNA recombination by other organisms, or human exposure to the antigen at low levels as another mechanism for inducing tolerance. However, the release of DNA and antigen to the environment already occurs through the presence and life cycle of the native pathogen. Much of the expertise to describe and measure these risks resides within the manufacturer, however at this stage in risk assessment much of that expertise can be duplicated by other stakeholders, or even nonpartisan consultants or agency (USDA) representatives on behalf of the greater community.

While the weight-of-evidence model would suggest that impartial contributions be provided wherever possible, it is likely that the manufacturer will have more data available directly related to the product in which it has invested time and effort to produce. Until the first PMV product comes under NDA consideration by the FDA it is unclear whether manufacturers will be required to submit this kind of analysis in support of the manufacturing strategy. These risks will be significant for USDA in any decision to allow field production, thus it is important for both agencies to be consistent in how this aspect of manufacturing should be reviewed.

What are the potential human health effects?: This question moves the focus from the environment and ecological diversity to the individual and our basic food and health safety. By design, PMVs have a known effect when provided to humans. Consistent with all other pharmaceuticals—excluding herbal and dietary supplements—the FDA requires that valid safety studies be conducted with PMVs in a phased manner through preclinical and clinical studies. These safety studies include pharmacokinetics of the vaccine components, formal toxicity studies in preclinical model species, and established safety in humans through experimental testing in phased clinical development.

In addition to most conventional vaccines however, PMVs represent a new combination of impure elements including the plant system, other transgenes, and resistance marker products, which must all be evaluated under the same criteria as a collective formulation. One of the most significant criteria for development of PMVs is associated with controlling the dose and the outcomes if dosage is not consistent. Heterologous gene expression in plants brings inherent variability in distribution of antigen within plant tissues.

If the volume of material administered does not contain the required dose of antigen, the resulting immune response may not be suficient to protect against an encounter with the disease. Such an instance would not only affect the individual who may become infected, but would also diminish confidence in the vaccine programme. If the vaccine is ingested too often then oral tolerance may be induced, whereby the mucosal immune system becomes desensitised to the vaccine and susceptibility to the natural disease can no longer be mitigated by vaccination. This strategy has been demonstrated by researchers interested in deliberately inducing tolerace as a means of treating autoimmune diseases, by feeding plant-made antigens within the diet for periods of multiple weeks.

In addition to high frequency of dose, oral tolerance has also been proposed as potentially being induced if dosage is either too low or too high. The different stimuli proposed for oral tolerance shows the incomplete understanding of this phenomenon. This risk is not only associated with deliberate use of the vaccine, but also with accidental exposure such as workers who touch or inhale PMV materials, exposure through the environment, or mixing of transgenic materials with food commodities.

Oral tolerance is perhaps the greatest risk in delivering vaccines by oral route, due to the potential for life-threatening consequences through perpetual risk of infection, although further research using adjuvants and optimising timing of delivery may provide a validated regimen for PMV administration. Development and approval of oral adjuvants will have a vital influence on the success or failure of PMVs. The main purpose of any adjuvant is to stimulate the immune system and thereby induce extra immunological attention to the vaccine.

Existing adjuvants based on oil emulsion technologies are important for injectible vaccines by causing local irritation and extended protection for the injected antigens, and can make substantial difference in product efficacy. Due to the lack of oral vaccines there are few adjuvant candidates available for experimental use with PMVs. Oral adjuvants such as enterotoxins or saponins have a systemic effect, where the mucosal linings are broadly stimulated.

One of the potential risks of this strategy is that other ingested proteins that normally are not immunogenic may become allergenic through hypersensitive responses. We are not aware of any study to date, which has evaluated this risk. It is likely that this situation occurs in nature when natural enterotoxin infections occur, or when plant saponins are consumed within the regular diet. Accordingly, while this risk is clearly acknowledged it applies broadly and beyond the scope of PMVs. Even without the use of adjuvants, there are several perceived risks of ingesting an antigen that has been produced in a plant.

One such concern is that post translational differences between plants and the native pathogen could infer new allergenic responses in the vaccine recipient when the transgene product is ingested. The second general concern is that long-term exposure to genetically engineered substances in a food crop may have unknown effects on gut microflora or epithelial tissues, or the general health of the population. Based on the widespread planting and consumption of transgenic crops, there is little evidence to conclude that this risk is significant for food crops. The nature of science is such that it can never prove a theory; so preclinical toxicity and safety studies are designed to evaluate the null hypotheses that the materials are unsafe.

Accordingly, risk assessment based on potential human health effects must consider both the nature of those effects, and the established estimates of their probability, which must be derived from clinical experiments. Although the manufacturer is responsible for providing these data formally to FDA, it is likely that some of the required studies will be completed by contract service organisations. Significant expertise resides within the FDA to evaluate the design and results of these studies and the FDA may be consulted prior to the study to ascertain the likely acceptance of the trial design.

What are the potential exposure scenarios?: Because the preceding question has sought to identify the potential effects in humans, it is necessary to evaluate the potential mechanisms for that exposure, and the dose-response relationships for components of concern. For other biotechnology products, this aspect is a major topic for debate, specifically caused by the variety of social and cultural concerns of transgenic foods and in light of differential perspectives on the physiological (in humans) consequences of genetically modified foods.

The obvious scenario for PMV technology is direct oral application of the vaccine as intended. As a regulated pharmaceutical, additional scenarios such as over-exposure or under-exposure are inherently addressed in the existing FDA structure, regardless of product. At the manufacturing site, accurate determination of dose exposure and hence product consistency is integrated within GMP requirements mandated by FDA. Release or approval of PMV materials for distribution will be dependent on meeting those criteria on a batch-by-batch basis.

While there are some technical and regulatory advantages for producing PMVs in food crops, and even though food crops may have greater risk of inadvertently reaching the food supply, these exposure scenarios apply regardless of the plant production system which is used. The role of risk management through GMP is to reduce the chance of both scenarios; however, within the science-based structure of risk assessment we must address the consequences of such an event. This analysis will differ for each PMV formulation depending on the active contents.

What are the potential routes of exposure?: The final question can almost be incorporated in the previous section, and specifically pertains to the methods of transmission that were described. For powdered PMVs, potential methods of transmission include oral, nasal, ocular, and dermal contact. The objective of risk assessment in this case is to determine whether suficient inadvertent exposure could ever occur at these exposure routes either acutely or chronically to induce an adverse immune or toxic response.

In the case of PMVs much of the risk assessment in this area must be based on models obtained through preclinical experiments, by estimating the volume required for an immune response of any kind at one of these sites. The final assessment from such models must also include consideration of the probability of such exposure with respect to GMP safety aspects that are designed to prevent this activity. An additional perspective that must be applied to these last two questions is the impact that such events have on the industry involved in developing PMVs and hence risk to the entire platform technology.

The potential for contamination of food or animal feed with transgenic products approved only for other uses has elevated the concern for stewardship of these materials. Stewardship is a deliberately proactive management position against unintended exposure, which could otherwise ultimately halt this technology if further events were to suggest unacceptable continuing probability of this risk. The manufacturer is also responsible to the appropriate government agency for all practices during technology development and for adhering to the standards, which are approved by FDA for manufacturing.

Failure to follow these standards can result in significant financial penalty from either agency. Ultimate penalty can include the revocation of product and facility licenses; something that would have significant impact on further relations between the manufacturer and the regulatory authority. In addition to the regulatory liabilities, failure to meet these standards during the manufacturing phase can result in liability owed to private individuals.

The precedence for public nuisance rulings reinforces the need for active stewardship of this new technology. The ability to control the potential routes of exposure falls almost entirely upon the manufacturer, with standards to be established by the regulatory agency. Monitoring is also possible by public interest groups, allowing all stakeholders to have potential roles in this aspect of risk assessment and management. However, unlike GM food crops, the acreage required for commercial production of a single PMV is likely to be quite small.

A basic model and cost sensitivity analysis for vaccine production using transgenic tomato is provided by Kirk & Webb and indicates a wide range in possible yield according to expression levels and dosage requirements. One billion doses could conceivably be produced on less than one hundred acres. The ability to control identified risks—especially contamination of the food supply on a single production site of this size is greatly improved compared to wide scale production of Starlink corn or similar transgenic crops. The high-value nature of pharmaceutical production also encourages additional measures to define how the crop is grown, harvested and processed, compared to commodity production which uses high-throughput facilities for multiple users.

Global Risks

The potential benefits of PMVs have been widely discussed and include heat stability, oral administration, and exclusion of contaminants such as prions. Advantages pertaining to cost of production have also been stated, but recent cost modelling suggest that this assumption may be premature for freeze-dried products. The conventional framework for risk analysis does not look outwardly from the technology to ask what external forces may risk the implementation or success of new opportunities, which in turn would deny the potential benefits.

The peril in controlling all risk associated with the technology itself is that valuable mechanisms for lowering global disease may become overly encumbered. Many current vaccines impose some risk either through chance of infection with the attenuated agent, contamination with another pathogen through unhygienic application of syringes (particularly in developing countries), through reactions to other ingredients such as the mercury-based preservative thimerosol, or through a lack of adherence to the vaccination schedule because of fear of injection.

The net value of replacing these products with PMVs that do not carry the same concerns must be considered alongside the potential risks. Additionally, the risks associated with production of PMVs in transgenic plants could be reduced if the technology was limited to non-food expression systems. Although this may solve many of the environmental risks however, it significantly reduces the utility of the technology, which is based on oral consumption of materials already known to be safe. A third example of over-regulating the technology would be mandating that production occur in a contained greenhouse.

Although this also reduces many of the environmental risks, and may actually provide controlled advantages to the manufacturer. This may be acceptable in high-margin products, but it is likely to unduly influence the economics of similar manufacturing in poorer regions of the world. One additional possibility is that PMVs are manufactured in one location (e.g. US) and primarily used in another location (e.g. developing countries). In that example, the aspects of how and where the materials are grown would be regulated by USDA, but the aspects of how the materials are used as pharmaceuticals would be regulated by the respective national agencies.

It has been suggested that the differential application of the Precautionary Principle, whereby a more subjective view may be adopted for developing countries, may increase the dificulty for academic and non-profit institutions to develop transgenic products, such as PMVs, for those locations. The risk of applying regulations designed for purified, injectible drugs are that cost and time of development may be unduly extended to meet criteria that are not specifically relevant to PMVs.

One example may be the requirement to regularly test microbial contamination of PMVs, despite production methods that are far superior to food commodities already consumed by the population. Another example may be the need to conduct extensive toxicology tests for a plant material that is already consumed at much higher doses in the regular diet without this testing. In both cases, the regulatory requirements are not cost-eficient given the background exposure to these materials that is already occurring routinely in the control population. Although most conventional criteria for injectible vaccines are relevant to PMVs, blanket adoption of all criteria will add undue development costs in the first instance.

14

Conservation of Medicinal Plants

Billions of people in the world rely chiefly on herbal medicine, while millions gain income from their wild harvest or cultivation, or are involved in their trading or processing. Medicinal plants are symbolically significant in many cultures, often being seen as sources of power. The significance of medicinal plants to people can be sufficiently great that arrangements made for the conservation and sustainable use of medicinal plants can lay important foundations for the conservation of natural habitats and ecological services more generally.

Therefore the 'biological beneficiaries' of 'medicinal plant conservation' are not necessarily only the medicinal plants themselves. This is nowhere more so than in those remoter parts of the world where cultural and biological diversity tend to be most concentrated, and where medicinal plants can assume high importance in cultures and for livelihoods. Because so many species of plants are medicinal, medicinal plant conservation is, in some ways, a microcosm of plant conservation as a whole. Similar questions arise concerning identification of the most significant issues and most effective approaches. This is especially so given that, just because a species has been used somewhere medicinally, it does not follow that it is so used everywhere and at all times.

There may be good reasons, for the purpose of genetic conservation, to conserve particular populations of 'medicinal plants', even though their designation as such carries little or no meaning to people living in the neighbourhood. The challenges facing conservationists are then similar to those encountered with other groups of plants singled out by 'plant conservationists' as special, but which lack any special significance to local people, such as, commonly, many 'threatened' species and wild crop relatives. There can be aspects of medicinal plant conservation which 'plant conservationists' can pursue, working largely outside the normal dynamics of people/ plant relationships. Work of this type can sometimes be found, for instance, associated with seed-banks, information systems or 'totally protected' nature reserves.

The fact that efforts are made in favour of medicinal plants, rather than plants of any other type, is incidental, except as regards the criteria used for the initial selection of species for attention. Most work by conservationists on medicinal plants should be with those people who own, manage or make use of these species, or else own or manage the land on which they grow. The special meanings of medicinal plants to people can best be 'exploited'. Working effectively with communities requires conservationists to have an appreciation of the cultures, economies and social structures and dynamics of local societies, in addition to the knowledge that they need about the biology and ecology of the plants themselves.

Similar 'lateral engagement' is also necessary for work with other classes of people involved with medicinal plants. For example, the main concerns of conservationists about manufacturers are likely to revolve around questions of the effects of their patterns of obtaining raw materials on the environment. However, manufacturers will often be more interested in other aspects of product quality than biological and ecological sustainability, especially those relating to quality control that involve species authentication, presence of active constituents, limitations to heavy metal content, and residues of pesticides and fertilisers.

Traditional Plants

It is estimated that 70-80% of people worldwide rely chiefly on traditional, largely herbal, medicine to meet their primary healthcare needs. The global demand for herbal medicine is not only large, but growing. The market for Ayurvedic medicines is estimated to be expanding at 20% annually in India, while the quantity of medicinal plants obtained from just one province of China (Yunnan) has grown by 10 times in the last 10 years. An example of increased pressure on collecting grounds is provided by the Gori valley in the Indian Himalayas, where the annual period of MAP harvesting has increased from 2 to 5 months.

Factors contributing to the growth in demand for traditional medicine include the increasing human population and the frequently inadequate provision of Western (allopathic) medicine in developing countries. There are many traditional systems of medicine. Some of them are;

— Traditional Medical Systems, with written traditions of documentation of knowledge, pharmacopoeias for doctors and institutions for training doctors;

— Traditional Medical Knowledge (Folk Medicine), which is orally transmitted and associated with households, communities or ethnic groups; and

— Shamanistic Medicine, with a strong spiritual element and which can only be applied by specialist practitioners (shamans). Traditional Medical Systems are especially concentrated in Asia. Some of the more widely familiar are Chinese Traditional Medicine, Tibetan Medicine, Ayurveda, Siddha, Unani and Western Herbal Medicine, the latter being rather ill-defined.

Herbal Medicine

Herbal medicine is becoming ever more fashionable in richer countries, a market sector which has grown at 10-20% annually in Europe and North America over recent years. In addition, there are many related botanical products sold as health foods, food supplements, herbal teas, and for various other purposes related to health and personal care. The extent to which herbal preparations are prescribed within conventional medicine varies greatly between countries, for instance being much higher in Germany than in the UK or USA.

Pharmaceutical Medicine

Plants have contributed hugely to Western medicine, through providing ingredients for drugs or having played central roles in drug discovery. Some drugs, having botanical origins, are still extracted directly from plants, others are made through transformation of chemicals found within them, while yet others are today synthesised from inorganic materials, but have their historical origins in research into the active compounds found in plants. There are undoubtedly many more secrets still hidden in the world of plants.

Global Use of Medicinal Plants

In terms of the number of species individually targeted, the use of plants as medicines represents by far the biggest human use of the natural world. Plants provide the predominant ingredients of medicines in most medical traditions. There is no reliable figure for the total number of medicinal plants on Earth, and numbers and percentages for countries and regions vary greatly (Table 1). Estimates for the numbers of species used medicinally include: 35,000-70,000 or 53,000 worldwide; 10,000-11,250 in China; 7500 in India; 2237 in Mexico; and 2572 traditionally by North American Indians.

Table 1: Numbers and percentages of medicinal plant species recorded for different countries and regions.

Country or region	Number of species of medicinal plants	Total number of native species in flora	% of flora which is medicinal
China	11,146	27,100	41
India	7500	17,000	44
Mexico	2237	30,000	7
North America	2572	20,000	13
World	52,885	297,000-510,000	10-18

The great majority of species of medicinal plants are used only in Folk Medicine. Traditional Medical Systems employ relatively few: 500-600 commonly in Traditional Chinese Medicine (but 6000 overall); 1430 in Mongolian Medicine; 1106-3600 in Tibetan Medicine; 1250-1400 in Ayurveda; 342 in Unani; and 328 in Siddha. The number of plant species that provide ingredients for drugs used in Western Medicine is even fewer. It was calculated for an article published in 1991 that there were 121 drugs in current use in the USA derived from plants, with 95 species acting as sources (more than one drug is obtained from some species).

Despite the small number of source species, drugs derived from plants are of immense importance in terms of numbers of patients treated. It is reported that ca. 25% of all prescriptions dispensed from community pharmacies in the USA between 1959 and 1973 contained one or more ingredients derived from higher plants. A more recent study, of the top 150 proprietary drugs used in the USA in 1993, found that 57% of all prescriptions contained at least one major active compound currently or once derived from (or patterned after) compounds derived from biological diversity.

The value of medicinal plants to human livelihoods is essentially infinite. They obviously make fundamental contributions to human health, and: "Is not health dearer than wealth?" Financially, the retail sales of pharmaceutical products was estimated at US$ 80-90 billion globally in 1997, with medicinal plants contributing very significantly. A study of the 25 best-selling pharmaceutical drugs in 1997 found that 11 of them (42%) were either biologicals, natural products or entities derived from natural products, with a total value of US$ 17.5 billion.

The total sales' value of drugs (such as Taxol) derived from just one plant species (Taxus baccata) was US$ 2.3 billion in 2000. The world market for herbal remedies in 1999 was calculated to be worth US$ 19.4 billion, with Europe in the lead (US$ 6.7 billion), followed by Asia (US$ 5.1 billion), North America (US$ 4.0 billion), Japan (US$ 2.2 billion), and then the rest of the world (US$ 1.4 billion). There is much trade in MAPs, on scales ranging from the local to the international. Much of this is unrecorded in official statistics or poorly documented—reasons why there is typically so little awareness among decision-makers of the significance of the trade to the healthcare and economies of their people, or about problems of unsustainability and the sometimes deleterious impacts of wild collection on natural habitats.

Large quantities of MAPs are traded into urban centres from rural areas in developing countries, and also regionally and internationally. China's production of medicinal plants from cultivated and wild-harvested sources, considered together, was calculated at 1.6 million tonnes in 1996, with a total value (excluding exports) in terms of finished products of US$ 3.7 billion. The reported annual imports of MAP material into all countries during the 1990s amounted to an average of 400,000 tonnes, valued at US$ 1.2 billion, showing a 100% rise between 1991 and 1997.

The three leading exporting countries are China (ca. 140,000 tonnes per year over 1991-1997), India (about one-third of the Chinese amount) and then Germany. Europe is the major trading centre for MAPs globally, with imports into one European country or another amounting to 440,000 tonnes in 1996. There are at least 2000 species of MAPs marketed in Europe, these originating from over 120 countries. It is guessed that the total number of MAPs in international trade may be about 2500 species. Although virtually everyone on Earth benefits from medicinal plants, it is the financially poorest who are typically most closely dependent on medicinal plants—culturally and for their medicines and income.

Only 15% of pharmaceutical drugs is consumed in developing countries, and a large proportion of even this small percentage is taken by relatively more affluent people. The poor have little alternative to using herbal medicine, which, anyway, they may prefer—at least for certain conditions. Both rural and urban dwellers, in developing countries, rely on medicinal plants, many rural people still depending largely on plants collected from close to their homes, while town folk depend, for the most part, on dried plants transported in from rural areas. Medicinal plants can provide a significant source of income for rural people in developing countries, especially through the sale of wild-harvested material.

The collectors are often herders, shepherds or other economically marginalised sections of the population, such as landless people and women. Between 50-100% of households in the northern part of central Nepal and about 25-50% in the middle part of the same region are involved in collecting medicinal plants for sale, the materials being traded on to wholesale markets in Delhi. The money received represents 15-30% of the total income of poorer households. Medicinal plants can be symbolically very important to people.

They can be held in special religious, nationalistic or ideological esteem. This can be advantageous for conservation efforts, given that it is an acknowledgement, well rooted in culture, of the worth of a sizable proportion of the world's flora. But it also carries challenges, in that this can result in dogmatic views about the medicinal properties of plants, resistance to accepting equally effective substitutes, and uncompromising attitudes towards the ownership of the plants and who should benefit from (or pay for) their continuing existence. The subject of 'medicinal plants' can arouse strong feelings, providing opportunities for bringing key conservation debates into the public arena. There is similarity to the emotions surrounding charismatic species, such as elephants and whales, with the difference that medicinal plants carry much more universal appeal.

Concerns of Medicinal Plants

Loss of biological diversity and the availability of resources

These concerns exist, for a large part, because most species of medicinal plants are collected from the wild. The total number of species of medicinal plants cultivated on any scale is few, although this does include some species of MAPs that are traded internationally in large volumes, as well as the many of the (small) number of species used as starting points for pharmaceutical drugs. As an example, the Rosy Periwinkle (Catharanthus roseus), a species which originated in Madagascar and which is the source of the anti-leukemia drugs vincristine and vinblastine, is widely cultivated in Spain and Texas.

China is probably the country with the greatest acreage of medicinal plants under cultivation, with over 300,000 hectares devoted to just one species—Sea Buckthorn (Hippophae rhamnoides)—with 10,000 people employed. However, even in China, only 100-250 species are cultivated and more than 80% of the 700,000 tonnes of medicinal plants reportedly used annually come from wild sources. Only 130-140 of the 1200-1300 species that are both traded in, and native to, Europe are derived predominantly from cultivation.

There are many parts of the world in which there is virtually no cultivation on any significant scale, including, by way of examples, Albania and Turkey in Europe, Pakistan and Bangladesh in Asia, and all countries in Africa. An estimated 99% of the 400-550 species currently sold for use in traditional medicine in South Africa originate from wild sources. There is no reliable estimate for the number of medicinal plants that are globally threatened, variously calculated as 4160 or 10,000.

There would seem little doubt from theoretical considerations that many medicinal plant species that have been listed as threatened, and indeed others that have not, must be suffering from genetic erosion now, or will do so in the near future. This is because populations of many species are in retreat, with outlying populations being destroyed, as the extent and quality of many natural habitats decline. However, genetic erosion among wild plants is very poorly documented.

The advantage of maintaining a pool of genetic diversity within a medicinal species can be illustrated with reference to Arnica (Arnica montana), a popular, but endangered, European medicinal plant, in which genes from wild populations have been used successfully to breed superior cultivated strains. Another example is African Cherry or Pygeum (Prunus africana), a forest tree yielding a medicinal extract from its bark in high demand in Europe. Varieties of P. africana are being tested in a breeding programme to select types that will take less time to reach harvestable age.

The number of species of medicinal plants known to have become globally extinct is very few and conservationists are advised to avoid exaggerated claims in this respect. One of the best advertised cases is Silphion, a plant apparently found formerly in the dry hinterlands of the Middle East and much prized by the Ancient Greeks. It is believed to have become extinct in ca. 250 BC, with over-harvesting thought to have been a contributory factor. It should be noted that many medicinal plants are rather widely distributed.

In the USA, only 121 of the 3214 plant species classified as of 'conservation concern' are reported to have been used medicinally or in any other way by native Americans. This low percentage suggests that it may be easier for people to recognise the useful properties of plants that are common than those that are rare. It has been estimated that over-exploitation threatens 150 species of MAPs in at least one European country, but it should not be deduced from this that many, if any, of these species are in danger of complete continental extinction. On the other hand, the seriousness of local, national or regional extinction, or, indeed, of commercial extinction should not be under-estimated.

There can be serious consequences for livelihoods and economies, quite apart from issues of genetic conservation. Many of the threats to medicinal plant species are similar to those causing endangerment to plant diversity generally. The most serious proximate threats generally are habitat loss, habitat degradation and over-harvesting (Hamilton, 1997). Medicinal plants can have other uses than as sources of medicines, and the threats from over-harvesting may be due, or partly due, to collection for purposes other than medicinal. This is so in the case of the African trees Acacia senegal, Boswellia papyrifera and Pterocarpus angolensis.

So far as collection for medicines is concerned, there is generally agreement that it is collection for commercial trade rather than home-use that is overwhelmingly the problem. One reason why medicinal plants have become increasingly threatened has been the weakening of customary laws that traditionally have regulated the use of natural resources. Such laws have proved often to be easily undermined by modern socio-economic forces. In at least one case, the collapse of customary institutions seems to have been connected directly to changes in the ways that a medicinal plant was exploited, and this may be a widespread phenomenon.

Commercial collection of Prunus africana commenced in Cameroon in 1972, being at first a monopoly of Plantecam Medicam, a company which took steps to promote its sustainable harvesting. Bark was removed from opposing quarters of trunks, avoiding girdling, the rotation time for bark recovery being 4-5 years. In 1985, the Government of Cameroon issued 50 additional licenses and the controlled harvesting system broke down. Complete girdling now became the norm, or else trees were simply felled so that all their bark could be easily collected.

In the case of one site, Mount Oku, it appears that this sudden injection of capitalist enterprise led to a great weakening in traditional customs that formerly helped to maintain a forest cover. The result was, not only destructive harvesting of P. africana, but a sudden massive loss of forest to agriculture, with stabilisation only becoming achieved through the intervention of an outside project, able to act as a mediator. Concerns about loss of medicinal plants, considered as material resources, relate to worries about healthcare, livelihood security and financial income. Among those for whom these problems are most acute are the rural poor, reliant on medicinal plants growing close to their homes for their healthcare and perhaps an income.

Manufacturers and consumers, higher up commercial systems, are less influenced by local scarcities of resources, often being insulated by manufacturers switching their sources of supply. Unsustainable harvesting practices result in spreading frontiers of resource-depletion, with the negative impacts of over-exploitation confined to the local level until such time as regional or global resource scarcity becomes critical. Poorer members of local communities can face additional problems of loss of access to medicinal plants due to the privatisation or nationalisation of land.

There is a major trend today in many developing countries towards stricter individual ownership of land and plant resources, replacing older forms of tenure and resource-rights in which poorer people could be less excluded. Loss of access through nationalisation can occur with the creation of more strongly protected types of conservation area.

Local knowledge and cultural survival

Knowledge of medicinal plants, as once embedded in tens of thousands of indigenous cultures, is rapidly disappearing. Every year, the sum total of human knowledge about the types, distribution, ecology, methods of management and methods of extracting the useful properties of medicinal plants is declining rapidly—a continuation of a process of loss of local cultural diversity that has been underway for hundreds of years. There has, of course, been a great growth in scientific information about medicinal plants in recent decades, but in many ways this has proved poor compensation, because such information is accessible, in practice, only to a very few people and, anyway, rather little of it is relevant to problems of management and utilisation, as encountered in the field.

Among those liable to suffer most from loss of indigenous knowledge are those who live in harsh places, such as mountain ranges, and who have high degrees of dependency on their local natural environments. The cultures and economies of such people must be closely adapted to the intricacies of their local environments, if they are to prosper. Knowledge of the natural world is typically a very important part of the knowledge-worlds of rural people following more traditional life-ways.

Further, medicinal plants tend to figure prominently in these galaxies. It is therefore not surprising that the revitalisation of traditional systems of medicine can be high on the agendas of those promoting local and indigenous cultures, a political trend in many parts of the world. The Foundation for Revitalisation of Local Health Traditions (FRLHT) is an example of an organisation, in this case working in India, which is engaged in many aspects of medicinal plant conservation and sustainable use, including—prominently—cultural aspects, as is clear from its name.

The adequate provision of healthcare is threatened by declines in traditional medical knowledge and related plant resources. There are many people, notably in developing countries who lack—and will continue to lack for the foreseeable future—effective access to Western medicine, while even those who do enjoy this privilege will be limited in their choices of alternative therapies. Traditional medical practitioners came under attack during the colonial era and the legacy of this widely persists. The spread of Western Medicine was aided in its supremacy by association with the political and economic power of the West.

Western Medicine became part of the 'civilising colonial mission'. Ayurvedic medicine was suppressed in state-funded medical colleges in India after 1835 and local medical traditions, with their 'witchdoctors', denounced in Africa. Even in China, never under full colonial rule, Western Medicine came to be seen as progressive. The Kuomintang Government decided that Traditional Chinese Medicine was unscientific and passed a law in 1929 making its practice illegal. The increasing nationalisation of medicine during the 19th and especially the 20th centuries and the rise in the power of pharmaceutical companies have given even further impetus to Western Medicine.

Until recently, and then only in some countries, national healthcare systems have devoted all, or nearly all, their resources to the promotion and delivery of Western Medicine, ignoring other traditions. This is now changing, more so in some countries (such as China and India) than others, but, even so, some medical traditions, such as Tibetan Medicine in India and Nepal, have yet to gain official recognition (unlike Ayurvedic Medicine which is officially recognised in both countries). Lack of official recognition and associated support has implications for conservation, because such recognition can raise the status of practitioners at village level.

Since such practitioners are generally the most knowledgeable people about plants in their communities and have an intrinsic interest in their conservation, an increase in their authority has the potential to greatly assist improved management of plant resources. From the point of view of efficient and effective provision of national healthcare, a problem facing those countries which acknowledge the value of traditional medicine is how best to utilise the resources available. One approach is to provide official recognition to traditional medicine, which is then permitted to operate as a separate sector parallel to and largely unconnected with the main Western medical services provided by the state.

Other countries, such as China, are attempting synthesis through trying to draw on the best of different traditions. Official recognition has several implications, including the desirability of registering authentic practitioners and supporting their training. There is also the question of how best to develop traditional systems to meet modern challenges. The environment in which traditional medical practitioners are operating today is not the same as in the past. Payment for treatment is now more frequently being requested, associations of traditional medical practitioners are being formed for networking and political lobbying, and there is a move towards professionalisation, including towards instruction based in schools rather than through lineages.

The development of traditional medicine to meet modern challenges can be resisted. For instance some Ayurvedic practitioners in India can be conservative and claim that their treatments have been authenticated through long tradition and should not be subject to research. Authentication of traditional medicine is both a cultural and physiological matter and requires more than just trials similar to those used to test pharmaceutical drugs. Sensitive techniques are needed to avoid unnecessary prohibitions. Due attention needs to be given to traditional standards of quality, which, in Ayurveda, for example, classically refer to cultural and tantric use as well as therapeutic qualities.

Concerns to the terms of research on medicinal plants

This has become the most publicised area of 'policy debate' relating to medicinal plants. It is a field in which "there has been a polarisation and we've ended up arguing over who is in the wrong". In part, the issues can be traced back to the Convention on Biological Diversity (CBD), agreed at the Earth Summit in Rio de Janeiro in 1992. Parties to the CBD accept that biodiversity is the property and responsibility of states, that the components of this biodiversity should be used sustainably, and that there should be a just sharing of the benefits arising out of the utilisation of genetic resources.

Some of the concerns have arisen because of knowledge, or suspicion, that some scientists, research institutes or commercial enterprises have taken samples of plants to test for new products, such as pharmaceutical drugs, without due permission or on ethically unacceptable terms. The worry is that there will be no, or inadequate, benefits accruing to the countries and communities from where the materials originate. There are also concerns about the theft of local or indigenous intellectual property, given that the traditional uses of plants as medicines can be useful guides for the development of new drugs.

Proponents of local and indigenous rights argue that traditional knowledge of the uses of plants can be based on years, perhaps millennia, of experimentation, and therefore it is not only scientists or pharmaceutical companies that can claim to be inventors (scientists do so through the filing of patents). There is also an argument that local and indigenous communities have acted historically as the keepers, or even developers, of biological diversity, and thus should be 'compensated' by those who benefit later from their care and labour. On the other hand, there are accusations that some countries and territories have over-reacted to the scares of biopiracy and theft of intellectual resources through creating such tight restrictions over research as to potentially cause serious setbacks to conservation and sustainable development.

It is highly likely that issues surrounding medicinal plants (especially) have been largely responsible for these alleged over-reactions. Probably, there are often misconceptions about the relative prominence that research aimed at bioprospecting should have (compared with research having other objectives), the extent of bioprospecting and the amounts of money to be made. There seems to be an unresolved conflict concerning intellectual property rights (IPRs) between the CBD and the Trade Related Aspects of Intellectual Property Rights (TRIPS) agreement of the World Trade Organisation (WTO).

It is not yet clear how a compromise will be reached between the commitments to accessibility and equity enshrined in the CBD and the pressures for private ownership and profit-based systems of reward represented by TRIPS. "There is no requirement on applicants (to TRIPS) to involve or consult with local communities or governments about patenting a compound based on a natural product from that country. Nor is there provision for sharing benefits or including the prior contributions of indigenous peoples to an innovation".

Different Approaches to Conservation

An ecosystem-based approach is endorsed by the CBD and is appropriate for conservation of medicinal plants. It encourages lateral thinking, inter-disciplinarity and prioritisation. The ecosystem-based approach of the CBD, as encompassed in its 12 principles, recognises that:

— humans, with their cultural diversity, form an integral component of biodiversity;

— the delimitation of ecosystems for conservation action needs to be defined conceptually on scales appropriate to the problems being addressed;

— work can involve all 3 objectives of the Convention, requiring the striking of a balance between them;

— there are uncertainties in managing ecosystems and, consequently, a need for conservation measures to contain elements of 'learning-by-doing' or feedback from research;

— the approach needs to be used flexibly, so that other approaches to management and conservation can be incorporated, such as protected areas and single-species conservation programmes;

— benefits need to accrue to those responsible for producing and managing the benefits derived from ecosystems, with a special emphasis on local communities; and

— networks are needed for the sharing of experiences and information.

In view of the inherent uncertainties, the CBD recommends an adaptive approach to interventions and management. This requires the establishment of indicators to monitor the effects of new measures, so that the need to make adjustments can be recognised. Conservationists should periodically take time to reflect fundamentally on their work, drawing back from deep immersion in particular matters. The desirability of changes in emphasis or taking on new types of activity may become apparent.

Activists (conservationists) will be essential to ensure the success of efforts to conserve medicinal plants. Their work (or 'projects') should be designed to influence the ways that resource managers, traders, manufacturers, consumers or members of other defined social groups go about their normal business. What is required is the institutionalisation of new activities in favour of conservation. The attainment of institutionalisation requires the taking of responsibility by the various stakeholders involved, and therefore conservationists need to be careful in how much they take a lead themselves, balancing this with encouraging the development of initiatives by those who are more fundamentally parts of the systems.

Conservationists can expect progress normally to be slow, though hopefully with occasional breakthroughs. They need to be persistent and imaginative. Inherent problems in this field of conservation, as in others, stem from the conservatism of human nature and the low priority that people normally give to conservation over more pressing day-to-day affairs. Conservationists must identify priorities if they are to stand much chance of being heard. The systems involved in medicinal plant conservation tend to be complex, with many variables and many types of actual or potential stakeholders. For the sake of presentation, 4 distinct sub-systems are recognised here, namely

— production systems and in situ conservation,

— commercial systems,

— ex situ conservation, propagation, domestication and the breeding of crop varieties, and

— new product discovery (Fig. 1), though actually all can be closely connected.

It is emphasised that the heart of medicinal plant conservation should be aimed at securing robust management systems in favour of conservation or sustainable production (or both) at the sites where the medicinal plants grow. Given the diversity of field contexts, most 'medicinal plant conservation projects' should be field projects rather than projects of any other type. It will be noted from the brief descriptions of approaches that follow that many measures, which can be taken in favour of conservation, are essentially indirect. They include changes in laws and in the purchasing practices of companies and consumers, the compilation of databases, the ex situ preservation of germplasm in seed banks, and so on.

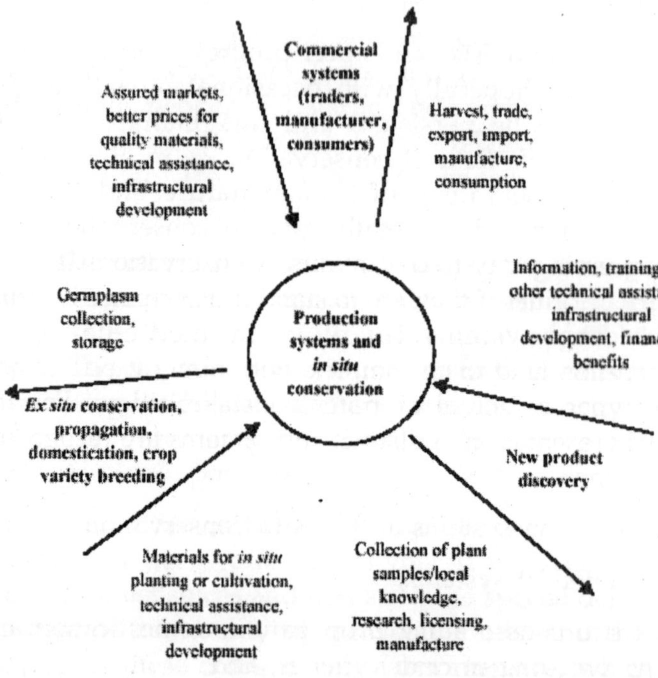

Figure 1: Some sub-systems involved in medicinal plant conservation.

What should be borne in mind is that all such measures will be essentially useless for supporting in situ conservation and sustainable development unless they 'feed back' positively to the field level. Unless due attention is paid, then 'distant' conservation measures, taken with good intent, may be ineffective or even backfire. Take the case of medicinal plants and Bwindi Impenetrable forest in Uganda. The upgrading of Bwindi from being a Forest and Game Reserve to a National Park in 1991 was a reaction to the rampant level of illegal activities, such as timber harvesting, hunting and gold-mining, that previously prevailed.

Following parks policy at the time, this declaration resulted in a total ban on the collection of all forest produce, including medicinal plants. What was not taken adequately into account, however, was the impact of this tough new regime on local livelihoods and attitudes. One of the items no longer legally available was the bark of Nyakibazi (Rytygynia spp.), a product so highly valued for medicinal purposes that, without it, declared the people, "they would die".

Conflict over this and other matters resulted in an increase in cases of deliberate burning of the forest and threats being made against the mountains gorillas, the flagship species of the forest. The conflict was later partially defused through the formulation of agreements on local rights and responsibilities allowing regulated collection of Nyakibazi and other natural products from the park. Another example of a good intention back-firing concerns a suggestion emanating from Europe in the late 1990s for the listing of the medicinal plant Devil's Claw (Harpagophytum procumbens) on CITES.

A proposal to list a species on CITES might be considered to be an entirely positive matter, but in this case this seems not to have been so, related probably to a lack of appreciation of the situation in the field. At the time, the non-governmental organisation CRIAA (Centre for Research Information for Action in Africa) SA-DC was just beginning to achieve considerable success in assisting rural communities in Namibia to harvest Devil's Claw in sustainable ways, also involving more direct access to markets and greater income for the harvesters. Even a mention of the idea of including the species on CITES was apparently enough to cause a fall in demand by the trade. This fed back to Namibia, causing a slump in sales and a general feeling of disappointment, threatening to undermine all that had been achieved through hard work on the ground.

Production and in situ conservation

In many ways, the approaches and methodologies used to promote the in situ conservation and sustainable production of medicinal plants differ little, in principle, from those used for conservation and sustainable use of plant diversity generally. In particular, there are many similarities to those used for other categories of wild plants that are harvested as resources, especially those subject to the pressures of commercial trade. The types and levels of activities that are possible will vary greatly between projects, depending on the resources of time and money available, as well as the particular interests and competencies of those involved.

In any event, it is desirable for project teams to be multidisciplinary, preferably with coverage of the biological, ecological, cultural, economic and political dimensions of ecosytems. At least some members of project teams should have an understanding of both the biological and social dimensions of the ecosystems. Interventions will stand less chance of being successful if conservation teams consist solely of different types of specialist, without such linking expertise. This is why a knowledge of applied ethnobotany is so desirable. (Ethnobotany is the subject that deals with the relationships between people and plants; applied ethnobotany is ethnobotany applied to conservation and sustainable development.)

The range of possible actions in favour of in situ conservation and sustainable use is vast. For example, the objective of a project could be the conservation of local populations of species of MAPs that are globally threatened. However, to achieve this objective might require engagement in a range of 'developmental' activities. Some of these might seem more obviously relevant, such as the strengthening of certain community institutions, but others might seem less so, such as measures to improve livelihood security, healthcare facilities or local income. It is a matter of judgement and experience how far conservation projects should include developmental matters.

The experience of FRLHT in southern India is that the involvement of communities in conservation of medicinal plants cannot be achieved without addressing the healthcare concerns of the people. The failure of many integrated conservation and development projects (ICDPs) in the past should not be interpreted as showing that conservation does not need to be integrated with development nor, indeed, that local communities should not be fundamentally involved in conservation projects.

Rather, their failure is thought to be due to a delinking of conservation and development and loss of a sense of purpose (and therefore authority) among some conservation agencies, which have increasingly seen their roles as taking responsibility for structural problems, such as poverty, market failures, corruption and the global economic order, rather than getting on with tackling practical problems on the ground. Current ICDP thinking tends towards an emphasis on building support for conservation based on local cultural and economic concerns, full use of traditional ecological knowledge, and negotiations about the rights and responsibilities of the various stakeholders.

The involvement of local communities will almost invariably be a fundamental ingredient of in situ projects aimed at medicinal plant conservation. One reason, crudely stated, is that it is not difficult, in many parts of the world, for collectors of medicinal plants (whether members of local communities or outsiders) to harvest medicinal plants unsustainably or illegally, if the only controls present are those associated with government officials. It is even easier to avoid detection in the case of many medicinals than with timber, which is illegally harvested on massive scales in some countries.

Conservation agencies, such as Park and Forest Departments, often suffer from shortages of resources and sometimes also work in conditions of political instability. Apart from the problems that they face in regulating medicinal plants, government agencies, acting alone, are liable to have little control over many other activities that can endanger medicinal plants, which may include excessive grazing by livestock, the harvesting of plants for other purposes apart from medicinal (for fuelwood, fodder, etc.) and excessive burning.

The forms of relationships between project teams, local communities and other local stakeholders, established at the onset of work, are critical. These relationships may well be unwritten and relatively informal, but the tone that they set is important if more precise agreements are needed later, including if possibilities of commercial opportunities emerge based on local biodiversity or knowledge. Projects are also liable to go through a period of confidence-building as trust is established. Whatever the initial purposes of a project, it is important that priorities are periodically reevaluated.

Successful conservation depends on the existence of rules and regulations, and a reasonable degree of compliance to them. Property rights and terms of access to resources are critical factors. It is especially important to ensure that the interests of those people in communities whose lives are most dependent on MAPs are properly accommodated. Despite reported successes of joint or participatory forest management in India and Nepal, the MAP sector has often been inadequately covered.

For instance, in Nepal there are frequent difficulties relating to a general neglect of NTFPs, excessive restrictions on access, heavy taxes and rent-seeking. Both customary and statutory laws will often be relevant to medicinal plant conservation. Each type of legal system has its merits and disadvantages, and a critical question facing conservationists will often be how they can best be combined so that their positive elements are strengthened, while avoiding a process of mutual undermining.

Analysis of the effectiveness of the two types of laws in India and Nepal shows that there can be considerable strength still remaining in customary institutions, but that they often need reinforcement today, as, for example, through their official recognition by government agencies. Protected areas, established through statutory law, can be very useful for the conservation of medicinal plants. There are many types (national parks, forest reserves, strict nature reserves, etc.), generally serving various purposes in addition to biodiversity conservation, and with various rules applying to the conservation and collection of medicinal plants.

Generally, medicinal plant issues have proved to be low among the priorities of the responsible agencies. In India, for example, the Forest Department is much more interested in timber than nontimber forest products (NTFPs) and, within the broad category of NTFPs, often in other types of products apart from medicinal plants (especially those regarded as being financially more lucrative). A study of the distribution and exploitation of 14 species of MAPs of high trade and conservation value in a high valley of the Indian Himalayas has started to reveal something of the details which local management plans must incorporate.

Research resulted in a classification of species according to their distribution (including in relation to altitude and habitat) and pressure (both as regards collection for local use or trade, and pressure from livestock). Recommendations, varying between groups of species, included the protection of particular populations, rotational harvesting, cultivation and development of improved marketing. The range of measures which can be taken to conserve medicinal plants in protected areas differs little from those that can be applied elsewhere, with the essential difference of an extra layer of legal protection. This means that the rights of communities and other 'outside' parties will be more circumscribed than they are in the general landscape.

Agreements between communities and agencies responsible for protected areas will be necessary if collection of medicinal plants is to be controlled. This legal necessity can create exceptional opportunities to strengthen biodiversity conservation generally—not just in favour of those particular species of medicinal plants which receive specific attention. This is because of the special status that medicinal plants can hold in local societies, related to their symbolic, healing and economic properties. Agreements on medicinal plants can form firm bases for improved management of protected areas generally.

If cultivation is introduced in the support zones of protected areas, then the provision of assistance by agencies to encourage this development can usefully be tied to agreements which enhance the participation of communities in conservation of the protected areas. Various, often isolated, initiatives are being tried to link conservation and livelihoods through a focus on medicinal plants. A project of the WWF-Nepal Programme with the

People and Plants Initiative, at Shey Phodsundo National Park, is developing community-based systems for the sustainable harvesting of medicinal plants, combined with the strengthening of local medical services as provided by amchis (practitioners of Tibetan Medicine).

The amchis are identified as key members of the communities for promotion of conservation, with their allied interests in plant diversity and livelihoods. The Forest Department of the Great Himalayan National Park, India, is promoting cultivation of medicinal plants as an income-generating enterprise linked to conservation. The emphasis is on women, in recognition of their economically marginalised status and their special interest in plant resources. By 2002, 92 Women Saving and Credit Groups had been formed involving 930 people.

The Foundation for Revitalisation of Local Health Traditions (FRLHT) is active across the southern cone of India with an integrated programme of conservation, health security and livelihood support, centred around medicinal plants and plant-based medicine. FRLHT encourages the foundation of micro-credit groups, and seeks to prioritise health problems and related local remedies. Species in demand, and also endemic and threatened species, are grown in nurseries, and planted out in demonstration plots, homegardens, and for enrichment planting in areas of degraded forest (ca. 200-300 ha in size). Steps are taken to encourage the transmission of medical knowledge between generations.

The FRLHT model is proving successful and becoming adopted elsewhere in India. Three levels of monitoring to guarantee that MAPs are used sustainably have been proposed for Prespa National Park, Albania. If implemented, they would involve collectors and collectors' organisations, the Forest and National Park Service and scientists, all working co-operatively. They would cover:

(1) the recording of the amounts of all MAPs collected, and associated information; (2) detailed population studies of rare species; and (3) monitoring to detect changes in the vegetation, especially on the landscape scale.

Actually, in practice, it is necessary to identify indicators in monitoring programmes and the selection of these is important. Certain species are of greater cultural or economic significance to communities or agencies, and there is a greater chance that monitoring programmes will give good results if these are included as indicators. The vulnerability of species to commercial collection depends on the parts of plants used and how they are collected. For example, the collection of underground organs, as is the case with many species in the Himalayas, is liable to be more damaging that if leaves are targeted, as is the case with many species used in tropical forest areas of Africa.

Populations of specialist species associated with habitats of restricted occurrence, as Mecanopsis spp. in the Himalayas, can easily be decimated. Some countries have laws specifically giving protection to wild plants, some of which may be medicinal. The UK Wildlife and Countryside Act prohibits the uprooting of any species of wild plant, except by landowners and other authorised people. In several Italian regions, Austrian Länder and Swiss cantons, not only is the uprooting or the collection of subterranean parts of plants prohibited, but there are restrictions on the gathering of aerial parts as well.

The number of flowering stems or branches that may be picked varies from 5 to 20, or a handful, according to local regulations. Only a few countries have laws specifically for medicinal plants. In Nepal, the collection, sale, transportation and export of Dactylorhiza hatagirea, Juglans regia and Picrorhiza scrophulariifolia are all banned, while other species are specifically banned for export. However, in many parts of the world, for instance Africa and India, laws protecting wild plants are little known by the general public or, indeed, even among those charged with their enforcement.

Cultivation is frequently advocated as a measure to take the pressure off wild stocks, especially for species collected in large quantities for trade. Cultivation can be commercially attractive to companies, because they then have greater control over quality and supply. Various factors influence the feasibility of cultivation, its impact on conservation and by whom it is best undertaken. If volumes required and market prices are both high, then cultivation is more likely to be economically feasible.

The introduction of medicinal plants into home-gardens is seen as a useful means of providing accessible cures for common ailments and supplementary income. Medicinal plants have been introduced successfully into traditional farming systems in Guatemala, providing regular incomes to farmers. If cultivation is to be introduced, then there can be many problems inhibiting success—for instance, in India, lack of knowledge of cultivation and post-harvest techniques for some species, and lack of availability of planting material of good quality.

If a species has not previously been in cultivation, then domestication may be needed, which can prove a difficult, expensive and lengthy process. There should be public funding for domestication programmes for those many species of MAPs which are highly endangered but which economically or otherwise are unlikely to become domesticated. It has been proposed for the Eastern Cape Province of South Africa that faster-growing species are most suitable for communities, but that the cultivation of slower-growing types of plants is best undertaken by statutory bodies, such as the Department of Water Affairs and Forestry, or by private companies. There can be advantages to wild collection over cultivation.

From the medical viewpoint, there is a widespread belief that wild-harvested material is more efficacious, as is sometimes reflected in higher prices. Asian buyers will pay up to 30 times more for wild-harvested roots of American Ginseng (Panax quinquefolius) than for those from cultivated sources. On the other hand, 82% of healers interviewed in the Eastern Cape Province of South Africa stated that they would readily make use of cultivated plants, possibly (according to the researchers) because they recognise that wild supplies are declining.

The social benefits of wild harvest too can be considerable, given that it is generally the most economically and socially marginalised members of communities that are so involved. Even if cultivation is introduced, then this may be adopted by relatively well-off people, with better access to land, financial capital or information. The landless and other disadvantaged sectors of society may fail to benefit, but rather continue to collect just as before.

Another important factor is that individual land-holdings can be very small and farmers are likely to adopt a high risk strategy in terms of livelihood security if they convet from food crops to MAPs. For example, in the Himalayas topographic and demographic factors limit the size of agricultural land per family often to only 0.4-1 ha. However, from the conservation viewpoint, perhaps the strongest argument for retaining or promoting wild harvesting is that this will then maintain links between people and the intricacies of their local natural worlds.

The successful conservation of biodiversity will always require the existence of people who know about such details and care enough for their existence that they will make efforts to retain them. Without this type of involvement, there is little cultural base at the local level on which to build support for national or global conservation goals. Some conservationists interested in MAPs should become engaged with the commercial sector, both because it is the pressures of trade that are responsible for so much MAP endangerment, and also, more positively, because of the opportunities which engagement with industry and consumers present. Various stakeholders are involved in commercial systems, including producers (collectors or growers), traders of various types, manufacturers and consumers (Figure 2).

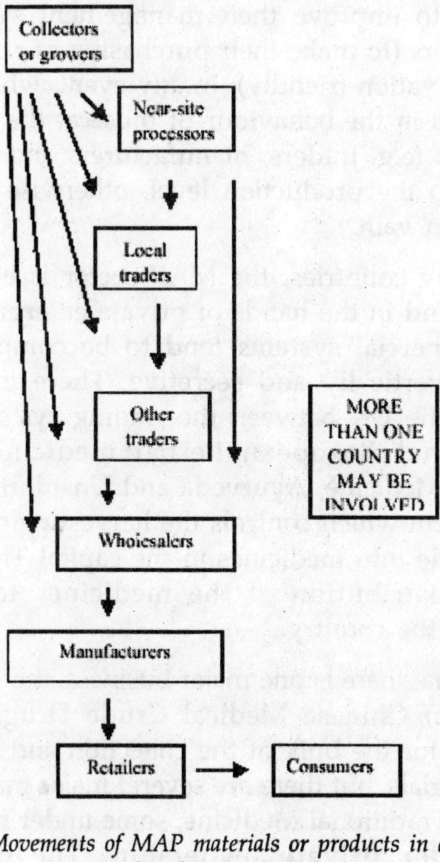

Figure 2: Movements of MAP materials or products in a commercial system based on medicinal plants.

Apart from self-regulation, commercial systems for MAPs are subject to many types of standard, statutory or otherwise. Conservationists can become engaged in various ways, including helping to formulate and promote appropriate standards, supplying relevant information to the parties involved, and also putting parties in touch which each other.

Because of the connections between different parts of commercial systems, it will often be productive to work simultaneously with different types of stakeholder. Thus, it can make sense to work simultaneously both with producers (to improve their management systems) and manufacturers (to make their purchasing of raw materials more conservation-friendly). In any event, what is vital is that changes in the behaviour of those at the 'top' of the trade chains (e.g. traders, manufacturers and consumers) feed back to the production level, otherwise efforts will have been in vain.

In many countries, the MAP sector is economically liberalised and in the hands of private enterprise. In such cases, commercial systems tend to be complex, poorly integrated vertically and secretive. There is very little overlap in the UK between the trading systems relating to traditional European herbal medicine, Chinese Traditional Medicine, Ayurveda and Unani. Bhutan has a central system which controls the harvesting of medicinal plants—made into medicines in the capital Thimpu—and then the distribution of the medicines to hospitals throughout the country.

In China, there is one major business, the state-owned Company of Chinese Medical Crude Drugs, which is responsible for the bulk of the collection and distribution of raw materials, but there are several major manufacturers of Chinese Traditional Medicine, some under national and others under private ownership. The collapse of

Communist regimes in eastern Europe resulted in considerable deregulation of statecontrolled commerce in MAPs and a weakening of pre-existing quota-controlled harvesting structures.

As a result, the number of traders in MAPs has increased and wild collection has grown in an unregulated fashion, with associated conservation concerns. In Bulgaria, an element of socialist centralisation remains. The main national dealer in MAPs is Bulgarcoop, a co-operative enterprise, but this is joined today by many small, largely familyowned, businesses. Both Bulgarcoop and 50-60 of the businesses (the latter acting collectively through the 'Private Herb Exchange') provide help to growers with cultivation and guarantees to purchase harvests.

Standard-setting with regard to MAPs is a complex business, more so than with timber (which will be a point of comparison for some conservationists). The complexity is due to the variety of harvesting and socio-economic circumstances, the complexity of the chains of custody through which materials travel, the wide range of markets (local to international) and the numerous types of product. The latter include not only medicines, but also foods, food supplements, fragrances and personal care products.

Quite a number of therapeutic products made from MAPs are marketed as food supplements or herbal tonics, rather than medicines, avoiding the stricter regulations that apply to the latter. The main concerns of the industry (and consumers) as regards standards normally relate to medical efficacy and safety (Pierce & Laird, in press). In terms of botanical ingredients, these concerns translate into specific requirements, most basically that MAP materials or products really are made from the right species, but also concerning the parts of the plants used, the times of harvest, the levels of active principles, and the contents of pollutants.

It is not unusual for species to be sold incorrectly labelled. Aside from these medical concerns, some enterprises (and consumers) are also interested in social justice, for instance relating to the distribution of financial benefits received from the trade, and the fair treatment of women and children. There are major questions of social justice in the MAP sector, because of the very low prices generally paid to collectors and, allegedly, the maintenance of artificially high prices by a monopoly of wholesale distributors.

Environmental concerns may not be restricted solely to matters strictly related to biological conservation or the sustainability of harvesting. Some environmental standards, such as those relating to organic accreditation, only relate partially to biological conservation. Many manufacturers, at least in some countries, are said to care little about the standards of quality of the material they purchase. If manufacturers actually are interested in conservation, then they are faced with the problem of knowing whether the raw materials that they purchase are derived from plants harvested or grown in ways that promote this objective.

Manufacturers commonly think about conservation in terms of sustainability. In general, even the most environmentally inclined manufacturers will find it impossible to guarantee that all their sources of medicinal plants are sustainable. Many manufacturers buy largely from wholesalers (some of the biggest of which, in Europe, are in Germany). They do so because they then can be more certain that stocks of reliable quality are available, prices are relatively low and purchasing is easy. Therefore, a problem for environmentally inclined manufacturers is how to learn about the origins of MAP materials on sale.

Some wholesalers are reluctant to provide information about their sources, fearing that manufacturers might use this information to side-step them in the future. It has been suggested that one way that manufacturers might be able to obtain greater assurance of sustainability is through the incorporation of conservation criteria in the specification sheets which they prepare for the formulation of products. They can then require wholesalers to confirm that they have met these standards or lose out to other suppliers.

Some manufacturers may be able to encourage higher conservation standards through their more direct sourcing of MAP materials. Likewise, ethical producers may be able to 'jump up' market chains, for instance selling MAP materials directly to manufacturers. Collectors and growers often benefit from being organised into associations of co-operatives, including to increase their negotiating power. The US-based Rocky Mountain Herbalist Coalition provides a list of ecologically conscious suppliers of botanicals.

Direct sourcing or marketing is not without its drawbacks. Manufacturers may be faced with higher costs and reduced reliability in supplies. For communities, social and economic problems can arise if traditional trading relationships are broken. Probably, direct sourcing is likely to remain a preferred option mainly for manufacturers of 'quality' products aimed at specialised markets, in which there is an ability to pay the higher prices required. Nevertheless, there are probably many unrealised opportunities for more direct sourcing awaiting discovery by enterprising communities and manufacturers.

Given the concerns of at least some manufacturers and consumers to produce, or use, medicines of good quality, there would seem to be opportunities for communities, perhaps motivated by NGOs, to seek market advantage for themselves through adopting higher environmental standards and establishing direct market linkages. An incremental approach is probably often realistic, starting, for instance, from first meeting organic standards, with full certification of sustainability (a complex undertaking) a more distant possibility.

If cultivation is attempted, then it is important to select suitable species from the agronomic and economic perspectives, the number of which may be quite limited for any particular site. An example, which so far is proving successful at promoting a socially and environmentally ethical trade, is the project, mentioned earlier, of the NGO CRIAA SA-DC on Devil's Claw (Harpagophytum procumbens). Devil's Claw has become a very popular remedy in Europe, but the plant has been unsustainably harvested in the past and it has even been held that it could be in danger of extinction. Between 10,000 and 15,000 harvesters rely on sales from its collection as their only source of cash.

In 1998, a sustainably harvested Devil's Claw project was established at one resettlement farm in Namibia and the scheme rapidly expanded. In 1999, the project covered some 307,415 ha of rangeland and 10,210 kg of Devil's Claw were produced, providing local people with a sustainable product at a guaranteed and fair price.

Compliance with sustainable harvesting techniques, i.e. leaving the tap-root undisturbed and refilling the hole, for example, has increased to between 80 and 85 percent. This is generally not the case in other areas where Devil's Claw is extensively harvested in Namibia. Another example of a project aimed at organising producers for market and conservation advantage is the Medicinal Plants Growers Forum (MPGF) in Uttaranchal, India. So far, 51 farmers in 4 valleys are members of the Forum, committed to growing medicinal plants to organic standards.

One lesson from this and other experiences is the need to involve a wide range of partners from the start, including not only the farmers, but traders, the government, NGOs and scientists, so that the necessary linkages and access to technical expertise are established. The involvement of industry from project inception can help ensure that products will be purchased at agreed prices, taking note of required species and standards of quality. Marketing is a critical issue for the success of organised collectors' or growers' schemes.

Obstacles to progress with the MPGF have included a cumbersome system of required permits (relating to permission to grow the plants and transport the products), lack of good quality planting material, problems with cultivation practices and access to markets. The Devil's Claw and MPGF projects are trend-setters, but throw up many challenges, requiring dedication and persistence. There is a wide range of laws, regulations and guidelines (with various degrees of official recognition) relating to MAPs.

Actually, biological conservation and sustainability rarely figure prominently in these standards, being, for example, mentioned with very little practical detail in recent proposals for Good Harvesting Practices (GHP) for Collecting Plant Material. Nevertheless, there can be significant opportunities for conservationists in commenting on standards produced by official bodies, recommending improvements in favour of conservation. The World Health Organisation (WHO) is currently developing Good Sourcing Practice guidelines, if so, they will provide a global point of reference for more local conservation efforts.

WHO first published guidelines for Good Manufacturing Practice (GMP) for medicines and herbal products in 1969, recommending these to member states. The aim was to guarantee the consistent quality of medicinal products. The guidelines contained no provision requiring proof of sustainable production, inclusion of which would have stimulated the development of sustainability criteria. In Europe, the European Herb Growers Association (EUROPAM) is currently developing Good Agricultural Practice (GAP) and Good Wild Harvesting Practice (GWHP) guidelines for MAPs.

These might be included in the European Union (EU) Directive on Good Manufacturing Practice for Starting Materials, if and when this directive becomes operational. The GAP guidelines are more or less finalised and have already been endorsed by the European Medicine Evaluation Agency (EMEA). They are weak from the sustainability perspective. There might possibly be a greater chance of incorporating sustainability criteria in the GWHP guidelines, since these are still under active development. There is an EU Directive on Traditional Medicinal Products nearing completion. This deals mainly with issues of efficacy and safety, and apparently will contain nothing on conservation and sustainable production.

In the case of China, a new law came into effect in June 2002 relating to the standards of traditional medicines. The main purpose is the regulation of products produced by larger enterprises. The law was introduced because of concerns about inadequate supplies, toxicity (pesticides in the case of cultivated plants; contaminants from plastic wrappings) and lack of standardisation of ingredients (medicines carrying the same name are not always formulated in the same way). The law will require various types of information to be supplied with each batch of MAP material, including the botanical name, the place of origin, the time of harvest and the level of insect contamination.

Material of cultivated origin will require information on the fertilisers and pesticides used, and on heavy metal content. Quotas will be set for the quantities of species allowed for wild harvest in particular areas. This is a framework law and regulations for individual species will follow. The current government target in China is to ensure that 50 species of MAPs are cultivated according to GAP by 2010. Promotion of GAP is regarded as the most important type of quality standard from the conservation point of view, because it applies directly to the source of the material, but other standards are being pursued in China, including Good Laboratory Practice (GLP), GMP, Good Clinical Practice (GCP) and Good Service Practice (GSP).

Some countries have laws that regulate the commercial collection or trade of MAPs. Poland lists species of MAPs that cannot be collected without permit. An Italian law of 1931 stipulates that permits for the commercial collection of species that are listed will only be issued to people who have degrees in herbalism from schools of pharmacy. Bulgaria has established a quota system for the gathering of certain MAPs that is reviewed annually, according to species and region. Countries may also ban exports, as did the Government of India in 1994 for 50 species believed to be endangered in the wild.

The Convention on International Trade in Endangered Species of Flora and Fauna (CITES) is the main global treaty regulating international trade in plants. Adherence to its provisions is mandatory on the part of its 157 signatory countries. To return to the matter of standards, it is known that there can be problems in adherence because there are so many types of standards and some of the requirements are cumbersome to meet. Furthermore, the expense involved in meeting some standards means that they can be discriminatory against small producers. Another issue is that conservation organisations have had problems in devising useful messages for consumers, related to the challenge of combining simplicity with accuracy.

A general warning that some medicinal plants are threatened (while most are not) is hardly helpful. There is no unified label existing today guaranteeing sustainability. Fortunately, there is a ground-swell in sections of the industry to improve their conservation standards, partly in recognition that, unless they do so voluntarily, they may well be forced to do so by law. There is also a sizeable market, especially in more affluent countries, for environmentally-friendly products. At present, the best that can be expected generally is that some manufacturers will gain just recognition for their environmental efforts and will accordingly be rewarded by concerned consumers.

It might also be useful for a few species which should be avoided by consumers to be identified and publicised, but these have yet to be authoritatively listed. Because presumably mostl consumers have some interest in the standards of efficacy and safety of medicines, and at least some of them are concerned also about social justice and the environment, it would be useful for conservationists to explore the possibility of establishing a unitary concept of 'quality', covering all of these matters. If so, this could be followed by the development of a system of labelling, with a chance of general recognition, guaranteeing the quality of products containing MAPs across the board. This would greatly help the ethical consumer. Such labelled products should be third-party certified.

Approaches to ex situ conservation, propagation, domestication and the breeding of crop varieties Plant species can be found away from the sites where they naturally occur in a range of contexts, including in botanic and other types of gardens, nurseries, seedbanks, tissue culture units, etc. In fact, ex situ conservation is not always sharply separated from in situ conservation. There are intermediates between the 'purest' forms of in situ and ex situ conservation, as represented possibly, on the one hand, by the total protection of wild populations of species without any other form of management and, on the other hand, by seedbanks with specialist scientists situated at a far distance from the places where the plants naturally grow.

The term circa situ conservation has been used for a range of practices commonly associated especially with more traditional (and biodiversity-rich) agricultural systems. They include the deliberate encouragement of certain species of 'wild' plants in 'natural' habitats, the retention of valued 'wild' plants when land is cleared for agriculture or crops are weeded, the growing of valued 'wild' plants in home gardens, and the selection and storage of seed at household level for later replanting. Circa situ conservation grades into both in situ and ex situ conservation.

Botanic gardens can play further major roles in medicinal plant conservation through developing propagation and cultivation protocols, and undertaking programmes of domestication and variety breeding. Such research can benefit from traditional knowledge. For example, the seeds of Paris polyphylla, a medicinal plant in China, have proved difficult to germinate in trials, but much greater success was achieved after following the practice of a farmer in Yunnan who mixed the seeds with those of another species.

Seedbanks offer a more attractive way of storing the genetic diversity of many plants ex situ than botanic gardens, at least in terms of cost. However, medicinal plants are poorly represented in seedbanks. In practice, most seedbanks are used mainly as repositories of the genetic diversity of agricultural crops and their main users are agricultural scientists—breeders of 'improved' varieties of crops. Seedbanks will remain of limited use for conservation of MAPs until, and unless, their fundamental purposes and modes of operation are rethought.

Bibliography

Akerele, O., Heywood, V. & Synge, H. *The conservation of medicinal plants*, Cambridge University Press, Cambridge, UK, (1991).

Arisawa, M., Ohmura, K., Kobayashi, A. and Morita, N. "A cytotoxic constituent of Lysimachia japonica Thrunb. (Primulaceae) and the structure-activity relationships of related compounds". *Chem. Pharm. Bull.* 37 (1989)

Droby, S., Prusky, D., Jacoby, B. and Goldman, A. "Induction of antifungal resorcinols in flesh of unripe mango fruits and its relation to latent infection by Alternaria alternata". *Physiol. Mol. Plant Pathol.* 30 (1987)

Ekola, A., Sutherland, J. & Wilson, E., "Ancient medicinal tree threatened with extinction: tree is leading remedy for prostate disorders worldwide", (2000).

Gellerman, J.L., Anderson, W.H. and Schlenk, H. "Synthesis of anacardic acids in seeds of Ginkgo biloba". *Biochim. Biophys. Acta* 431 (1976)

Ghosh S, Malhotra P, Lalitha PV, Guha-Mukherjee S and Chauhan VS "Expression of Plasmodium falciparum Cterminal region of merozoite surface protein (PfMSP119), a potential malaria vaccine candidate, in tobacco". *Plant Sci* 162: 335–343, (2002)

Goklany I, "Precaution without perversity: a comprehensive application of the precautionary principle to genetically modified crops. *Biotechnol Law Rep* 20: 377–396, (2001a)

Gomez N, Wigdorovitz A, Castanon S, Gil F, Ordas R, Borca M.V and Escribano J.M, "Oral immunogenicity of the plant derived spike protein from swine-transmissible gastroenteritis coronavirus". *Arch Virol* 145: 1725–1732, (2000)

Grazzini, R., Hesk, D., Heininger, E., Hildebrandt, G., Reddy, C.C., Cox- Foster, D., Medford, J., Craig, R. and Mumma, R.O. "Inhibition of lipoxygenase and prostaglandin endoperoxide synthase by anacardic acids". *Biochem. Biophys. Res. Commun.* 176 (1991)

Haq T.A, Mason HS, Clements JD and Arntzen CJ "Oral immunization with a recombinant bacterial antigen produced in transgenic plants". *Science* 268: 714–716, 1995.

Howard J.A and Donnelly K.C., "A quantitative safety assessment model for transgenic protein products produced in agricultural crops". *J Agr Environ Ethics* 17: 545–558, (2004)

Ja.e G "Regulating transgenic crops: a comparative analysis of different regulatory processes". *Transgenic Res* 13: 5–19, (2004)

Kozubek, A. and Tyman, J.H.P. *Resorcinolic lipids, the natural non- isoprenoid phenolic amphiphiles and their biological activity.* Chem. Rev. 99 (1999)

Orabi, K.Y., Mossa, J.S. and El-Feraly, F.S. "Isolation and characterization of two antimicrobial agents from mace (Myristica fragrans)". *J. Nat. Prod.* 64 (1991)

Registan, G.I., Stoyanovich, F.M., Lille, Y.E. and Ostrovsky, D.N. "Structural-functional changes in bacterial and model membranes induced by phenolic lipids". *Biol. Membr.* 4 (1987)

S.Shibata, O.Tanaka, J.Shoj i and H.Saito, "Economic Medicinal Plant Research" 1, ed. by H.Wagner, H.Hikino and N.R.Farnsworth, Academic Press, 155-284 (1985).

Index